LANGUAGE, RACE AND EDUCATION

Printing Corrigenda:

Page 10 — Last line — the word 'swapped' should read 'swamped'.
Page 22 — Paragraph 3, 20th line — the word 'later' should read 'latter'.
Page 23 & 30 — the words 'chinese' & 'jews' should be 'Chinese' & 'Jews'.
Page 63 — 11th line — the word 'that' should read 'than'.
Page 66 — Paragraph 3, 10th line — the word 'by' should read 'be'.

Occasional Papers on Education
by Gurbachan Singh

LANGUAGE, RACE AND EDUCATION

Gurbachan Singh

Foreword by Dr. Gajendra K. Verma

JAYSONS AND COMPANY

©Gurbachan Singh 1988
Foreword© Dr. Gajendra K. Verma 1988
First published 1988

British Library Cataloguing in Publication Data

Singh, Gurbachan, 1988 —
Language, Race and Education
1. Great Britain. Ethnic Minorities
   Native languages. Teaching
I. Title
   418' .007

ISBN 0-951304-90-9

Cover design by Bernard van Lierop, Wolverhampton

Published by Jaysons and Company
265a-267a Soho Road, Birmingham, B21 9SA.
Telephone: 021-523-6851

© 1988, G.Singh. Telephone: (0332) 764064
          'Gurjas', 5 Albrighton Avenue, Stenson Fields,
          Derby, DE2 3BP.

Typeset in 11/12pt Times Roman by Graham Hales, Derby.

Printed and bound in Great Britain by
Pear Tree Printers, Units 3&4, Kingsmead Industrial Estate,
Noel Street, Derby. Telephone: (0332) 41982

Mother-tongue is the
basic human right
of every person
and its safeguard
is the duty of
the society and the state

To my wife Surjit
and our children
Gurmeet, Gurjit and Jason Jagdeep

Contents

Ethnic, racial, linguistic and religious differences among the population are not novel in British society, but it is only over the last 30 years that these differences have generated discussion and arguments amongst educators, policy-makers and politicians. This has arisen as a response to the presence of visible minority groups who are differentiated from the indigenous population in terms of language, religion, life-style and skin colour.

A major part of the debate has been centred on or around education. In this process a number of questions have been raised about how the educational system and the school curriculum can best be modified to meet the needs of changing characteristics of society. The philosophy of dealing with such changes has been widely debated, but very little progress has been made with regard to educational policies and practices.

Some LEAs and schools have moved slowly and grudgingly in recognising and adapting to the idea of multicultural and anti-racist perspective of educational practice. One of the issues still being debated is the place of the mother-tongue within the system of education. Many educators, administrators and policy-makers view language differences in terms of cultural deficiencies. They tend to make judgments that what is different is less desirable or bad. This book, based on evaluation of LEAs' policies and practices, raises some serious questions about the way the language retention programme is being implemented. The response of LEAs to the existence of linguistic and cultural minorities has been patchy, piecemeal and lacking in sound strategy.

In a plural society, children should have opportunity of access to formal instruction in their first language and/or that which best conveys the cultural traditions of their ancestors. The teaching of English, the lingua franca in British society should be introduced when the child starts school, but this should not imply the subordination of the child's home language. It should be fostered in the educational system and incorporated into the curriculum, formal and informal, of the school. It is clear from the findings that the British educational system has failed to meet the legitimate expectations, aspirations and needs of ethnic minority pupils, denying them opportunity to share fully in their communities' cultural life and traditions.

Education in a plural society must address the way of life, the beliefs and values, the linguistic and religious dimension of the individual, and the way these are expressed from day to day. It must also deal with the institutionalised racist practices and procedures which have a negative impact upon the growth, development and progress of certain social, ethnic and linguistic groups. It is from this point of view that Gurbachan Singh's research makes a useful contribution to the current debate about language and education. One may not agree with all the aspects of Mr. Singh's research to appreciate the force of his main findings.

(Dr.) Gajendra K. Verma

Reader in Education and Director of Centre for Ethnic Studies in Education, University of Manchester, Department of Education.

Preface

This publication is based on a research work for a Master of Philosophy thesis at the University of Bradford International Centre for Inter-Cultural Studies. This study examines the development and implementation of mother-tongue/community language teaching and of related educational policies with special reference to ethnic minority groups in Britain. It takes an empirical descriptive approach whilst utilising multi-method research strategy. The thesis provides an account, in the first instance, of the historical dimension of Britain as a multi-cultural and plural society, tracing the initiatives put forward by different agencies for pluralistic development and their effect on education.

In the context of multi-culturalism and multi-lingualism, the contribution of wide-range of literature is examined to add to our understanding of the social, psychological and educational implications of the development of these phenomena. An attempt is made to analyse the patterns of immigration to Britain over the centuries, the related problems of racism of British society and their effects on the education of multi-ethnic, multi-lingual society in general and that of the minorities in particular. The concepts of bilingualism and multi-lingualism are discussed in relation to the effects of these phenomena on the social, cultural, cognitive and educational developments of bilingual/multi-lingual children.

Major documents — the European Economic Community Directive (77/486) on the education of children of migrant/immigrant workers, the D.E.S. Circular 5/81 in this connection, together with statements and reports put forward by various agencies are examined in order to establish the present position of such development. The study of the development, formation and implementation of mother-tongue/community language teaching policies is approached using a case study model. A number of conclusions are subsequently offered on the basis of data collected from the ten Local Education Authorities representing different regions of England, Wales and Scotland.

Whilst policy formulation and implementation represent different approaches by the different L.E.A.s, there are undoubtedly strong elements of similarities among them to reflect a national trend. The study thus incorporates a unified approach to account for the common thread of policy process both at local and national levels.

The study offers a number of provisional conclusions, educational implications and recommendations with reference to the development of ethnic minority community language teaching as an integral part of the curriculum i.e., supply of teachers for minority languages and teachers' in-service training, teaching resources for mother-tongue teaching and bilingual education, public examinations for minority languages, language awareness courses for all concerned, vocational aspects of ethnic minority languages and suggestions for further research in mother-tongue teaching and other related aspects of inter-cultural education.

Gurbachan Singh

Acknowledgements

Any study which is based on the resolutions and activities of individuals and their reactions to events owes a debt of gratitude to those who gave their time to the author to provide much needed and often vital information. This study is no exception.

It is impossible to thank them all by name. However, my special thanks are due to the Derbyshire County Council Education Committee for granting me full-time study leave to carry out this piece of research; Mr J.H. Booth, Headmaster, St James C.E. School, Derby, for his constant inspiration and academic advice; and Mr. A.R. Neasham of International Centre for Inter-cultural Studies, University of Bradford, for his valuable thoughts and comments on the manuscript.

I am also grateful to the staff and teachers of ten Local Education Authorities in England, Wales and Scotland for their willing co-operation in allowing the study to take place; my wife for her perseverance with me throughout this research project, Jean Willoughby for her expert help in typing and arranging the manuscript, and Michael Tranter for his professional advice on the printing aspects of this work.

Finally, I am indebted to my research adviser, and mentor, Dr. Gajendra Kishore Verma, Reader in Education, University of Manchester, for his on-going support, encouragement and counsel in the completion of this publication.

Any errors, omissions and inaccuracies remain, of course, with the author.

Gurbachan Singh

Abbreviations

'A' Level	Advanced Level
B.Ed.	Bachelor of Education
B.I.C.S.	Basic Inter-Communication Skills
BL	Bi-lingual
B. & T.E.C.	Business & Technicians' Education Council
C.A.L.P.	Cognitive Academic Linguistic Proficiency
C.I.L.T.	Centre for Information on Language Teaching and Research
CLT	Community Language Teaching
C.N.N.A.	Council for National Academic Awards
C.R.E.	Commission for Racial Equality
C.S.E.	Certificate of Secondary Education
D.E.S.	Department of Education and Science
E.E.C.	European Economic Community
E.F.L.	English as a Foreign Language
e.g.	For Example
ESL or E2L	English as a Second Language
E.S.N.	Educationally Sub Normal
G.C.E.	General Certificate in Education
G.C.S.E.	General Certificate in Secondary Education
H.M.S.O.	Her Majesty's Stationery Office
I.B.A.	Independent Broadcasting Authority
i.e.	that is
I.Q.	Intelligent Quotient
L.E.A.	Local Education Authority
L.M.P.	Linguistic Minorities Project
M.P.	Member of Parliament
N.A.H.T.	National Association of Headteachers
N.A.L.A.	National Association of Language Advisers
N.A.M.E.	National Anti-racist Movement in Education
N.A.S./U.W.T.	National Association of Schoolmasters & Union of Women Teachers
N.C.L.E.	National Congress on Languages in Education
N.C.W.P.	New Commonwealth & Pakistan
N.U.T.	National Union of Teachers
'O' Level	Ordinary Level
O.P.C.S.	Office of Population Census Survey
P.E.P.	Political and Economic Planning
P.G.C.E.	Post Graduate Certificate in Education
R.E.	Religious Education
R.P.	Received Pronunciation
R.S.A.	Royal Society of Arts
S.C.D.C.	School Curriculum Development Committee
S.E.D.	Scottish Education Department
S.E.S.	Socio-Economic Status
S.N.P.	Scottish National party
T.E.F.L.	Teaching English as a Foreign Language
T.E.S.L.	Teaching English as a Second Language
U.S.	United States
U.S.A.	United States of America
Vol.	Volume

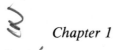

Chapter 1

Introduction

During the last two decades there has been an increasing awareness that Britain is a multi-cultural, multi-lingual society. However, the multi-cultural, multi-lingual dimension is not a new facet of British society; pluralism has been ever present in Britain since the earliest days of its history. What is new is the awareness of this dimension specifically in education and generally in all walks of life.

Most societies are multi-ethnic in composition, this is the result of migration over the centuries and, in particular, of the migration that has followed in the wake of the Second World War. What has emerged is an increased consciousness of personal identity which has challenged the assumptions on which many established societies have been built by seeking proper recognition of individual difference and worth. This has far reaching implications for society and, in particular, for the education of young people. In this technological age, it is vitally important that they be given an education that will equip them to play a full part in a society that is cohesive yet has sufficient flexibility to take account of the realities of pluralism. These bear on the conduct of the individual and on that of society itself.

The Department of Education and Science Green Paper (1977) 'Education in Schools: A Consultative Document', states: "Our society is a multi-cultural, multi-racial one, and the curriculum of schools must reflect a sympathetic understanding of the different cultures and races that now make our society ... the curriculum of schools must reflect the needs of this new Britain." The Green Paper has emphasised the importance of all schools giving their pupils an understanding both of the multi-ethnic nature of British society and Britain's place in an inter-dependent world. It stresses that: "We live in a complex world and many of our problems in Britain require international solutions. The curriculum should, therefore, reflect our need to know about and to understand other countries and people." Obviously, languages spoken by different people are vehicles for such mutual understanding. The linguistic diversity is one of the most important features of Britain today.

As we always have lived, and will always live in a plural society, we need to examine the aims and objectives of the mainstream curriculum in order to enable all pupils to understand:

(i)   the nature of our plural society;
(ii)   how to gain from the benefits of cultural and linguistic diversity;
(iii) how to cope with and reduce the conflict and the tension inherent in such a society. Otherwise such conflict and tension can have disastrous effects on social harmony. The 'race' riots in Nottingham and at Notting Hill, London, in the 'fifties and the eruption of riotous tension in the British cities in the 'eighties are only a few examples of such conflicts.

The philosophy of multi-cultural education necessitates the making of far reaching changes in the school curriculum. The translation of that philosophy into a workable and effective programme poses many problems, not the least of which is the elimination of existing confusion which surrounds the concept of multi-culturalism. Verma (1984), in a recent publication 'Race Relations and Cultural Differences' states that: "Terms without clear-cut meanings have blind-alley implications taking us away from moral and social realities and leading us to conceptual confusion". He points out that one such term is "multicultural education with a number of meanings which vary from one society to another". He writes that use of other apparently synonymous terms like 'multi-racial' 'multi-ethnic' and 'multi-lingual' education in Britain, Canada, the United States, Australia and, more recently, Sweden, have led to confusion particularly in the classroom.

Some teachers assume that 'multi-cultural' education refers to only what needs to be done in order to meet the special needs of pupils from the ethnic minority groups — especially language support for bilingual children in learning English as a Second Language. Some imply that this includes ways of getting to know ethnic minority pupils in terms of their family backgrounds and cultures, and at the same time of supporting their self-esteem and cultural identity. There are some who see 'multi-cultural education' as something for all children in all schools laying the emphasis on ways of revising the whole curriculum to reflect a global perspective rather than the traditional Eurocentric focus. Verma (1984) in his paper 'Multi-Culturalism and Education' strongly reiterates this theme: "There is then, a need to generate a firm frame-work of **inter-culturalism** in education, looking not only on the nature of ethnicity, culture, and power in relation to a changing social structure in which children of all ethnic groups have new and changing needs, but also at an eductional philosophy, method and practice which will be international, fostering interaction and understanding between ethnic groups both within and between different social systems across the world."

The professional bodies representing teachers in Britain have also shown their support for educational practice appropriate to the changing needs of British society. In 1978, the National Union of Teachers, in its document 'All Our Children' strongly argues the importance of all schools giving consideration to the implications for their curriculum of a wider multi-ethnic society. It has stressed that: "We live in a multi-racial society. Although this fact is self-evident, it has taken the agencies and institutions of our society some time to awaken to its implications for social and educational provision . . . This concern does not extend simply to schools in areas of great cultural diversity; It includes schools all over England and Wales." Viewed in these terms, it is apparent that current developments are scant, patchy and haphazard. The label of multi-culturalism is being used in a fragmented and superficial way at all levels from primary to higher education without regard to the relevance of particular strategies to the needs and aspirations of the overall community (Verma, 1984). Eggleston (1983) writing about 'ethnic naivety' urges teacher educators in their approach to multi-cultural education, to avoid premature emphasis on difficulty, differentiation and disadvantage especially when they are presented in a theoretical way seems unrelated to the classroom. The conceptual confusion surrounding the philosophy and practice of multi-cultural education is not peculiar to Britain alone. As Gibson (1976) and Chipman (1980) have noted that this problem of untested and sometimes unsupportable assumptions regarding goals, strategies and outcomes, seems a universal one. In the British context the lack of a national policy for multi-cultural education has hindered progress towards a truly plural society.

One of the many functions of the school is to develop in pupils an understanding of the society in which they live. Given the multi-cultural nature of British society, the curriculum in schools ought to reflect the differing backgrounds and cultures of its members. The mere inclusion of elements such as Black Studies, Asian Studies and Ethnic Studies etc., in the curriculum is unlikely to be satisfactory to promote a harmonious and well-integrated society. Rather, the development of such a society depends on the fostering of tolerance, an acceptance of different customs and traditions other than British, and above all an understanding of the nature and often debilitating effects of prejudice in our society.

As far as ethnic, cultural, religious and linguistic aspects are concerned, multi-cultural education ought to be concerned with promoting the maximum educational potential of all pupils. It has to meet appropriately and effectively their particular needs in terms of maximising their educational performance and developing their understanding of the plural society in which they live.

Events during the last decade in various parts of Britain have contributed to the need for a cogent response to the cultural and racial diversity of society (Scarman, 1981). Even without such events, however, there would still have been a need in schools and other educational and social institutions to formulate a coherent approach to this aspect in order to equip young people effectively for life in a multi-cultural society. Multi-culturalism should not be confined to a liberal ideology as reiterated by Verma (1984). He writes: "The term 'multi-culturalism' today comes rapidly on the lips and pens of those who wish to be seen as 'progressive' in the field of education, media, social welfare and police/community relations".

Therefore what is at issue is not just the provision for special needs such as teaching English as a Second Language or supporting children's bilingualism but a more fundamental development in the curriculum reflecting the pluralistic practice in all aspects of schooling. This is an area which has received little attention until recently and developments have tended to rely on local and individual initiatives. While one can come across several examples of goodwill and genuine practice, developments in this respect have been rather fragmentory and, in the main, confined to schools with a multi-ethnic intake. If the education service, as a whole, is to respond to the changing needs of a multi-cultural society, a co-ordinated approach is necessary for all educational institutions whether or not they have pupils or students from ethnic minority backgrounds.

Multi-cultural education seems to be confined to 3S's i.e., Samosas, Saris and Steel-bands (Newsom, 1983). Its success depends not on the mere promotion in schools of fringe activities such as Asian festivals and multi-national costume displays, although such activities have a part to play in contributing to an awareness of cultural pluralism in a wider society. A multi-ethnic dimension should permeate both the everyday learning experiences of all pupils and the thinking of all those responsible for formulating policies. Thus, it presents a new challenge to researchers, administrators, and educators to make provisions for such inter-cultural experiences.

Some schools, particularly those with no pupils from ethnic minority backgrounds, may question the relevence of this concept to the needs of their pupils. Some may even wonder whether, at a time when schools are subject to so many pressures such as the new GCSE examination and the proposed National Curriculum, they can find the time and the resources to carry out such an exercise. There are others who believe that the British ethnocentric approach is the best solution to present problems, that is, they wish to take the assimilationist standpoint. Confirming this assimilationist orientation, Bagley and Verma (1982) in their study 'Self-concept and Long-Term Effect of Teaching about Race Relations in British Schools' write about the opinion held by the majority of the indigenous population who believe that the British Way of Life is the best and that the newcomers should conform to this. This is a dilemma of British multi-culturalism. By implication, any significant effort towards a multi-cultural curriculum would require a measure of attitudinal change on the part of the Department of Education and Science, the Polytechnics and Colleges Funding Council (P.C.F.C.) the Manpower Services Commission, universities, Local Education Authorities, Examination Boards, colleges and school governors, the community and the teachers along with many other agencies and educational bodies.

Despite the caveats which have been expressed above, and the need for some form of attitudinal change, few educational establishments are likely to argue with the basic principles under discussion. The following extract from the National Union of Teachers policy statement (1983) 'Combating Racism in Schools' reinforces this view:

"Teachers should show by their own attitudes that cultural diversity is welcomed in schools; this can be done by adopting a multi-cultural curriculum which does not contain racial stereotypes and is not narrowly ethnocentric; by according status to minority group languages in our schools, in the curriculum and in notices and by messages sent home, by assemblies and displays of arts which represent other cultural values and faiths. Even more important, teachers should overtly show that they value the achievements of their ethnic minority pupils, and should have just as high expectations of their academic standards as they do of their other pupils."

It goes on to say:

*"Only by adopting such a positive stance by using opportunites to replace ignorance with factual information about minority cultures and the reasons for immigration to this country, teachers will show that they are actively anti-racist, thus countering the charges of 'unintentional racialism' levelled at the teaching profession (**Also see Rampton, 1981; Swann, 1985)**...only by examining their own attitudes will they be properly equipped to combat racialism in schools and the Union will continue to support its members through dissemination of its positive policy on multi-ethnic education, without which sanctions will be ineffective. A curriculum which celebrates multi-cultural awareness and encourages positive attitudes towards different ethnic groups is the other side of the coin".*

The general aim of multi-cultural development must be to foster respect for oneself and others in the context of an educational system and society which adhere to the values implicit in the principles of equality and opportunity. This may require:

a)   the fostering of mutual tolerance among different cultural, ethnic and linguistic groups;

b)   the inculcation of fairness and objectivity in our dealings with and treatment of all the members of a society;

c)   an understanding of the nature of prejudice of the dominant group towards the subordinate groups;

d)   an awareness of the importance of personal identity to individuals belonging to different groups.

These aims can be achieved in general by developing a quality of open-mindedness which encourages:

i)   an active awareness of others points of view in relation to different social problems;

ii)   a willingness to explore others points of view for the same;

iii) a readiness and ability to distinguish facts from personal opinions and stereotypes;

iv)   an awareness of the importance of relevant reasoning, knowledge and information for the opinion forming process;

v)   a willingness and ability to discover evidence before making judgements;

vi)   the readiness and abilty to evaluate such evidence;

Given the right kind of social climate and carefully planned educational practice the above broad aims may be achieved by adopting the following strategies that will enable young people:

a)   To know about the customs, values, beliefs and languages of different ethnic minority groups mainly represented in Britain and, particulary of those forming the local community.

b)   To know the reasons for the presence of different cultural and linguistic groups in the United Kingdom and particularly how the local community has come to acquire its present ethnic and social composition.

c)   To be able to evaluate one's own culture objectively in relation to that of others.

d)   To be able to recognise stereotypes when they occur in what one does, hears and reads.

e)   To recognise the uniqueness of each individual human being.

f)   To appreciate the underlying humanity we all share.

g)   To accept the principles of equal rights and justice.

h)   To value the acheivements of other cultures and nations.

i)   To accept strangeness without feeling threatened.

j)   To accept and appreciate that Britain always has been and always will be a multi-ethnic plural society.

k)   To appreciate that no culture or language is static and that constant mutual accommodation is required for all cultures and accompanying languages which are part of an evolving multi-cultural, multi-lingual society like Britain.

l)   To be aware that there is prejudice and discrimination in society and to understand the historical and socio-economic contexts which have given rise to this.

m)   To appreciate the possibilities of developing multiple loyalties towards different groups of a society.

n) To be aware of the virtues of various cultures, and of what man is capable of, and to recognise points which are common to different cultures, religions and languages.
o) To be able to read, write, talk, listen, and think effectively and efficiently in English and other languages.
p) To develop a positive self-image and confidence.
q) To develop confidence in ones own sense of identity.

Some schools would claim that they already incorporate many of the objectives listed above in their schemes of work. However, in order to adopt a multi-cultural, multi-lingual curricular approach as a major policy priority, steps will have to be taken to monitor and evaluate, so far as possible, that these objectives are reflected across the whole curriculum.

Multi-culturalism and Multi-lingualism in Britain:

There is an apparent need for the establishment of 'norms' if there is to be a suitable development in educational practice so that it can meet the needs of a plural society. At the same time evaluation is necessary of the actual progress being made in the field of positive multi-cultural development. The gradual acceptance of the fact that Britain is a multi-cultural, multi-lingual society may be an institutional response to a long-standing social reality. Perhaps the multi-racial demographic structural development during the recent decades also stirred the conscience of politicians and educationalists prompting them to respond to the changing demands and needs of British society. This response occurred long after the arrival in Britain of people with different cultures and languages. When the assimilationist model proved unsuccessful in absorbing the new minorities, the multi-cultural, multi-lingual model was put forward. The 'assimilationist model' is one of the concepts advocated by contemporary sociologists and educationists to deal with the diverse components of the population of a society. 'Integration' and 'pluralistic development' are other models in the context of social and educational progress of diverse groups of society. Some assimilationists believe in the complete absorption of minority cultures and languages into the dominant culture and language by the passage of time. The Huguenot culture, for example brought to Britain by eighteenth century refugees gradually filtered into the mainstream British culture (Mason, 1966). However, this sort of process operates like a steam-roller and has little regard for the cultural and linguistic identities and sensitivities of those on whom it operates.

By the mid-'sixties there was a new definition of social aims, i.e., 'equal opportunity accompanied by cultural diversity in an atmosphere of mutual tolerance' (Jenkins, 1966). There began a shift in thinking and policy making, away from the 'assimilationist' approach towards one of 'integration'. A limited positive action took place by the creation of the Race Relations Board and the Community Relations Commission. The year 1976 saw a new Race Relations Act and a reappraisal of the whole situation. The Race Relations Board and the Community Relations Commission were merged into the new Commission for Racial Equality. The Government's White Paper (1975) noted that strengthened anti-discrimination legislation was not sufficient. It pointed out that a more comprehensive structure was needed to deal with the related and at least equally important problems of disadvantage associated with being a member of an ethnic minority. The White Paper emphasised that the policies and attitudes of central and local governments were of critical importance in this respect. It suggested that a broad strategy was necessary to combat 'a cumulative cycle of disadvantage' exacerbated by racial discrimination whereby 'the entire groups of people are launched on vicious downward spiral of deprivation'. The disadvantage and deprivation are perhaps more true in the educational context and this was confirmed in the **Interim Report of the Committee of Enquiry into the Education of Children from Minority Groups** (Rampton, 1981).

The dilemma lies with British Society which finds it difficult to accept those people, cultures and languages which are foreign particularly if they happen to be non-European. Account has to be taken of the racialism present in British society when considering the advance of multi-culturalism. Multi-culturalism in Britain was mistaken by many as a 'compensatory' measure to alleviate the educational and linguistic deficiencies of children from minority groups (Anderson, 1969; Kagan, 1969). The responses of academics, government, local authorities and head-teachers reflect this 'compensatory' or 'deficient' notion of multi-culturalism put forward by some theoreticians. A progressive philosophy of multi-culturalism for the whole society at all levels is long overdue. The negative attitude of the mainstream society to foreign languages and cultures may have serious consequences for the children from ethnic minority groups. A case study conducted by Alladina in 1979 indicated that speakers of minority languages in British schools suffered psychologically, socially, academically and linguistically. This may be due to the fact that there is a lack of cohesive official policy to support home languages of those from the ethnic minorities. This has also been the concern of recent educational research in North America, Australia and Europe (e.g. Lambert and Tucker, 1972; Swain and Cummins, 1979; Garner, 1981; Smolicz, 1980 and 1981; Cummins, 1978(c); Skutnabb-Kangas and Toukamaa, 1976 and 1977).

British Prologue:
Starting from the arrival of Anglo-Saxon, Nordic, Roman and Norman newcomers, there has always been inter-penetration and co-existence of languages and cultures in Britain. The language of the rulers and its imposition through political and economic power, and linguistic and

cultural domination, produced what later became the English language and culture. The expansion of English society in Britain made the Celtic languages of Ireland, Scotland, Wales and Cornwall the languages of the ruled and English as the language of the rulers. Although there were always families who spoke a Celtic language in their homes, it is only for the last twenty years that these languages (i.e., Irish, Gaelic, Welsh and Cornish) have been given recognition in education and local governments. Broadcasting time and space have been allocated to them. Today, Cornish is a relic language with only about 300 people who can still speak it.

The arrival of the Jewish people and later on of East European refugees, right up to the Second World War and after, brought many languages and cultures to the shores of Britain, However, the trend so far, has been the attempted assimilation and integration of these groups of people along with their diverse languages and cultures into the mainstream language and culture. The significant factor has been the possibility of assimilating these particular groups because of the homogenous racial dimensions. In most of these cases, the maintenance of languages and cultures was in the realms of sub-cultures. The British interest in languages other than English is a recent phenemenon and it should be seen in the light of growing political, cultural and linguistic assertions by groups of people in many parts of the world. They have been pressing for proper recognition to be given to the legitimacy of their languages and cultures. For instance, Romany the language of the gipsies or 'travellers' as they are called today, had been accorded, until recently, only the status of an argot.

In the 'fifties, people from the British colonies and ex-colonies started coming to the metropolitan areas of Britain in search of employment. Some came for further and higher education and eventually decided to settle here. People from India, Pakistan, Bangladesh, the Caribbean Islands, East and West Africa, Cyprus and the Far East differ culturally and linguistically from one another. Each of these groups has its own attitudes and experiences in relation to the English Language. The one common denominator of their experiences was that English was the language of the ruler, the language of education and the educated and that it had status and power. Their own languages had been treated (by the British rulers) as inferior to English. For example, an arrogant English baron ridiculed the Indian languages in his minute-book by asserting that the whole shelf of Indian vernacular literature is not worth a single book in English (Macaulay, 1856). Even now the newcomers' languages are seen as irrelevant. They are ridiculed and are considered as a hindrance to the integration of those who speak them.

However, if languages are socially relevant and have social functions to perform, they should continue to be used. They have what is called 'linguistic vitality'. This is precisely what is happening in relation to homes and communities. Adult speakers of such languages presented no serious problems on the factory floors and at work places where their menial labour was in earnest demand (Brown, 1970), but their children seem to have become a 'problem' for schools and education authorities. If the children come from a different language background, there is said to be a 'linguistic mis-match' or a 'linguistic interference' (Darcy, 1953; Macnamara, 1966 and 1967, Tsushima and Hogan, 1975).

During the 'sixties and 'seventies, efforts to deal with the situation ranged from putting those children in reception classes or concentrating them in one school, i.e., 'ghettoisation', to spreading them out to many schools, i.e., 'bussing' (Ministry of Education Circular 7/65; Boyle, 1965). In these reception classes, very often the teachers had no idea of these children's linguistic, cultural, social and psychological backgrounds. In the schools the ethnic minority children are considered as a main cause for a decline in academic standards. There is insufficient support for their educational progress in an atmosphere of equal opportunities. It is not surprising that a large number of these children are being labelled as 'Educationally Sub-Normal (ESN)' and are consigned to special schools with all the attendant undesirable social consequences (Coard, 1971;. Tomlinson, 1981). This is particularly true with children from a West Indiam Background. Their variety of English is considered as 'bad English' (Rosen and Burgess, 1980; Rampton, 1981). Their Creoles and Patois, the home languages of many Caribbean families in Britain, are dismissed as being no language at all (Whittingham, 1982).

The entry of Britain into the European Economic Community provided opportunities for a large number of Italian, Portuguese, Spanish, Greek and North African people to come to Britain in search of employment and in pursuit of business and commercial interests. Obviously, many of these groups wish their children to learn their mother-tongue for a variety of reasons. Firstly, they want to keep in touch with their home-lands. Secondly, they may hope to return to their countries. Finally, they wish to maintain their languages and cultures within their own homes and communities. Most of them arrange private tuition at their homes; some organise themselves in the communities to teach their languages and cultures through religious instructions while others receive support for such programmes from their own governments (Alladina, 1982).

It is clear that minority languages have relevance, vitality and social functions to perform both at domestic and community levels. Yet no satisfactory provision has been made for teaching minority langauges within the mainstream education. Thus, the present system of education has denied minority languages the recognition and the social status necessary for a pluralistic development. The linguistic and cultural minorities in Britain receive negative attributes from the national politicians and policy makers. For example, the Prime Minister during a national broadcast speech expressed her fears lest the British culture and values be 'swapped by people with different cultures' (Thatcher, 1978). A similar view was expressed by the then Labour Party Whip, Robert Mellish (Sivanandon, 1982).

The two major political parties in Britain still have public debates on restricting immigration despite the fact that the figures show that in the last ten years more people have left Britian than have entered. Politicians have also made racialism respectable by discussing at their conferences the motions to stop immigration and to encourage repatriation (The Conservative Party Annual Conference, 1983). Given the climate, it is not surprising that 'racial disharmony' in Britain still exists. It is in this context that multi-culturalism has to progress. Some sociologists and educationists put forward the pluralistic model of multi-culturalism and multi-lingualism in response to the failure of the assimilationist model. At the same time other theoreticians and policy makers do not seem to offer whole-hearted support for the minority cultures and languages particularly the non-European ones. The ethnic minority groups in Britain have adapted themselves to the new environment and are making further adjustments to life within a multi-cultural, multi-lingual society. Multi-culturalism and multi-lingualism are concepts to which British society seems to find itself difficult to adjust.

It should be pointed out that the deficiency theory of multi-culturalism and multi-lingualism, is still in the minds of some writers. They assume that intellectual, psychological, and social deficits of minority groups hinder their educational achievement (Putnam, 1961; Shuey, 1966; Eysenck, 1971 and 1973; Jensen, 1973). The concepts of multi-culturalism and multi-lingualism have not yet received sympathetic attention from education policy makers. This can be illustrated by the responses of the three important groups in the British educational field concerning the teaching of 'community languages' in schools and colleges.*

Institutional Response:
a)   The Headteacher: In the British Education System, the headteachers have power, authority and freedom to influence the curriculum contents of their school. French, German, Spanish and Russian languages have traditionally been offered in the school curriculum. These languages are seen to have had immediate economic benefits. This may not have any bearing upon the educationally enlightened ideas as expressed by Goethe and endorsed by Vygotsky (1934) that:

> *"Success in learning a foreign language is contingent on a certain degree of maturity in the native language. The child can transfer to the new language the system of meanings he already possesses in his own language. The reverse is also true – a foreign language facilitates mastering the higher forms of the native language. The child learns to know his language as a particular system among many, to view its phenomena under more general*

*The term 'community language' is proposed because 'mother-tongue' or 'home language' has failed to take into consideration the question of a variety of languages, the standard form of languages, the appropriate register, the relationship between dialects and languages, and a variety of scripts used for a particular language and so forth.

categories and this leads to an awareness of his linguistic operation."

Goethe believed that, "He who knows no foreign language does not truly know his own". The attitudes of headteachers in British schools with regard to minority languages vary from total rejection of a child's mother-tongue to gradual and, in some cases, grudging acceptance by allowing it to be taught after school hours (Saifullah-Khan, 1980; Alladina, 1982). There are very few schools in Britain that have introduced Asian languages or support West Indian Creoles and Patois in their time-table.

b) The Government: The Council for the European Economic Community (E.E.C.) on 9th February 1976 in its resolution on Education, decided that the Education of migrant workers and their families should be the first priority for consideration and action (Ref. NOC 38-2 IV). On 25 July, 1977 the Directive (Ref: 77-486-EEC) on the Education of Children of Migrant Workers was passed by the Council for the European Economic Community. The first draft of this directive was circulated to the member countries in the same year. The spirit of the document stresses that the maintenance of home languages and cultures is the basic human right of all migrant workers and their children in the E.E.C. Countries. However, after some opposition mainly from Britain, the draft was amended to read that this teaching would be provided according to "the circumstances and the legal systems of the member countries." To begin with, this provision was applicable only to the migrant workers of the member states. The situation is rather complex in the British context. A considerable number of minority language speakers are not 'migrant workers' but are British citizens.

This led to a peculiar situation. A Portuguese, Greek or Italian child can expect to get teaching in his/her home language and culture in any of the E.E.C. countries but a British child who may speak Gaelic, Welsh, Panjabi or any of the minority languages in his/her home could not expect the same privilege under the terms of the Directive. This anomaly was rectified by the D.E.S. (1980) through extending this provision to all minority groups in Britain. In his opening speech at the E.E.C. Colloquium on the Bedford Pilot Project on Mother-Tongue Teaching, Carlyle (1980), then Secretary of State for Education, clarified this further: "First, let me stress that we intend to apply the E.E.C. Directive without regard to the country of origin of the children concerned." Paradoxically, if education in Britain were truly multi-cultural and multi-lingual, this situation would not have arisen. The provision of education that values, encourages and teaches other languages and cultures should ensure that minority cultures and languages are reflected in the teaching syllabuses. For example, Arabic has been available in France for many years. A school in Stockholm provides teaching in Gujrati for six pupils although Sweden is not in the Common Market, nor has it had any colonial contact with Gujrat or any other parts of India (Alladina, 1982). Perhaps this is why Sweden can provide home language teaching for her migrant workers without any legal, economic or moral traumas.

c) The Academics: The majority of educational theorists in Britain come from monolingual backgrounds. A sense of mystification regarding multi-lingual performance and competence is in their minds and this is projected or reflected in their theories (See Lamy, 1974). That is why the existence of other languages and the presence of children from other lingustic backgrounds are seen as 'problems' rather than 'assets'. Many of the theorists and academics seem to be preoccupied with compiling statistics about lingistic minorities. Very little is being done to find ways of making minority languages part of the British school curriculum. Whilst the reality of multi-lingual Britain remains ill-defined, children from minority groups suffer socially, pyschologically and academically. This is highlighted by Alladina (1979) in his research into the question of 'The Relationship Between the Degree of Bilingualism among Gujrati/English School Children and their Academic Performance'. The findings of his study indicate the pressure towards conformity that his subjects experienced from their peer groups; the negative stereotyping that the members of the majority British society hold towards people of other cultures and races particularly towards the South Asian Minorities and their languages; the lack of awareness on the part of teachers and educationalists, the hostility from the host society and constant reminders from the media and politicians that their presence is a 'problem'. The study further suggests that such a climate leads to a decline in the self-image of 'people from other cultures' who are often speakers of minority languages. As a result some children from linguistic and cultural minorities may abandon, conceal and even disown their language and culture.

The issue of identity and self-image among minority group children has long been the interest of the present writer who is a practising teacher. He has been involved in the controversy surrounding mother-tongue teaching provision for ethnic minority pupils. There is some evidence that pupils who are well versed in their native home language use the others more effectively (see Vygotsky, 1934). It should be noted that there is still a poverty of educational research into this aspect of the curriculum. A great deal of lip-service has been paid and cosmetic policies are being tried for supporting minority pupils' bilingualism or multi-lingualism. In the light of the some educational reports (e.g. Bullock, 1975; D.E.S., 1981; Rampton, 1981; N.C.L.E., 1983; the Swann Report, 1985) and the E.E.C. Directive, there is a need to examine the actual progress of multi-cultural, multi-lingual initiatives being made in different parts of the country in order to ascertain the national pattern.

A great deal has been produced in the form of reports, statements and circulars but very little has been done in terms of practice to promote multi-culturalism and multi-lingualism in British schools. It should be recognised that we are moving towards the acceptence of pluralism as a British way of life. Even the British Monarch acknowledged this trend during her Christmas Broadcast Message to the British Commonwealth. She condemned the notion of nationalism and the inward-looking attitude of British society and stressed the need for interdependence in a plural World (Her Majesty Queen Elizabeth II, 1983 and 1987).

Contextual Research and Reports:
A committee was set up by the Department of Education and Science in 1972 to enquire into the teaching of reading and the use of English. The committee's findings received wide publicity (Bullock, 1975). Chapter 20 of this report 'Children from Families of Overseas Origin' is of special interest to teachers and administrators committed to multi-cultural education and its practice. It would be relevant to examine its recommendations and conclusions at a later stage; it was the first government document highlighting the importance of bilingualism and mother-tongue teaching to the children from minority groups.

The second most important landmark was the E.E.C. Directive (1977) on the education of children of migrant workers. It has far-reaching implications for the education of children from ethnic minorities in the United Kingdom.

The Schools Council's Pamphlet 18 — Multi-ethnic Education: The Way Forward (Little and Willy, 1981), Schools Councils Programme 4 Individual Pupils: Supporting Children's Bilingualism (Houlton and Willey, 1983), and schools Council's Programme 4 — Community Languages at 16+ (Broadbent et al., 1983) are other sources for generating discussion of the issues.

Since 1977 a number of projects relating to multi-lingual issues have been commissioned by the Department of Education and Science:
1.   Investigation of the languages of Inner City Pupils (Rosen and Burgess, 1980);
2.   Mother-Tongue and English Teaching for Young Asian Children in Bradford (Rees and Fitzpatrick, 1981-82);
3.   Linguistic Minorities in England: A project to establish the range of linguistic diversity in schools in a small number of local education authorities (Saifullah-Khan, 1983).

The Council for the European Economic Community has sponsored the following British-based projects:

1. Bedford Mother Tongue Pilot Project for teaching Italian and Panjabi Languages (1976-80);
2. Schools Council Mother Tongue Project (1981-1984): Jointly run by the Schools Council and the Inner London Education Authority, the project was to develop material for bilingual teachers of Greek and Bengali speaking pupils.

In addition to the above initiatives, other establishments and individuals have also made important contributions to this field of education. The Runnymede Trust has published 'Briefing Paper: Linguistic Minorities in Britain' (Campbell-platt and Nicholes, 1983), 'Bilingualism and Linguistic Minorities in Britain' (Saifullah-Khan, 1979), and 'Ethnic Minority Languages and the Schools' (Russell, 1980).

The Commission for Racial Equality has produced its own statement 'Ethnic Minority Community Languages (1982)' in additiion to its relevant occasional papers following the E.E.C. Directive.

The Centre for Information on Language Teaching and Research (C.I.L.T.) Reports and Papers 14 'Bilingialism and British Education: the dimension of diversity (1976)', the National Union of Teachers Policy Statement 'Linguistic Diversity and Mother Tongue Teaching' and the current research and studies at home and abroad are further sources for an up-to-date evaluation of the issues and developments.

Reports, directives, projects and research findings on educational issues have implications at local and national levels and even internationally. One would not expect the situation to be any different so far as the community languages of minority groups are concerned. In Britain education is the responsibility of local education authorities. Given the local circumstances and the political climate in relation to ethnic minorities the developments of community language teaching on the whole are far from satisfactory. This study was designed to examine developments in mother-tongue teaching and bilingual education in Scotland, England and Wales with special reference to ethnic minority groups. The terms 'mother-tongue' and 'community language' have been used interchangeably throughout this study.

Chapter 2

Immigration, Race Relations and Education in Britain

Immigration is not a twentieth century phenomenon in Britain; it started with the arrival of Anglo-Saxon, Nordic, Roman and Norman newcomers centuries ago. There has been interpenetration and co-existence of people of different cultures and languages since time immemorial. Britain has absorbed large numbers of immigrants in the course of history. The medieval Jewish population was estimated to be approximately 16,000 i.e., one per cent of the total population, prior to the expulsion order initiated by King Edward 1 in 1290 (Wilson, 1970). In addition to internal migration from Scotland and Ireland, historians have noted the influence of Italian bankers, Flemish and German weavers, Dutch bankers and dyke builders, and Huguenot silk manufacturers (Cunningham, 1969). From the Napoleonic Wars to the late nineteenth century the belief existed that immigrants had, by and large, made a beneficial contribution to British society (Wilson, 1970).

The presence of Negroes in Britain as early as the late sixteenth century is evidenced by a deportation order made by the Privy Council during the reign of Queen Elizabeth I. Under the order a number of "Blackmoores" were expelled because of food shortages. After that the number of negro slaves and domestic servants increased considerably. Lord Mansfield's famous judgement in 1771 in the case of James Somerset indicated an estimated 20,000 negroes in London (Little, 1947).

Immigration from Asia also started on a small scale at the beginning of the nineteenth century when the East India Company employed 'Lascars' i.e., Indian seamen. Some of them were discharged on their arrival in Britain. It was not until the end of the nineteenth century that black immigrants began to settle in the dockland areas of the ports of London, Liverpool, Cardiff and Tyne-side.* It may be argued that because of the small number of black immigrants towards the end of the nineteenth century, there seemed no cause for anxiety at the time.

Governmental policy in nineteenth century Britain has been

---

* The term 'black' is used in this study to denote all non-European immigrants from the New Commonwealth and Pakistan (NCWP) unless specified otherwise. It should be noted that many Asians do not consider themselves 'black' and the West Indians and Africans do not like to be called 'coloured'. These 'terms' have emotive racial under-tones for a variety of reasons.

characterised as being one of laissez-faire. This would be no less true, as far as immigration was concerned. During the middle years of the nineteenth century, the famine and poverty in Ireland led to a mass exodus from that country. Many Irish people went to the United States and Canada but some took the shorter journey across the Irish Sea. The Irish population in Britain rose from 400,000 in 1841 to 727,326 in 1951, i.e., 3 per cent of the population in England and Wales and 7 per cent of the population of Scotland (Rees, 1982). The same source of information shows that the Irish population, at present, constitutes 10 per cent of the British population but it is classified as 'internal migration'. The Irish sectors of British cities such as Liverpool date largely from the last century. Unlike many of the Huguenots, most of the Irish immigrants came from poor backgrounds and were forced to form a sub-stratum of society.

During the early part of the eighteenth century, there had been a number of anti-Irish riots in Britain caused mainly by religious differences but during the nineteenth century discrimination against Catholics gradually ceased. Irish navvies played a major role in building railways and roadways in Britain through the years and even now the Irish people form a substantial proportion of Britain's workforce (Jackson, 1963; Rees, 1982).

The Alien Restrictions Acts of 1914 and 1919 had a marked impact on emigration to Britain. As a result that period saw West Indians migrating to the United States of America rather than to Britain. When American restrictions on immigration were introduced the pendulum began to swing the other way. Strict quota restrictions on Irish migration to the United Staes led to increased Irish migration to Britain. During the Second World War many Irish came to work in Britain's war factories and in post-war era many took advantage of the British economic boom to leave the poorer economy of southern Ireland.

People from the Republic of Southern Ireland might have strong feelings about the division of Ireland into North and South. Most of the people in Britain regard the Irish as part of, or bound together, with the British way of life. Perhaps there is a common purpose for working together. Economic necessity has forced both communities together and the 1949 Irish Act recognises this (See Webb, 1969; Jackson, 1963; Wilson, 1970).

English, Scots and Welsh Catholics accept the Irish people in church, schools and public life on religious grounds. At places of work there is no separation of Catholics and Protestants as is found in Northern Ireland. Atheists and non-religious liberal workers in Britain have understood something of their Irish colleagues' religious ways. This feeling is clearly illustrated when a prominent Catholic Conservative Member of Parliament told his Labour counterpart jokingly: "I preach love and you practise it" (Bidwell, 1976). Irish immigration is an integral part of British society because they have lived in Britain before 1200 A.D. (Jackson, 1963). Yet, they are regarded as aliens by the majority of mainstream British population. In the nineteenth century Irish immigrants were often blamed for the 'plague, pestilence and poverty' in the large cities of London, Liverpool, Manchester and Glasgow. Wherever the Irish congregate in large numbers, they found themselves driven to the poorest accommodation in those areas which acted as a vortex of poverty and degradation (Jackson, 1963). Advertisements for accommodation and employment prospects stating unashamingly "No coloured or Irish need apply" were not a distant reality to humiliate foreign workers before it became illegal under the Race Realtions Act of 1968. In a curious way, this has perhaps helped the development of good relations between Irish and New Commonwealth inhabitants of Britain. They have developed some fellow-feeling because both groups have been stigmatised by the mainstream indigenous population.

The other important immigrant group, the Jews, have been in Britain for centuries, The Board of Deputies of Jews was established as early as 1760 (Cunningham, 1969). However, there was no large-scale entry of Jews to the British Isles until the late nineteenth century when the Russian pogroms of 1881 and persecution of Jews in Central and Eastern Europe forced many to migrate. The period from 1880 to 1905 saw a substantial immigration of Jews, many of whom settled in the East End of London and mingled with other immigrant communities . In 1900 an estimate of the Jewish population in Stepney put the total at 80,000 (Richmond, 1973). The Jewish Pale, stretching through the border lands from Ukraine to Poland and Lithuania, witnessed the exodus of its population with serious results for the social, political and economic structure of the area. These people found it hard to adapt to life in Britain.

Unlike the Irish migrants, the Jews did not speak English and had a noticeably different culture. Many of them were skilled workers but were unlikely to find it easy to practise their trades. As a result they were forced to find different types of work that have since become associated with this group i.e., tailoring, shop-keeping, banking and merchandising. White-Chapel and Stepney districts of East London became well-known for hard working Jewish settlements. Migration from Europe increased and became the source of concern. The antisemitic pogroms in Russia and Eastern Europe forced the movement of Jewish families to the United States, Britain and other countries in Europe. In the East End of London, Jews were the victims of hard labour enduring appalling working conditions (Webb, 1969).

The experience of persecution in many countries of Europe helped the Jews to become anti-racist. One does not have to be a Jew to be aware of the strong arm of Jewish anti-racism in the present struggle. The Jews who came to Britain tended to keep largely to themselves because of local hostility. Their success in business and other enterprises led to outbursts of anti-semitism from the indigenous population as well as other immigrant groups. These feelings were exploited by politicians such as Johnson-Hicks and Evans-Gordon (Steel, 1969). A campaign aimed, mainly, at Jews culminated in the passage through Parliament of the Aliens Act of 1905 to prevent destitute Europeans from entering Britain. 'Dirty Jews' was a phrase much in use as 'nigger' or 'Paki' is currently used. There are many points of similarity between the past antipathy to Jews and the present antipathy to black immigrants (See Richmond, 1973).

By 1910 Jewish immigration had passed its peak and anti-alien feeling had declined. The Liberal Government in Britain adopted a softened attitude towards Jews. The arrival of Jews was followed by the rise of facism in Germany and Austria, and Hitler's accession to power in 1933. First came the exiled Germans and Jews from Germany — they proved useful material for Oswald Mosely in his facist ranting in Britain during the years immediately before the War (Steel, 1969). The exodus continued as Hitler's Nazi armies advanced through Europe, establishing extermination camps and shipping millions to their deaths. By 1943 there were 114,000 civilian refugees in Britain from Europe and large numbers of foreign troops had become attached to the British Army (Rees, 1982).

At the end of the War, there came a large number of Eastern Europeans who chose to come to Britain rather than risk their lives through political persecution in their homelands. Most of them were Poles who had fought with the Allies in the Second World War. They fought in France and had made up General Anders's army in Italy. Twelve thousand of these soldiers settled in the United Kingdom (Steel, 1969). At the same time, many others came to Britain under the government-sponsored European Voluntary Workers Scheme. It included 30,000 Ukrainians, 14,000 Poles, 12,000 Latvians and 10,000 Yugoslavs who had been prisoners-of-war, or who had been forced to work for the German Reich (Bidwell, 1976).

The majority of the European voluntary workers stayed here for only a short period of time and returned to their own countries. In contrast more Poles and their dependants, who feared a return to a 'Stalinised' Poland, stayed in Britain. Most of these European workers found work in the mines, in the woollen mills of the then West Riding of Yorkshire and the Borders of Scotland, and the cotton mills of Lancashire. They endured very hard restrictions and lived under appalling conditions like earlier immigrants (Patterson, 1968). They suffered all kinds of industrial and social discrimination. The fourth session of the United Nations (1945) made strong criticism of Britain's treatment of her European migrants. As a consequence, the British Government took some action to help these these people to adjust to their new environment by providing special language courses. The British economy needed an increased work-force immediately after the War and further immigration was considered necessary. The trade unions were not in favour of such a decision. At the Trade Union Congress in 1946 some hostility was expressed with regard to the presence of Poles in

Britain. This attitude was partly the result of a Stalinist-Russia hangover, and partly because of the fear that foreign workers would under-cut the employment prospects of British workers.

In spite of all the difficulties and the trade union opposition the post war Labour Government worked hard to achieve Polish settlement. The Resettlement Corps was set up and a planned campaign was initiated to find jobs and homes for the Poles in order to smooth the transition from army to civilian life . A large number of Poles remained anti-socialist because of their total distrust of Russia. It was hoped that their children would think not only in terms of Russo-Polish relationships but also of what would best aid their progress in Britain (Bidwell, 1976).

The need for added man-power to prop up the British economy after the war prompted Cyril Osborne, a new Conservative M.P., to call in 1947 for a relaxation of restrictions on the former Italian prisoners-of-wars wishing to return to Britain. By June, 1948, not suprisingly, he changed his tune and began his long campaign demanding the suspension of the European Voluntary Workers Scheme. It was wound up soon afterwards but in the same month the 'Empire Windrush' sailed from Kingston, Jamaica with 400 West Indian passengers emigrating to the United Kingdom. This, perhaps, marked the beginning of a large-scale immigration from the Commonwealth to Britain. In view of the new-comers' visible racial differences, this was considered as a new dimension to the existing immigration phenomenon.

Black people were not new to Britain, indeed they had been present in London and other British cities since the seventeenth century (Little, 1947). When slavery ended in the nineteenth century they drifted into the poorer industrial areas mingling with the local population and existing immigrant communities. When the Colony of Sierra Leone was established in the nineteenth century, some black people from Britian emigrated there. Thus by the middle of the century the black population of Britain was very small well integrated with the mainstream society (Steel, 1969).

Towards the end of the century, black seamen started to base themselves in British ports, thus beginning to reverse previous trends. This process was accelerated by the First World War when some seamen chose to stay in Britain rather than to return to their native countries. The black groups already in the dockland areas received a new infusion of strength and they could be seen once again as separate communities in ports on Tyneside, Merseyside, and in London and Cardiff (Tiger Bay).

In the period between the two World Wars the increase in the numbers of black immigrants was slow and largely the result of black seamen deciding to settle in Britain. However, not all of them remained seamen. No doubt, there was some overt discrimination towards these black immigrants. Disturbances over the employment of black people broke out in Liverpool and Cardiff during the 'thirties and 'forties and these newcomers fell victims of the discriminatory legislation governing the shipping industry (Little, 1947). Initially the trade unions were opposed to the black workers until they had established themselves as a labour force. The right wing forces that emerged in the great depression and during the years before World War II showed a lot of hostility towards the black population. At the same time there was an increasing cohabitation between black men and white women resulting in mixed marriages. In 1919 'Association for the Welfare of Half-caste Children' was established to look after the offsprings of mixed marriages. This association changed its name to the 'Liverpool Association for the Welfare of Coloured People'. A study carried out in 1936 showed that black families in Merseyside were living under the poorest housing conditions and suffered discriminatory treatment in all walks of life (Caradog-Jones, 1946).

The second World War led to a considerable growth in the numbers of black people settling in Britain. One of the contributory factors was the increased war-time recruitment of seamen. They were joined by more West Indians who were recruited as ground personnel for the Royal Air Force or to work in forestry and other war-time industries. There were also colonial soldiers who entered Britain. Although most of their operations took place in the Mediterranean i.e., for the Africans and in the Far East for the Indians, some of them chose to come to England. In transit many black American soldiers stayed in Britain. Therefore, the British population was more likely to meet black people during the war than it had before. Moreover, black people were confined to small areas before the war and now they were able to move about the country. They were no longer an oddity in the eyes of the indigenous population.

Most of the New Commonwealth personnel drawn to Britain by the war effort, returned to their own countries afterwards. The soldiers went home where they were to play a significant role in the emergent political systems of the colonies. Many West Indians returned to the Caribbean hoping that they would establish themselves better at home. In the immediate post-war period, immigration began to build up again. This began with seamen leaving their ships and with stowaways in search of a higher standard of living in Britain. Others came to further their education since colonial subjects considered Britain a centre of culture and learning.

As mentioned before, the sailing of the 'Empire Windrush' from the Caribbean marked the beginning of a new phase of black immigration. Now began a flow of fare-paying immigrants, who, forsaking the traditional avenue of seamanship, sought employment in the wider fields of British industry. This new flow of immigration came from the Caribbean Islands, initially from Jamaica. Those islands had been over-populated for decades and had been accustomed to exporting some of their population to relieve pressure on land and employment. The former outlets to Cuba, the United States, and Central and South America had been closed in the pre-war period. Those who wished to emigrate turned their attention to the United Kingdom. Their education and the values of their society led inevitably to their way of life being modelled on that of Britain. In his study Collins (1957) states "West Indians tend to be oriented towards British society". The chronic unemployment in the West Indies was worsened in the immediate post-war period and there was a steep rise in the cost of living. All these factors contributed to emigration from the Caribbean Islands.

When recruitment for labour began in the West Indies, there was a pool of potential emigrants willing to accept the preferred opportunities. Those who had been in Britain during the war were dissatisfied with the conditions back home, and remembered the better living standard they had enjoyed here. They made up a considerable proportion of the early immigrants. Others had often been in contact with those who had spent some time in Britain and were therefore influenced by the impression of better life in Britain. Moreover, many of the early immigrants from the West Indies had been accustomed to urban life in their homelands and had reasonable industrial experience. Banton, viewing the situation in 1954 wrote that "these migrants were mostly skilled and semi-skilled workers".

The process of immigration from the West Indies continued for some years but there was a perceptible shift in the background of the migrants. Among the West Indian newcomers to Britain, there was a steadily increasing proportion of people from rural areas. This section grew to sizeable number during the 'fifties. After the initial flow of immigrants in the late 'forties, the base in the United Kingdom had been established and prospective West Indian immigrants to Britain could be assured of a warm welcome by their fellow ex-patriates. The West Indians were the first group of black immigrants to come to the United Kingdom in significant numbers in the post-war period. They were followed by two other groups. The West Africans, as mentioned earlier, began to arrive immediately after the war. They came largely from the coastal tribes of Nigeria, the Gold Coast (now Ghana) and Sierra Leone. When they arrived in Britain they tended to concentrate in the same areas as their fellow-tribesmen for various reasons. For instance, they could use the machinery of the tribal network to maintain themselves in terms of social relationships and other cultural activities. Again, once the initial groups had established themselves, the process speeded up and by the early 'fifties a significant number of West Africans had entered the country. Their attitude towards British society was slightly different from that of the West Indians. Whereas the later had a British outlook in the education system, language, and political and social institutions, the former came from a background of colonial society that had its own distinct identity. The impact of colonial rule had, of course, altered African society but it had been unable to destroy it in the way that slavery had destroyed the native heritage of the West Indians (Steel, 1969). Modern education had tended to orientate them towards the British ways of life but they also maintained values of their ancestral past.

The third group of black immigrants consisted of Asians, mainly from India, Pakistan and Bangladesh. There was also small-scale immigration by people of chinese extraction from Hong Kong, Singapore and Malaya, and, more recently, by the so-called 'boat people' from Vietnam. The tight-knit structure of Indian and eastern societies meant that close links were maintained between those who had settled in the United Kingdom and those who were at home. Although there were occasional protests from the indigenous population, Britain badly needed their labour and allowed them in without undue restrictions (Brown, 1970).

Asian immigrants came to Britain for a variety of reasons. Some had tied themselves too closely to British rule in the Indian sub-continent and could not survive its disappearance. This was true of the Anglo-Indians and the Parsees, as well as of the East African Asians (Parekh, 1978). Parekh comments:

> *"Some Asians had acquired love of the British way of life and felt that they would be happier in Britain than in their own country whose physiognomy was bound to alter under indigenous rule. Many, however, immigrated because, like the British and partly because of the British encouragement, they had developed a tradition in search of better prospects. They came to Britain not immediately after the independence of their countries, but several years later when the economic structures of their countries, gravely distorted and lamentably underdeveloped under British rule, offered them little hope for the future."*

The employment opportunities in Britain led to the migration of more and more people from the Indian Sub-continent, mostly from the same areas, and even the same villages, as those who were already in this country. They were usually unskilled and came looking for employment, while seeking to maintain links with the home countries.

There were many differences between these separate groups of immigrants in terms of their ethno-cultural backgrounds, their relation to British society and their motives for immigration. They tended to be grouped together by the British population who knew little of their different places of origin. Moreover, the experience of British rule varied from colony to colony and this gave rise to differing assumptions and expectations as to what life in Britain would be like among the new imigrants.

The position of the West Indians as an immigrant group has already been mentioned. Although their colour marked them out as different, their outlook on life was similar to that of the British (Collins, 1957). They came to Britain with the belief that they would be accepted as an integral part of British society. They spoke dialects of English — though their Creols and Patois are not considered fully-fledged languages in their own right

(Whittingham, 1982). They followed the Christian religion, although of a more demonstrative kind than the relatively sombre British varieties. The heritage of slavery had destroyed their old African traditions and they had been taught to orientate themselves towards the British way of life. As there was no firmly established indigenous society with fundamentally separate traditions in their own islands they were taught to look towards Britain for further progress. Indeed they thought that it was their right to expect favourable or at least equal treatment in terms of opportunities in Britain. Collins (1957) and others noted that West Indians illusion of 'mother country' of Britain was shattered when they met discriminatory treatment on racial grounds from the indigenous people.

The Africans who came over in comparatively small numbers, had a similar position to that of the West Indians, though their indentification with the ideals of the British Society was different. Those who were educated, had received their education through a system which was British orientated. Others who had adopted a religion were usually drawn towards a form of Christianity preached by the British. The heritage of British colonial rule meant that the English Language was fairly widely known among those who immigrated to Britain. Many of them had either come over with the intention of continuing their education or had come from low-grade office jobs that required some knowledge of English language (Hancock, 1979; Patterson, 1968). Their tribal connections proved valuable in preventing any individual from becoming completely destitute, since they could easily call upon relatives or fellow-tribesmen for assistance. This was sometimes formalised by the creation of tribal societies in Britain among immigrants from Ibos, Yorubas and other large tribes (Steel, 1969). The political stirrings in the African colonies and the continued existence of their indigenous societies meant that the African immigrants in Britain were more allied to their home countries. They were not usually prepared to identify themselves with their host society to the same extent as the West Indians. They were, however, to a considerable degree still committed to making a success of their life in the United Kingdom in more than purely short-term economic gains (Wilson, 1970).

The Asians, however, were completely different in their attitudes towards British society. They came from countries which had achieved independence by the time the flow of immigrants began to reach large proportions. Their attitude towards Britian was inevitably different from those whose countries were still under colonial rule. Moreover, most of them came from well-established societies with long histories and highly elaborate cultural and social systems. Their religious traditions were neither animistic nor Christian, but Hindu or Moslem which could not be challenged merely by the impact of Western society. The typical structure of society in the Indian Sub-continent was based upon the loyalty of the individual to the family unit and the community rather than the individual's own role. Therefore, when others came to Britain from the family or the same village, they concentrated in the same area, much as did their West Indian or African counterparts. This tended to strengthen their links with their home countries.

The nature of life in the Indian sub-continent is different from that in Britain. Naturally, the communities from India, Pakistan and Bangladesh that established themselves in Britain continued to maintain their own ways of life. There was a very slow attempt to adapt to the new environment. The South Asian languages were completely alien to Britain yet their development over the centuries was such that they had produced substantial literatures of their own. Thus the need to form any close relationship with the native society was minimal.

Most of the South Asians immigrated chiefly for reasons of employment. They were prepared to take almost any job to earn enough money to return home which was, perhaps, never practical. A considerable amount of what was earned was sent back to their home countries and some of it was used to pay for their families to join them in Britain. Their relationship with British society remained largely on economic levels at the initial stages, in contrast to the attempts at social and cultural integration by some groups of immigrants (Parekh, 1978). If they had not adapted themselves fully to British society they had, at least, tried to accommodate themselves to their new environment.

There were three main groups of immigrants from the New Commonwealth and Pakistan, whose attitudes towards British society differed considerably. The two ends of the scale were marked by the West Indians and Asians. The West Indian wished to establish themselves as an integral part of British society. Asians, on the other hand, had sought to live more in a symbiotic relationship by maintaining their cultures and languages. The Africans fell between the two. These differences in attitudes can be accounted for by an examination of the backgrounds from which they came. There is a tendency in Britain to lump different nationalities and ethnic groups together. Any assessment of the problems of immigrants and their integration in Britain should take into account these differences.

The arrival of immigrants from the New Commonwealth began in the late 'forties and early 'fifties and was marked by a consistent lack of fore-thought or planning by British governments. The legal position was that anyone from the Commonwealth and the Empire could enter the country and it soon became apparent that a considerable number of people wished to do so. However, successive governments in Britain took no action to help integrate or adjust those who had arrived, or even to make them aware of the type of society they had chosen to come to. With the European Voluntary Workers' scheme some action had been forthcoming from the administration, though it was by no means sufficient. No such elementary steps were taken to help black immigrants despite the warnings from sociologists, educationalists and even some members of parliament.

In the last year of the First post-war Labour Government Reginald Sorenson (Later Lord Sorenson) introduced a bill to outlaw racial discrimination and provide for positive action to aid the integration of new-comers. This bill was not given time for debate and fell by the wayside. The Labour Government and its Conservative successors showed no imagination or appreciation of the problems that were building up in the fields of employment, housing, social services and education. There was no central policy for the reception of immigrants at their ports of entry to give them an elementary introduction to the country. There was no help with finding accommodation, even though it was soon apparent that this was a major source of discontent. No extra educational provision was made either for the children who so obviously needed some special tuition to enable them to compete on equal terms with the mainstream children, or for adults who needed language classes. They could not understand those with whom they were working. No help was offered to acclimatise the wives to the mores of British society and they continued to follow entirely different ways of life resulting in tension between them. All this was attributable to a lack of awareness in the mainstream population which a positive policy from the Government might have been able to dispel.

The tasks which the government declined to take up were, therefore, handed on to the local authorities. The local authorities throughout the 'fifties and early 'sixties, struggled to tackle the problems raised by black immigration without any extra financial support or other aid from the central government. In housing, education and social services local councils were faced with a great burden on their services, and one for which they lacked the resources to handle effectively. The political structure of Britain during the 'fifties i.e., Conservative Party's strength at the national level and Labour Party's control of the large towns and cities with most of immigrants compounded the problem. In this connection Paul Foot (1965) stated: "The bulk of immigrant problems fell on the shoulders of Labour controlled local authorities". While these authorites were struggling at the local level, the Conservative Party remained isolated from the difficulties . The propaganda of those within its ranks, who were conducting a virulent campaign against the immigrants was not countered by those who had any real understanding of the nature of the problems (Steel, 1969).

New Commonwealth immigrants, therefore, came in to a country that was not prepared to help them adjust to life in the new society except in a few isolated instances. When they arrived, they were left to their own devices. This strengthened their tendency to turn to relatives or friends who had already settled here. Instead of dispersing gradually over the country, they began to concentrate on particular quarters of the industrial towns. They were forced to establish themselves in the strange environment and find employment with little help from the host society.

Some people came over with specific jobs already arranged for them. This was true, for example, of some of the West Indians who were recruited by the London Transport Board. For others, the finding of employment was a serious problem. There was still a need for more labour in the British economy and immigrants filled up the gap in jobs particularly those of menial nature and/or involving unsocial working hours. There were many instances of discrimination against black people both in terms of employment and promotion. One was the Birmingham Bus Strike of 1954. A trade union official encouraged the men to come out on strike in protest against the employment of black immigrants. The Birmingham Bus Corporation, however, stood firm and the strike soon collapsed. By the autumn of the same year officials responsible for the strike admitted that their action had been a mistake. One of them was quoted in the Birmingham Post (19th October, 1954) as saying "Before the black staff started work with the department, I thought the whole thing a big mistake. I thought they would not be able to do the job. I had been proved wrong!" There have been isolated examples of this nature up and down the country.

When black immigrants began to appear in the labour market, there were examples of different industrial actions too. It soon became apparent to native workers of liberal persuasion that immigrants did not provide a threat to their position. Most of the black workers joined the trade unions and supported their actions aimed at improving the conditions of all workers. Where large groups of black immigrants made up a significant section of the labour force in a particular work place, there was occasionally a continuation of the early suspicions but discrimination in the field of employment tended not to survive the initial period of ignorance. Foot (1965) writes: "In the main, throughout the numerous engineering factories and mills into which the immigrants were absorbed, the degree of hostility and bitterness at work was remarkably small". The same was true of such occupations in the National Health Service as the HEALTH SERVICES which soon came to rely on immigrants. The transport system in the whole country also depended on the black work-force. But this should not imply that there were equal opportunities for employment and promotion in all spheres of life for black immigrants.

It was in other spheres that it became apparent that discrimination was a serious problem. Cyril Osborne was soon joined by other Conservative Members of Parliament in his stand against immigration. In addition to his previous concern with European immigrants, he now decided that black immigration from the New Commonwealth produced a bigger threat to his conception of British society. He remarked that "This is a white man's country and I want it to remain so" (Osborne, 1961). This was his constant refrain throughout the 'fifties and he preached virulent racialism during the 'sixties. He and another Conservative Member of Parliament, Ronald Bell, have been singled out for praise by the National Front, the latest of the right-wing extremist groups to have emerged on the British political scene (Frost, 1965). The Spring 1968 edition of the periodical 'Combat' called them "the only two members of Parliament who have consistently opposed the policy of mass immigration and warned of its dangers".

In 1950, for example, Cyril Osborne, called upon the Home Office to provide separate figures for black immigration. The numbers game of black immigrants will be discussed later in this chapter. Osborne launched a campaign in 1952 calling for controls on New Commonwealth immigration. He did not receive much support in the House of Commons, nor from the Government. Nevertheless, there were areas in which his ideas were well received. Although most of the Tory local councillors did not accept his ideas, those in the West Midlands boycotted the Commonwealth Welfare Council for the area from the time of its inauguration in 1955. A Conservative Councillor in Birmingham campaigned openly on an anti-immigrant platform from 1956 (Foot, 1965) and it had a devastating effect in the field of race relations of that city.

It was not only in the overt political field that resentment towards immigrants was shown. The problem of housing was made worse by the refusal of many building societies and banks to grant mortgage facilities and loans to black immigrants. The people who were prepared to work hard to improve their social position and wanted to move out of the areas of bad housing were hampered by the lack of credit facilities, more freely available to others.

In schools the immigrant children with limited knowledge of English language, and of different cultural backgrounds were faced with problems at the more basic level than many of their parents. The education system was geared to teach attitudes towards the colonies in line with the imperialist tradition. Stories of the savagery of the black tribesmen that had no relevance whatsoever to the immigrants' new surroundings in Britain, played a damaging role. This created stereotypes and negative images of the Africans in the minds of mainstream youngsters who had never come into contact with black people before. Banton (1954) writes of the impact this caused on a Stepney black child and his relationship with his class-mates. He also describes the effect which a short period of teaching by student teachers from the West Africa had created among the native children.

Outside schools the mainstream children lived in an environment in which their parents continued to express their own prejudices, born out of ignorance, but reinforced by their impression of the immigrants around them. The situation of 'Contact and Prejudice' under these circumstances in an inter-racial community is confirmed in a study by Verma and Bagley (1979). The lack of government action, therefore, created a situation in which immigrants were forced to live under conditions that strengthened prejudice against them. Had there been a concerted positive action to aid immigrants in their attempt to adapt themselves to British society, there would not have been the undesirable growth in overt and covert prejudice and discrimination that characterised the 'fifties and thereafter (Banton, 1970).

Had the Government taken a firm stand, it might have been able to create a favourable climate for the integration of the newcomers. Leaving the immigrants' problems to the local authorities represented an unjustifiable shuffling of the responsibility that should have been taken up by the central authorities. The overt discrimination that became more apparent in the 'fifties (e.g., The Birmingham Bus Strike), can largely be attributed to the previous record of indifferences on the part of the Conservative Government and the weak attitudes of the Labour Party in drawing attention to the problem. Warnings were given repeatedly from different sources (see Foot, 1965; Steel, 1969). For example, from 1953 onwards Fenner Brockway, Member of Parliament, attempted to introduce legislation every year to outlaw racial discrimination and incitement. He called upon the findings of researchers like Banton (1954), Montagu (1952) and Merton (1949) to show the existence of the problem. Politicians, in general, chose to adopt an ostrich-like attitude. When they began to wake up, they acted in a painfully slow manner, and rarely with the wisdom and calm that the challenge demanded.

Immigration and Race Relations:

British society has been based upon the perennial arrival of different groups of immigrants. An examination of British history reveals that over the past two thousand years there has been steady inflow of people from different countries with different ethnic, religious, linguistic, cultural and racial backgrounds. Therefore, Britain of today can be described as a multi-ethnic, multi-faith, multi-lingual. multi-cultural and multi-racial society. The process of immigration has continued up to the present time. Although there are legal restrictions on new arrivals, this process of immigration seems likely to continue. After the Second World War a great man-power shortage notably in the Health Service, agriculture, coal-mining, engineering, building and textiles provided the opportunity to issue work permits to European Voluntary workers. The work permit scheme did not apply to the subjects of the British Commonwealth countries. The latter were allowed to enter Britain freely to find work, to settle and to bring families under the British Nationality Act of 1948. A substantial number of immigrants from the Caribbean territories, Guyana, the Indian Sub-continent, Africa, Malyasia, Singapore, Hong Kong and the Far East have entered Britain since 1948.

As outlined earlier the increasing number of newcomers from the new commonwealth led to social unease about immigration. There were continuous political manoeuvrings of an unusual nature seeking to bring about the imposition of controls (Cyril Osborne and his colleagues, 1961).

These political protests led to the passing of the Commonwealth Immigration Act of 1962. It was the first measure to control the black immigration to Britain marking the racialist policies of the British Government of the time. It was confirmed by Gaitskell (1962), then Labour Party Leader:

"There has been over the years . . . an almost precise correlation between the movement in the number of unfilled vacancies, that is to say, employers wanting labour, and the immigration figures. As the number of unfilled vacancies goes down, the immigration goes down, and as the number of unfilled vacancies rises, the immigration figures go up. It is, in my opinion, an utter and complete myth that there is the slightest danger or prospect of millions and millions of brown and black coming to this country. Anyone who is trying to put that across is only trying to frighten people into believing that".

This portrays the sound economic principle of "demand and supply". He added: "It (the 1962 Bill) is a plain anti-Commonwealth measure in theory and a plain anti-colour measure in practice". He warned that: "It has been said that the test of a civilised country is how it treats its jews. I would extend that and say that test of a civilised country is how it behaves to all its citizens of different races, religions and colours".

In 1969 it was estimated that nearly a quarter million British-born and educated whose phenotypical characteristics or ancestry led them to be classified as part of the 'black' population. According to the 1971 census the total number of immigrants born in the New Commonwealth was 1,157,170, i.e., about 2.1 per cent of the total British population. This figure slightly rose to 1,516,422 in the 1981 Census showing 2.79 per cent of the New Commonwealth citizens in Britain (Registrar General, 1981). They are likely to constitute between 3 and 3.5 per cent of the total population by the end of the century. It is an insignificant number in a real sense and ought to refute the fear and anxiety of racialist propagandists. Nonetheless the presence of different groups of immigrants makes Britain a multi-racial society. Ethnic diversity has been part of countries such as Canada, France, Holland and the United States. Britain at first sight appears to be culturally homogeneous. If the United Kingdom of Great Britain and Northern Ireland is taken as a whole it becomes clear that nationality, language, religion and class have given rise to a considerable diversity (Richmond, 1973). One American political scientist has gone to the extent of describing the United Kingdom as 'a multi-national state' (Rose, 1970).

Do the ordinary native Britons think in these broad terms? The British imperial and colonial past distorts the ordinary Britons' behaviour towards immigrants of ex-colonial origin. They have been prone to unquestioning acceptance of notions suggesting variations in the capacities and potential of people from different races. Their contemporary racial attitudes have been shaped by the colonial experience forged in the crucible of imperialism. As a consequence, a sense of innate superiority, by virtue of being British, has become endemic in the national conciousness. Thus have grown up many Britons nurtured by the press, the literature and the education that have promoted notions of 'being on a civilising mission' and of paternalism with regard to those from other races (Katznelson, 1973).

The situation of 'racism' i.e., the philosophy, ideology or theory of racial superiority or inferiority with their discriminatory implications of racialism, i.e., the practice to reinforce such thinking, can be described in its crude form as institutional and scientific racism (Bagley, 1975). Banton (1977) illustrated an example of nineteenth century's crude racial philosophy. He portrays Charles Kingsley's (1819-1875) views of 'white supremacy' when in 1848 the latter wrote a placard at the time of London riots 'Englishmen! Saxons! Workers of the Great cool-headed, strong-headed nation of England, the workshop of the world, the leader of freedom for 700 years'. At one point he said, "The black is more like an ape than a white man ... Men and races are unequal in nature but equal in Christ. Only by recognising this can a man realise himself". What a narrow view of religion and capabilities of human race! In an address to the Ladies' Sanitary Association he misinformed his audience saying:

"Of all the races on earth now, English race is probably the finest ... that there are congenital differences and hereditary tendencies which defy all education from circumstances. I have seen, also, that certain races e.g., the Irish Celts, seem quite unfit for self-government".

Kingsley's version of the Norse-Saxon race as 'Our Caucasion Empire' ... Our race ... Our fore-fathers were mystics for generation; they were mystics in the forests of Germany and the dales of Norway ...' seems nothing more than arrogant self-indulgence and subordination of races other than the Anglo-Saxon Stock.

Such racist ideas were reinforced by successive writers and thinkers in Britain. The Conservative Government set up a Commonwealth Immigrants Advisory Council in 1963 and in its second report (1964) it included:

"There is a further danger that educational backwardness which, in fact, is due to environment, language or different culture may increasingly be supposed to arise from some inherent or genetic 'inferiority' presumably among ethnic minority children".

It is another example of institutional racism instead of following the positive role of advisory nature.

At this stage it would be relevant to examine the relationship between the host community and immigrants in the context of the above background which is based on the colonial encounter of unequal economic and political power with its educational implications. Colonialism can also be seen from other two dimensions i.e., economics and culture. By its very nature colonialism was basically based on a master-servant relationship of a fundamentally exploitive nature. Colonies were largely suppliers of raw materials and consumers of British industrial products; and the native bourgeoisie played a role subordinate to imperial interests. Not only did colonies remain poor, but also their economic systems, closely tied to that of Britain, were seriously distorted (Parekh, 1978). It is a simple fact that even after decades, and in some cases centuries of colonial rule they were still very poor and underdeveloped when granted independence.

The second cultural factor turned economic subservience into cultural and moral inferiority. A nation cannot subjugate others without convincing itself that it is right to do so, and that it is gifted with qualities that others lack. The British draw a fairly neat contrast between themselves and their subject races. It is clearly reinforced in an Independent Broadcasting Authority's soap opera entitled 'The Jewel in the Crown' (Granada Television, 1984). In this series an English police officer in India (Ronald Marick) tortures an Indian subject (Hari Kumar) by stressing that their relation is based on 'hatred' and 'fear'. One can trace plenty of such examples from the public media, broadcasting and English literature. The British ascribe to themselves qualities the native lacked and declared themselves free from vices and weaknesses which the latter seemed to possess in plenty. Such a contrastive mode of self-definition meant that the British eliminated from their self-image a large class of qualities and attributes. The natives were emotional, like women and children, whereas the British were unflappable. The natives were spontaneous, the British cool and calculating; the natives were tribal, communal and depended on others; a Briton stood on his or her own feet — and so on.

The familiar bourgeois view of individual, suitably sharpened during the colonial encounter gave rise to a view of individual that became the standard by which the British judged themselves and other societies, and worked out a neat scale of society. Since the standard was derived from their own modes of thought and life, the British naturally found that of all people they most closely approximated to it and accordingly placed themselves at the top of the human hierarchy. The Europeans came to be placed below the English. The Asians, pejoratively called the Asiatic people were placed third and the African (negroid) were placed the lowest. Since different people occupied different rungs on the human scale, different values were placed upon them. For example, the lowest value placed upon the life of an African, who could, therefore be bought and sold like a chattel. In contrast the Highest value placed on a Briton's life. By virtue of his or her birth and breeding the Briton was not aggressive and militant like the Frenchman, nor strident and murderous like the German; such attitudes were inconsistent with being British. Thus the character of British racism was calm, arrogant, secure in its self-righteousness and self-confident (Parekh, 1978).

Non-European societies found these ideological definitions of man very difficult to resist. There was some obvious resistance and scepticism in the beginning but it collapsed before the systematic British indoctrination carefully carried out by educational, legal, political and economic means. Parekh (1978) puts it like this: "Once the native's soul was conquered the stage was set for a racist belief that he/she was lacking in those essential qualities that made a person fully human".

Race and Social Development:

Because the term racism is widely used, it is appropriate to explain what is meant by this term only in the context of its use in the present discussion. Racism is not the same as racial prejudice. Prejudice is a partial rejection of a man or woman on the basis of his or her real or supposed, specific or specifiable characteristics (Hartmann and Husband, 1974). For instance, a white person may be prejudiced against a black person because the former thinks that the latter is unintelligent, mean, unclean, lazy, dirty and so on. A black person may be prejudiced against a white individual because in the former's view the latter is selfish, inhumane. merciless, devious, emotionally undeveloped and the like. Since prejudice is based on some assumed characteristics of the victim, it can be countered by showing that he or she does not in fact possess these characteristics, or that these are not really obnoxious, or that he/she can be helped to get rid of them. Racism belongs to a very different categorty. It involves a total refusal to accept the victim as a full human being entitled to the respect and treatment due to a fellow human being. It implies that his or her belonging to a particular race has so corrupted his or her humanity that he or she belongs to an entirely different species (Banton, 1977, quoting Kingsley, (1848).

The term 'racist' would not be used to refer to an individual who believes that mankind is divisible into different races, each one distinctive, without drawing any moral or political conclusions from this, nor is the term used to refer to a person who holds that some races are intellectually or in some specific respect inferior to others. The person holding this view might go on to advocate policies designed to remove their inferiority or deficiency. The term 'racist' is used to refer to an individual or body of people holding the view that some races, however categorised, are inferior not in this or that respect but as human beings altogether, and that, therefore, their interests and feelings do not deserve to be regarded as of equal importance to those of the other superior race. So the term 'racism' should refer not merely to a body of beliefs but also primarily to the type of conduct it generates. At the same time attempts have been made by different writers to differentiate 'racism' and 'racialism' — former as an ideology and the latter as a practice to operate such ideology.

To simplify the concept of 'racism' it can be said that a person who believes that the black people are intellectually inferior, and then goes on to propose discrimination in their favour, is not a racist. A racist person on the basis of such belief argues that they should be treated as less than full human and may be expoited with a clear conscience. It is with these predicaments that one has to look at the immigration of black, brown and yellow people to British Isles with the consequent impact on race relations and overall social developments.

Most people would agree that racism exists throughout the world. The literature concerning race and race relations contains no consensus regarding a definition of the term 'racism'. One writer puts it, "there exists as many definitions in the literature as there are specialists and experts in the field" (Mullard, 1980). Many writers have utilised a concept of racism based upon the notion of racial prejudice at the level of personal feelings (Harmann and Husband, 1974). In this formulation a definition of racism involves two elements. First of all the belief that the world is composed of different 'races' in the sense that the human population can be compartmentalised into different types on the basis of some immutable biological characteristics transmitted genetically from one generation to the next e.g., caucasian, mongoloid and negroid etc. Historically, colour of skin has been taken as the crucial biological characteristic (Tierney, 1982). Secondly, there is the notion that some of these 'races' are biologically inferior to the others, this being manifest in inferior intellectual performance, moral qualities or forms of social behaviour (Eysenck, 1971, 1973; Putnam, 1961; Shuey, 1966; Jensen, 1973). In other words one's potential as a human being is biologically determined according to one's racial membership.

Such discussions of race have entered into day to day conversation to the extent that there is often an implicit assumption that races exist as easily measurable entities. For this reason anthropologists have in recent years attempted to stress the problematic nature of the discussion of race. This point is illustrated by an anthropologist:

"All but a few persons that take it completely for granted that scientists have established the 'facts' about race and that they have long ago recognised and classified the 'races' of mankind . . . It is not difficult to see, therefore, why most of us continue to believe that 'race' really responds to something which exists" (Montagu, 1942).

Montagu's argument is an important one as he emphasises the actual classification of people on this basis of social endeavour. It is social in the sense that races are created by theorists processing empirically gathered data relating to physical differences into some sort of classificatory scheme or social gradation. Some anthropologists, as quoted by Bohannan (1966) have moved away from the anachronistic reliance on phenotypes towards the use of genotypes. These are types of individuals which are described in terms of composition of genes and chromosomes in their cells. He goes on to say: "Physical anthropologists are fast forsaking the phenotypes and becoming qualified geneticists. To do otherwise would be to reduce their science to the level of alchemy".

However, whether using phenotypes or genotypes, researchers come to terms with the fact that human population cannot be sectioned off into neat and discrete categories. It is confirmed by another anthropologist:

"Hence to embark on the discussion regarding the inter-mixture of a number of hypothetical pure stocks is unprofitable, and there is no direct evidence for the existence of 'pure' racial populations. To claim any purity of stock for a living European group is therefore ludicrous" (Firth, 1958).

Thus, a whole range of factors outside the simple biology — geographical, social, religious, cultural, political, economic — has been at work for thousands of years. This is not to suggest that scientific research in this field should be censured but rather proper care should be taken to guard against the politically distasteful use to which such research has been and can be put.

Racism and Culture:

The second element of the popular definition of racism is manifest in the belief that some races are inferior to others. Here racism is considered and viewed as a personal feeling that certain 'races' and their accompanying cultures are inferior as a result of immutable biological factors. This sort of sentiment is illustrated by the following statement:

"It is based on the simple principle of white leadership . . . while every race may have its particular skills and qualities, the capacity to govern and lead and sustain civilisation as we understand lies essentially with the Europeans" (Tyndall, 1977).

Washburn (1966) puts forward the same idea of 'white supremecy'. Banton (1970) argues for a definition which also stresses the element of personal feeling:

". . . the doctrine that a man's behaviour is determined by stable inherited characteristics deriving from racial stock having distinctive attributes and usually considered to one another in relation of superiority and inferiority".

Examination needs to be made of racism as an ideological phenomenon and racism as manifest in the treatment of and status accorded to racial minorities in a particular society. As has already been mentioned, different writers have attempted to draw a distinction between the concepts of 'racism' and 'racialism'. Banton (1970) refers to the 'relative distinction' between racism and racialism made by Nicholson (1957) saying that: "Racism is more often applied to the doctrine and racialism to the practice of that doctrine". This is also confirmed by Rex (1973) who states that "Racism is the doctrine of racial differences between men, and racialism is the practice which derives from this doctrine".

In Britain, the belief in the immutable biological inferiority of black people is in strong evidence within the ranks of certain right-wing groups such as the National Front and the British Movement. Nor can it be said with any degree of confidence that the Conservative Party is entirely free from racism, as defined by Banton (1970) and Rex (1973). Racism shows its unacceptable face even at the Conservative Party Conference where a motion was tabled demanding control of immigration and repatriation (Blackpool Conference, 1983). In 1971 the Chairman of the Sussex Monday Club told the Daily Mirror, "I accept I am a racialist. If you read Mein Kampf you will see it has been wrongly derided. I personally am an admirer of Hitler" (Walker, 1977).

The concept of 'biological inferiority' has been taken further in the form of scientific racism. In the work of Putnam (1961), Shuey (1966), Eysneck (1971, 1973) and Jensen (1973) attempts have been made to show 'scientifically' that apparent differences in measured Intelligence Quotient (I.Q) between blacks and whites in America are the result of genetic factors. I.Q. tests used in this and other contexts have been criticised on many counts and from many quarters. Criticisms range from the technical to the political, from testing and sampling procedures, test and sampling validity to the use and misuse of test data for political propaganda. Critics too have been at pains to point out the degree of cultural and other 'biases' implicit in test construction and which is likely to affect adversely the scores of those not fully versed in the 'mainstream' culture (Bagley and Verma, 1975, 1979; Flynn, 1980).

Another problematic issue is the consistency or otherwise with which policy-makers, politicians and commentators make the distinction between biological and cultural determinants of measured intelligence. Basically, what is meant by a 'culturally based' doctrine is a variant of the 'culture of poverty' concept as suggested by Lewis (1959). According to him black culture is seen as being different/inferior not as a result of genetically determined characteristics, but as a result of members of that group being socialised into specific cultural patterns. Black or brown people thus generate their own different/inferior culture and any negative features of this culture can, therefore, be blamed on these people (Lewis, 1961). In the same way the 'culture of poverty' concept postulates that poverty can be blamed on the poor. It is worth noting that sometimes, although not made explicit, there is a tacit belief in the biological basis of these differences (Lewis, 1966). For instance Enoch Powell (1968) is more concerned with the 'biological basis' of the ethnic minority British-born children when he states: "The West Indian or Asian child does not, by being born in England, become an English man. In law he becomes a United Kingdom citizen by birth, in fact he remains a West Indian or an Asian."

Racism is embedded as a structural feature in British society. One has to look beyond psychological and ideational definations in this context. Hodge, Struckman and Frost (1975) put forward the notion of 'racial domination'. They argue for a definition of racism which goes beyond 'prejudice'. What is required they say, is a definition which embodies a condition whereby those defining themselves as superior also believe that they should put this belief into practice and so create and sustain a set of relationships based on domination and subordination. The harm occurs not only when a group believes that its superiority entitles it to rule and control but also on the prediction of decisions and policies for the purpose of subordinating a racial group and maintaining control over that group. It seems that the problem of racism then, is not prejudice but domination.

One can analyse the validity of the above philosophy in the context of Britain and its minorities. During the colonial era immigration was one-sided. The British migrated to different parts of the world. They were not invited by the natives, they simply stormed their way into other people's lands and turned them into either colonies over which they ruled or made them their new homes to settle. Their relationship with the 'natives' was that of the victor and the vanquished or the dominant and the subordinate. This is the background from which the present race relations are emerging in Britain. They have their historical roots in the development of western capitalism and colonialism. We can relate contemporary examples of racism to the historical fact of British colonialism and it's long-term pervading influence, social and cultural interaction, among different groups. John Rex (1973) has written in this context:

"... The inequalities between men of different nations, ethnic groups or religions, or between men of different skin colours which resulted, were often justified in biological racist theories or some functional equivalent".

The migrant workers have frequently had to contend with widespread hostility and discrimination in Britain and other European countries. The verbal and physical excesses of contemporary right-wing groups represent only the more recent examples of a long and inglorious line of racist reaction. Foot (1965) gives an account of the latest situation, saying that "Since the problem crashed into British politics with the Smethwick result in the 1964 election, race relations in Britain have steadily deteriorated". He stresses that racial differences arising from immigration from the New Commonwealth had in the past been exploited with disastrous results. He also examines what he calls the 'chauvinism, cynicism and neglect' in the Conservative Party's attitude to immigration and exposes the strange somersaults of the Labour Party's policies. He calls for an end to sloppy thinking and vicious propoganda which could present Britain with a racial tension of American proportions. Along with the prediction made by other commentators, (e.g. Parekh, 1978; Little, 1978) about the potential unrest and violence, Foot (1965) was perhaps right in foreseeing the riots of the 'eighties in the cities of Britain.

The emigration figures were also exploited against black immigrants. The figures from Britain of 1971 and 1981 Censuses show the trends of larger emigration from Britain compared to the immigration from the New Commonwealth and other parts of the world. Foot (1965) cites an example of the situation by quoting an extremist, Harvey Jones (1961), Secretary, Birmingham Immigration Control Association:

> *"Emigration figures are rising. Of those I have spoken to, all have told me that their reason for leaving their homeland is that they could no longer live in a multi-racial community. There are now 419 lepers in this country (he means black immigrants). These people could be sitting next to you on the buses handling the same money as you and their children could be going to schools with your children. West Indians are prolific breeders. Soon our children will be getting education on a rota system – in the morning one day, in the afternoon the next. These people do not know the basic principles of hygiene . . . Most of them come to batten off the social services . . . We are harbouring one of the biggest fifth columns in the world".*

This appears to be nothing more than blatant propaganda, born of ignorance and racial hatred. On the contrary Brockway (1965), a Member of Parliament countered the charge in favour of healthy multi-racial developments in Britain.

Considering these contrasting views one can say that the cause of racial prejudice is in the subject, not in the object of such prejudice. It is an irrational, pathological phenomenon, rising from an individual's own inadequacy and resulting in displaced aggression (Banton, 1954). Robb (1968) has described racial prejudice as a 'fulfilment of human need'. Perhaps it is not difficult to find such 'human needs' and inadequacies in contemporary Britain. Racial discrimination, housing shortages, over-crowded schools, inadequate education, insufficient hospitals, inefficent transport service and now the economic recession are certainly not caused by immigration but on the other hand immigrants were the first victims of such inadequacies. Moreover, at the time of economic recession racist ideology can break out in its most virulent form looking for scape-goats.

Any kind of discriminatory situation can lead people to conflict of one sort or the other. Various kinds of conflicts between the immigrants and the mainstream British population have predictably been generated both at individual and group levels. These conflicts have mistakenly been classified under the label of 'cultural conflict' on all occasions. For instance, every time a child displays insecurity or appears to be aggressive, he is diagnosed by social workers, headteachers, judges and others as a victim of 'cultural conflict' or 'educational subnormality' and they hasten to refer him to a special school (Coard, 1971). The experts fell over each other trying to find an impossible answer. What is often referred to as 'cultural conflict' includes a wide variety of situations, some of which cannot be subsumed under its capacious umbrella. Sometimes this cultural conflict is more than intergenerational conflict endemic in all societies. Sometimes it is little more than a rejection of a specific custom, for example, arranged marriages in Asian societies, rather than parents' culture as a whole. Sometimes it is a conflict not between two cultures but between colour and culture. For example, a black or brown child may have fully adapted to the British way of life but because of his colour he is not accepted as British by the white community. Some of the acute cases of the 'so called' cultural conflict arise because of the sense of 'self-rejection generated by the white society's denigration of the immigrants' culture' (Parekh, 1978). The Dewsbury Parents' reaction (1987) was one such example.

Often the dominant white culture encourages ethnic minority children by subtle or not so subtle means to despise their own cultures. They, then, develop attitudes of self-rejection, self-contempt and with them a contempt for their parents. There are countless cases where minority group children at an infant age call their parents "You niggers or damn Pakis" and then run away in tears; where boys or girls of ten and eleven are ashamed of walking in the street with their parents or being heard speaking in their own languages (as quoted by Milner, 1975); where adolescents describe themselves not as Asians but as Italians especially during the 'sixties and 'seventies (Alladina, 1979). Again there are cases of children struggling to wash themselves white, persuading their mothers not to wear saris or their national costumes and asking their parents to give them new names. It seems no more than a crisis of identity. Many of these cases are extremely tragic and cannot be solved unless Britain recognises itself as a multi-ethnic society and takes firm and positive steps to encourage a sense of positive identity in its cultural minorities (Hicks, 1981).

Education of Ethnic Minorities in Britain:

Immigration from the New Commonwealth countries brought the racial/ethnic issues to their forefront for which initial ground has been covered earlier in this chapter. Ethnic minority populations are the direct result of immigration to any country. The history of Britain records the arrival of many ethnic groups i.e., from the Romans, Saxons, Danes and Normans to the Irish, Jews, West Indians and Asians. There are many minority groups within most contemporary societies. Pupils need to be made aware of cultural diversity, something from which they can benefit. Provision ought to be made within the school curriculum in order to offer them experience of that diversity. The school curriculum should reflect the plural nature of society even when there is no significant ethnic minority presence in the immediate locality. If it does not, then it fails to reflect the reality of the pluralistic social development

The phrase 'education of ethnic minorities' raises a variety of questions. In the present research the word 'minority' is used not only to refer to relative numbers but also to 'the conditions of being inferior or subordinate' as discussed before. The term minority could be taken to include pupils with a variety of handicaps i.e., physical, intellectual, socio-economic, cultural, pupils with low literacy, and victims of race or sex discrimination. However, the present study concentrates on the problems of pupils who are disadvantaged through differences of cultures and languages. They include ethnic minority groups which do not possess the background, attributes and skills of the dominant group and are, therefore, distanced from the source of power, status and equality of opportunity.

In recent years, consciousness of ethnic identity and awareness of minority status have been growing rapidly all over the world (Hicks, 1981). In countries like Canada, America and Australia where this has been recurring, the problems have been underscored by politically vocal and even violent protests. In Britain, long-standing assumptions of ethnic homogeneity have been challenged by the growth of separatist political parties (e.g., S.N.P. and Plaid Cymru) and linguistic groups in Scotland and Wales, escalation of sectarian violence in Northern Ireland and the recent eruption of racial tension in Bristol, London and Toxteth (Liverpool). Deeper and more widespread problems underlie these signs on the surface and they recur in different forms in different parts of the world. In his publication entitled 'Minorities', Hicks (1981) has suggested that we should deal with the whole situation in terms of majority/minority issues rather than 'minority problems'.

It should be pointed out that cultural, linguistic, psychological and sociological disadvantages are all closely connected. The cultural and linguistic strands are the strongest themes to emphasise in the context of multi-cultural, multi-lingual British society. Language is not only a clearly visible identifier of many minority groups, but it is also more reliable than physical characteristics. It is also the vehicle by which human beings persuade, manipulate and exercise power over each other. As one begins to find the nature of majority/minority issues, it may be more appropriate to look at the problems presented by the entrenched attitudes of the majority group rather than solely concentrating on the minority groups. We may be aware of the importance of identifying ourselves with a particular group, but often are less aware of the ways in which inter-group perception leads to prejudice., steroetyping, scapegoating and discrimination. It can be easily illustrated by an example of a politician who tries to inflame the sensitive issue of immigration in a racial tone. Pannel (1965), a Conservative Member of Parliament writes:

> *"The fact that the coloured immigrants congregate in urban areas and generally in particular districts, is creating considerable difficulties in educational establishments. Their total ignorance of the English language is posing further difficulties for their speedy integration . The indigenous people want to move their children to other schools under their right of choice provided by the 1944 Education Act. In*

fact it is a sort of Education Gresham's Law in operation i.e., the bad children driving out the good".

He discusses the implications of the Ministry of Education Circular No. 7 (Boyle, 1965) which allows 30 per cent of ethnic minority pupils in any school without changing its character. He argues that:

"It is too high a number and the experience in the U.S.A. shows that if coloured children exceed 15 per cent, parents of white children endeavour to get them transferred ... the placement of immigrant pupils for employment is another serious problem. If immigration were to be suspended, the educational situation would correct itself... In the short term, the danger of all-immigrant schools in some areas is a real one".

The above exemplifies one of the hurdles of racism or racialist practice that ethnic minorities have to overcome. This is an evidence of scare-mongering fostered by an influential and supposedly responsible member of the society.

Reference was made earlier to the scale of racist thinking among ruling nations during the colonial era. The racism and economic exploitation developed during this period did not disappear when ex-colonial people began to arrive in Britain. Perhaps, they were not exposed to the ugly forms of racism to which their ancestors were subjected by their colonial masters. Britain had always maintained an important distinction between its domestic and colonial policies. In the territories of the United Kingdom a tradition of relatively humane liberalism was maintained and insisted upon, whereas crude forms of racism were allowed in relation to the British rulers and their colonial subjects abroad. The laws passed by the British Parliament with regard to immigration have been relatively free from overt racism. This, though, conveniently overlooks the covert control exercised by the machinery of entry certificate issue, taking place in British diplomatic missions abroad (Parekh, 1978).

The racialist attitudes developed during the imperialist era did not decrease simply because the colonial natives, now settled in Britain were also British citizens. They have continued to dominate the white society's approach to the black immigrants' problems. This has been abundantly made clear by various Political and Economic Planning (P.E.P.) Reports, Community Relations Councils and research findings (See Daniel, 1968; Smith, 1974, 1977, 1981). One of the issues with a vocational emphasis is taken up by Verma and Ashworth (1981). They look at the relationship between cultural conflict, self-esteem and the education system among South Asian adolescents in Britain. It is believed that the concept of vocational choice presupposes both opportunity and aspiration. They have documented how cultural, social and personality factors offset the individuals, even in the absence of overt or deliberate discrimination.

"An ethnic minority's estimation of its worth not only influences its members' individual self-image, but also affects its valuation by the rest of the community in the job market and as citizens" (Megarry et al, 1981). It would be pertinent to point out the relatively new feelings of resentment against the black immigrants that have developed over the past two decades and have given racist attitudes a rather peculiar orientation (Simpson and Yinger, 1972). The feeling of resentment has never been clearly expressed, but it is fairly powerful and widely held. Parekh (1978) has described it in these words:

"The coloured immigrants should not really be here and they do not belong here and are an undesirable nuisance".

This feeling can be ascertained from the graffiti slogans 'No coloured', 'Get out niggers' or 'Paki Bashing' etc. The host community thinks that black immigrants stealthily sneaked into the country when the nation was not alert. Once immigrants are considered to have entered the country while the nation was in a chronic state of absent-mindedness, it is implied that they could be sent back home as soon as the nation, thanks to Mr. Powell and his right-wing counterparts' strident alarm bell, comes to its senses. This feeling of resentment of being tricked, hurt and duped which, in fact, has no basis. It has become a rather convenient ideological device and a subtle psychological defence-mechanism with which to cover up the full horror of discriminatory policies and to put the nations conscience at ease (Parekh, 1978).

Whatever the explanation, the fact remains that immigrants from the New Commonwealth and Pakistan have been subject to varying forms and degrees of discrimination and abuse. This is evident in the widespread discrimination in housing, jobs, promotional and educational opportunities and in the persistent refusal to recognise the special and cumulative disadvantages arising from colour (Smith, 1977). It is also true in the refusal to recognise the special educational and cultural needs of minority group children. Indeed, almost every minority demand for the appreciation of its distinctive problems and requirements is resented and construed as a plea for privelege.

According to politicians and policy makers black immigrants cannot have problems because they are themselves a problem. The fact that they bring problems to the authority is itself sufficient indication that they are a problem. Let us take a simple example. South Asian immigrants have a distinct cultural and linguistic heritage which they wish to preserve. There is nothing wrong in their suggestion that at least in those schools where they constitute a substantial number of student population, some provision should be made for the teaching of their mother-tongue, history and culture, and the inclusion of their religion in the daily school service (Ref: E.E.C. Directive, 1977; Carlyle, 1980). Such provisions not only give minority pupils a positive sense of cultural identity but also, what is equally important, secure its recognition from their white peers. While some local education authorities have recognised these simple demands, others have not. The two following fairly typical remarks shed some light on the thinking behind this:

A headmaster, quoted in the School Council's Working Paper No. 50 (1973) says "I do not consider it the responsibility of an English state school to cater for the development of cultures and customs of a foreign nature. I believe it is our duty to prepare children for citizenship in a free Christian democratic society, according to British standards and customs". It is interesting that the headmaster concerned could not acknowledge the simple fact that what he calls foreign customs are not foreign customs to a sizeable section of British society. It is no less interesting that he could not accept the equally obvious fact that Hindus, Muslims, Sikhs, Jews and some others are not Christians.

Consider another remark made by the Director of an Education Authority in his evidence to the House of Commons Select Committee on Race Relations and Immigration (1974). According to him, the immigrants general education problems could be summarised as follows:

i) "Communication — inability to speak and write English.

ii) For Asians — Lack of cultural support at home. Of course, this is understandable. 'Strangers in a strange land'. Their Asian culture means too much to them. However, undeniably it makes the work of the schools difficult.

iii) For West Indians — They present the greatest problem. They make a point of honour of learning West Indian Patois and set out deliberately to emphasise cultural differences. Therefore, they produce some 80 per cent of the disipline problems in schools. The cultural differences are more obvious in bad time-keeping, lack of ambitions, antagonism and a natural tendency towards violence as a solution to their problems."

Similar racist sentiments are reflected in the way black immigrants are referred to in the press and in private conversations. One can see how the truth is distorted: "While a white couple has a large family, black immigrants breed like rabbits; while white immigrants come in large numbers, the black immigrants come in hordes and waves; while the whites living together constitute a community, the immigrants form a ghetto" (Parekh, 1978). When through bureaucratic mismanagement an immigrant couple from Malawi was temporarily housed in a four-star hotel near Gatwick Airport, it was not the local authority concerned but the immigrant couple that was hounded by the press (The Daily Mail, 24 September, 1976), and the immigrant community as a whole became a target for racist attacks and abuse by the media.

The racist resentment does not always take the aggresive forms discussed earlier. It may also take defensive and negative forms which may be difficult to detect. For example, John Sparrow in a letter to the Times (18 March,

1973) asked why it should be considered wrong or racist to want to live with one's own people and to wish to keep out men of different cultures. His question was perhaps well-intentioned and reflected a genuine puzzle resting on at least three assumptions.

First, he assumed that it was right for Britain to invade other lands but not for her colonial subjects to come to Britain. Of course what Britain has done cannot be undone. History cannot be judged in convenient and arbitrary terms. A nation is a historical entity and each generation benefits from the deeds of its predecessors. One cannot therefore accept the benefits accruing from Britain's occupation of other lands and deny the inhabitants of those lands a right to benefit from Britain. Second, when he asked why the British should be critisised for wanting to live with their own people, he rather conveniently uses 'we' and 'the British' to refer only to white Britons. He denied the black and brown their right to have a say in determining national policies for the benefits of majority and minorities. Third, if the assumptions underlying the question was carried out to its logical conclusion, the countries of the New Commonwealth could legitimately object to the British having settled there on the ground that they represented a different culture and an alien way of life. This is a formula for massive international expulsion and unwitting endorsement of Dada Amin's (1971) outrageous hard-line against settlers of Asian origin. On the contrary there is a need both for a policy of non-discrimination and of positive action in favour of ethnic minorities, not with a view to give them privileged status but rather to counteract the results of previous practices of gross discrimination.

Some of the British citizens have their distinct minority cultural and linguistic identity. Whilst playing their full part in British society, they wish to preserve their heritage. This is an understandable desire and can do no harm to Britain. Indeed, as a liberal democratic society we should value and cherish cultural diversity as an enrichment. We should explore what we, collectively, can do to enable immigrant minorities to preserve and enrich their heritage in the framework of a national policy. Once immigrants begin to be considered as part of a British society, it should be possible to deal with common problems in a spirit of good-will and reciprocity of obligation. In this way many issues of mutual concern could be resolved more easily and effectively and without the anxiety of ill-feeling generated by the present 'separatism'. This view is endorsed by Little (1978) when he writes:

"Our schools now are educating black children born in this country, and this is the first idea to put absolutely at the centre of public, political and professional attention. This means that our problems, our needs and our opportunities are to enable people to grow up as black and British. To enable them to develop with a positive sense of their worth and with a sense of their place in this community because this is the community they were born into ... One ought to stop talking about 'minorities'. We are no longer talking about

immigrants. We are not talking about small minorities, we're talking about large slices of the school – or the potential school population in some areas".

The second point — no less important — is the fact of disadvantage. The areas where black people live in large numbers are amongst the most disadvantaged in Britain. The Department of the Environment analysed the 1971 Census and listed the twelve areas of Britain as highest in an index of social and economic deprivation; ten of these were the areas with the heaviest concentration of people from the ethnic minorities. The same report reveals that in the districts where 80 per cent of the black communities live, the instance of over-crowding and of amenity-sharing are three times greater. The black communities live in the run-down areas. Therefore, there is a need to analyse the fact that problems of race and race relations overlap with the problem of poverty in the context of all spheres of life including schools. This is the double bind, or the double jeopardy of minority communities i.e., the issue of colour and culture on the one hand and the issue of poverty on the other.

Kelmer Pringle (1971) conducted a study to establish the proportion of the child population suffering from multiple disadvantage in terms of their social development and educational potential. Calculating disadvantage on the basis of factors like an over-crowded home, level of family poverty, single parenthood, she found that 6 per cent of all children suffered from multiple disadvantage. When Little (1978) carries out a similar study among West Indians in the London area, the figure for the West Indians was 18 per cent — three times the figure for the mainstream population. Therefore, the issues of race relations and education are a combination of the racial issues and the problems of disadvantage, deprivation and poverty (House of Commons, 1974, 1977, 1978; Rampton, 1981; Swann, 1985).

It has been established that one of the main causes for such deprivation, disadvantage and poverty is discrimination (White Paper, 1975). The education system in general and school in particular neglect these issues. The minority pupils are exposed to discrimination and racial prejudice at all stages. Little (1978) in his work on 'Schools and Race' refers to a government inquiry which showed that black youngsters fully educated in this country compared to their white peers (i.e., matched for age, school performance, job aspirations, and for what the teachers expect them to do in the world of work) take four times as many interviews with the careers officer for their placement than the white. This situation is confirmed by further research (Verma and Ashworth, 1981; Ashworth, 1983; Verma, 1986). It showed that employers discriminate heavily against black youngsters.

In addition there is also prejudice and discrimination within schools. 'New Society' published an article in 1978 which suggested that 25 per cent of adolescents in two East End London Boroughs were at that time active supporters of the National Front. This sort of attitudes, beliefs and steroetypes that led them to support the National Front were all in the classroom in the form of books and literature, and the black and brown children are exposed to these. There is a lot of research to suggest that the children are exposed to it at a very young age. One particular piece of work showed that at the age of five certainly, and may be even before that, racial stereotypes were already found amongst children (Little, 1978).

The Schools Council Multi-racial Education Project 1973-76 confirmed this syndrome when Lucy Hodges (1978) reviewed it in her report entitled 'Multi-racial Reality'. In the introduction to this report she wrote, "The most significant feature of this reality is racism". Hundreds of schools were visited in 25 local authorities and the project team spent most of their time working in conjunction with teachers, assessing what the children needed and developing ideas for a multi-racial curriculum. The material was then tried on pupils. The project team's findings highlighted that:

"One of the manifestation of racism is the education system – the under-performance of minority race was a motivating force behind the establishment of the project . . . we have found many schools and teachers around the country reluctant to concede that this is so, either they fear that intervention will be interpreted by outsiders as 'political' rather than 'educational' or because they feel they can achieve nothing against the battery of hostile forces in the wider society".

The report cited the example of a classroom of seven-year-olds from a multi-racial inner-city school who were taken to the sea-side. A local child said to another, "I do not like those Sambos on the beach. They dirty it up". A teacher was asked by a girl "Ganhar says honky houses stink. But it's not true, Miss, is it, that the Paki houses stink?" The authors point out that these examples show an early awareness of race "which in some cases takes the form of open hostility based on a confused version of the facts".

Children also pick up attitudes from teachers. The same report quoted the following incident reported by a teacher: "I was teaching a small withdrawal group of West Indian children in a West Midlands boys secondary school. A senior member of staff passed by the door, paused and looked in. He opened the door, grinned at me and said in a voice loud enough for all to hear, "Excuse me, is this the Dudley Zoo"? Perhaps the most difficult fact for the teaching profession to handle is that teachers themselves may reflect some of the attitudes and beliefs found in the wider community. This fact is confirmed in the Rampton Report (1981) entitles 'West Indian Children in our Schools'. Teachers too, may be prejudiced and may actively discriminate. They may have lower expectations for the black youngsters. Little (1978) refers to an interesting study done by the National Foundation for Educational Research. Teachers were asked how they responded to certain questions about children from different backgrounds. The teachers as a group saw West Indian children as being 'stupid' and being 'trouble makers' — a clear negative stereotype.

So long as the stereotypes exist and are communicated to black children, these will influence their response to the school, their attitudes towards the society and their images of themselves. The extent of teachers' professional knowledge and experience is profoundly important as a determinant as to how well or how badly a child will do. This is what the present investigator has tried to argue. The focus of our attention ought to be the cultural and linguistic needs of minority children in our schools. The school has a responsibility and has a potentiality to do something about these needs which has now been politically accepted. What is not known is how to translate them into positive action. There is some evidence that, so far as the West Indian community is concerned, there is a gross and disturbing level of under achievement among its youngsters (Rampton, 1981). The Swann Committee of Inquiry (1985) has also confirmed this situation drawing attention to the special educational needs of pupils from ethnic minority backgrounds.

The British education system has missed an opportunity to meet the genuine and legitimate needs of minority pupils. If we continue to miss this opportunity we may be sowing the seeds of racial disharmony and racial discontent and certainly reinforcing racial injustice (Scarman, 1981). We are producing situations in which young people leave school unemployed and unemployable. Wasted opportunities mean wasted lives; without justice between groups, harmony is a fiction. Without special educational effort neither justice nor harmony can be achieved; that is both the educational challenge and the warning (Wren, 1977).

An understanding of what is called the 'minority experience' necessitates some prior considerations. What exactly is a racial or ethnic minority group? Is it merely a question of statistics? a group that is numerically in the minority or does it involve other characteristics as well? Wirth (1945) suggests that:

> "We may define a minority group as a group of people who, because of their physical or cultural characteristics are singled out from others in the society in which they live for different and unequal treatment, and who therefore regard themselves as objects of collective discrimination. The existence of a minority in a society implies the existence of a corresponding dominant group enjoying higher social status and greater privileges. Minority status carries with it the exclusion from full participation in the life of the society. Though not necessarily an alien group, the minority is treated and regards itself as a people apart".

Given the range of different ethnic minorities settled in Britain, is it possible to speak of a common minority experience as far as social status is concerned? Investigation seem to suggest that despite the magnitude of the differences, because of the shared minority status of these groups. some common or parallel experiences do exist. It is these parallel circumstances that make up the minority experience.

As discussed earlier, most if not all members of such minority groups occupy a disadvantaged socio-economic position in the society. In comparison to the dominant group they are often deprived of full social, economic and political equality. According to Wirth (1945), the effects of such deprivation and disadvantage are far reaching. He goes on to say:

"These deprivations circumscribe the individual freedom of choice and self-development. The members of minority groups are held in lower esteem and may be objects of contempt, hatred, ridicule and violence . . . . There subordinate position becomes manifest in their **unequal access to educational opportunities** *and in their restricted scope of occupational and professional advancement."*

In the United Kingdom, the objective disadvantage suffered by the minority groups was studied by the Political and Economic Planning Unit (P.E.P.) between 1972 and 1975 and the findings of this research were published under the title 'Racial Disadvantage in Britain'. In this report David Smith (1977) sets out quite clearly the extent of racial **discrimination in employment, housing and education.**

The objective characteristics of the 'minority experience' outlined above are closely related to subjective characteristics associated with the feelings that members of a minority groups may have about their own status. One cannot long discriminate against people without generating in them a sense of isolation and persecution leaving them with the impression of being more alien than is warranted by reality. In the face of such treatment people may come to suffer from a sense of their own inferiority or to develop feelings of being unjustly treated to the point where the only outlet is to rebel — by exaggerating their own ethnicity, or even by making overt displays of hostility. This sort of outcome may depend in part on the length of time that they have been subject to the suppression of their aspirations, and in part upon the total social setting in which the 'differential' treatment occurs (Wirth, 1945).

The above description is an example of the psychological internalisation by minority groups and born out of their helplessness. Frideres (1974) gives a live example of such a situation when he quotes Wilfred Pelletier saying that "Being surrounded by an aggressive and confident majority has made me somewhat defensive. I have spent a lot of years trying to convince myself, after being told all my life that I was no good, because I was an Indian, that I am really all right". Such experiences may be very common to many members of minority groups. In large part it is a question of imposed identity e.g., Pelletier had internalised an image of his own worthlessness in society.

'Internalisation of the image of the oppressor' as Freire (1972) has called it, 'is of course not only limited to the experience of minority groups but can be equally applied to colonial subjects'. Wren (1977) has also explored these issues and their educational implications with great clarity in his book 'Education for Justice'. According to him one of the most important characteristics of subjective deprivation in the context of majority/minority issues is the sense of powerlessness. There is not only powerlessness to define one's own identity in the face of majority prejudice but also the powerlessness to define one's socio-economic status and to act to remedy the situation. In his work in 'The Social Psychology of Minorities' Tajfel (1978) has explored many of these dilemmas including the need for many minorites to 'acheive a new group distinctiveness' in the face of hostility and prejudice. Simpson and Yinger (1972) have discussed such prejudice in ethnocentric terms. These ethnocentric attitudes can thus prevent the minority experience from being seen as valid or even relevant for any positive action.

However, ethnic minority families and organisations cannot alone ensure the cultural under-pinning for positive minority identity. In a plural society each ethnic group whether majority or minority, ought to have a wide range of cultural and structural supports. One of the most important of these is a school system which would allow individuals to achieve literacy in their mother-tongue and mainstream language to develop intellectually within their native culture. In a multi-cultural society with a set of shared values that include a positive evaluation of ethnic diversity, the national government in liaison with the local authorities might be expected to provide educational support for all ethnic groups. The state education system would thus accept responsibility for making courses in ethnic minority languages available to all interested students. In a plural society it is essential to extend the range of educational coverage to embrace the values of both majority *and* minority groups.

In a society where the Anglo-ethnic group is dominant, minority ethnic identity has been, largely, maintained through voluntary efforts with little underpinning from the state institutions and the education system. Britain is no exception to this. As a result, young people from ethnic minority groups seem to have been denied the opportunities to learn their native tongue and study the intellectual aspects of their culture. Perhaps minority languages have suffered the most. Linguistic studies in this context reveal that there has been a marked decline in the levels of literacy and language usage among young people from minority backgrounds (Fishman, 1966; Baetens-Beardsmore, 1977). In Australia where migration is still quite recent and mostly of the post-World War II period, many ethnic minority children learn to speak their native tongue during the pre-school years but do not master the art of reading and writing it. Among children of their own age, they almost invariably speak in English and balanced bilingualism is a rarity (Smolicz and Harris, 1977; Smolicz and Lean, 1978). The situation in Britain also, seems to be far from satisfactory in this context.

The lack of retention and strengthening of ethnic identity accompanied by the denial of the means for its cultural expression represents a potential threat to social cohesion. Failure to provide support for minorities to maintain and develop their cultural and linguistic heritage does not result in their increased identification with the mainstream population. Instead it may lead to frustration, perhaps conflict and fragmentation. However, Canadian Surveys provide evidence for another view, i.e., minorities' increased identification with their ethnic groups is reflected in their enhanced identity with Canada as a permanent homeland (Richmond, 1974). This suggests that conflict and division arise not out of differences but rather out of denial of the right and opportunity to be different.

Cultural pluralism that is internalised at a personal level is not likely to be achieved unless the state makes provisions for the transmission of ethnic minority languages and cultures within its education system. The school is an agency which can fulfil the function of reinforcing and developing the culture of the home for children both of minority and majority groups. Indeed, all children irrespective of their ethnic origin could have access to more than one cultural heritage. It seems that schools could help to ensure the social stability through programmes based on shared traditions which are upheld by all groups in a society. Curriculum planning that takes into account the literacy in both majority and minority languages can avoid the cultural devisions (Muller, 1979).

Chapter 3

The Concept of Bilingualism and Multilingualism

Bilingualism may be defined in terms of an individual's ability to use two different languages, whereas the term multi-lingual is usually reserved for the individual possessing the ability to use more than two languages. This simple definition of bilingualism may seem adequate for general usage; however, it leaves open several issues that have been a constant source of confusion and lack of clarity both in the theoretical and research literature on this topic. Various attempts have been made to define bilingualism which have proved exceedingly difficult when examined under different circumstances. There seems to be more than one kind of bilingualism and any definition must take into account a number of psychological, social, cultural and linguistic variables. According to Charbonneau-Dagenais (1979) bilingualism means that an individual is able to communicate with speakers belonging to two different language groups by means of two distinct linguistic systems without having necessarily attained a high level of linguistic competence; it is open to all.

Some writers, like Bloomfield (1933) maintained that the term should be applied only to those individuals who possess 'native-like' ability in both languages. Others (e.g. Haugen, 1956) take the opposite view that bilingualism should be characterised by minimal rather that maximal qualification. Weinreich (1953) takes a more neutral position in defining bilingualism as the 'practice of alternatively using two languages'. The best way to deal with this variation in definitions would seem to recognise that bilingualism is an individual characteristic that may exist to degrees varying from minimal competency to complete mastery of more than one language. Therefore, the evaluation of the degree of bilingualism is an extremely important consideration in research dealing with bilinguals. Such evaluation is complicated by the fact that any system that is intended to be employed for evaluating bilingual competence must take into account the degree of competence in both comprehension and production in the spoken as well as the written mode (Mackey, 1962; Hornby, 1977). This type of evaluation system would also have to consider the relative competence of an individual in the numerous stylistic variations in the speech code that characterises a native speaker (Joos, 195). Some clarification has been brought to this aspect by the introduction of the term 'balanced bilingual' (Lambert, Havelka and Gardener, 1959) which is intended to be used to refer to individual fully competent in both languages. This is, perhaps, more of an ideal than a reality as most bilinguals are probably more fluent and more at ease in one of their languages than in the other. For this reason, the convention of listing the dominant language first is commonly employed in the literature on linguistics. For example, a Panjabi/English bilingual should not be confused with an English/Panjabi bilingual.

Methods of evaluating the degree of dominance (Lambert et al., 1959; Mackey 1962) as well as consideration of the factors that may contribute to determining such dominance have frequently occupied researchers in this area. Many factors may potentially affect the relative status or strength of an individual's amount of opportunity for communication, degree of emotional involvement, social function, as well as literary and cultural values (Weinreich, 1953). This situation is clarified by Prashar (1980) in her study on 'Mother-Tongue—English Diglossia'. Her paper documents the function of English vis-a-vis Indian mother-tongue in respect of a sample of 350 educated Indian bilinguals. Her findings show a pattern of use of languages. The mother-tongue or first language is the most dominant language in the domain of family, while English dominates the domains of education, government and employment. Although English is dominant in the domains of friendship and transactions, the mother-tongue, the regional language and Hindi are also used in certain situations in these domains. No language emerges clearly as the dominant one in the domain of neighbourhood. The pattern that emerges is that only one of the co-available languages in the bilingual's speech repertoires tends to be used in a particular situation type.

A second issue regarding the problem of defining bilingualism is the question of what constitutes 'different languages'. A variety of factors relating to historical, socio-cultural, political and geographical considerations are usually employed in attempting to determine whether two linguistic varieties should be considered as distinct languages or whether certain variations might be characterised as dialectal variations (Lyons, 1968). In addition, distinct codes (Bernstein, 1961) or simple stylistic differences (Joos, 1959) within a single language have often been taken as signigicant linguistic variation (Hymes, 1974). These issues are explained further by Bhatia (1982) in his study of 'English and the Vernaculars of India'. None of the Indian states is linguistically homogenous; linguistic diversity is compensated for by a complex network of bilingualism i.e., Pan-India bilingualism and State bilingualism. The two main sources of the former are English and Hindi whereas Hindi speakers prefer to learn the state or local language of the region they move to. English is associated with prestige and modernisation; it is employed in scientific, medical, technological, sporting and other registers. Bhatia discusses the anglicisation of the Indian languages in the context of phonology, syntax, code-mixing and the emergence of Hinglish (Hindi and English). At one extreme an individual might be fluent in two languages from distinctly different language families (e.g., English and Hindi) or he might simply possess more than one stylistic variation of the same language (e.g., casual versus formal English). Bilingualism has sometimes been defined to include the latter group. For instance, Taylor (1976) defines a bilingual as a person who speaks two or more languages, dialects or styles of speech that involves differences in sound, vocabulary and syntax. Under this definition, most normal adult speakers of any language would be considered bilingual. The most important question, however, is whether or not a single theoretical model such as that suggested by Hymes (1967, 1974) should be applied to all such code variations. Many of the phenomena and effects related to bilingualism are equally charcteristic of other forms of language code variations as suggested by Bernstein (1961) and Labov (1966). However, the present discussion is mainly concerned with bilingual situation in which two or more distinct language competencies are present in the same individual, what Hymes (1974) has decribed as 'bilingualism par excellence'.

One of the ways in which bilingualism par excellence (e.g., speakers of both French and English in Canada or Welsh and English in Wales) may differ significantly from stylistic variation is related to the question of the degree of cultural variation or cultural duality associated with the differences in linguistic codes. As pointed out by Pride (1981), there is an important distinction between bilingualism and biculturalism and although they may normally occur together, they can also occur separately. The possession of two stylistic variations of English or two dialectal variations of Dutch are not necessarily associated with significant cultural variation. As in majority of cases possession of two languages does reflect interaction and knowledge of distinct cultures, it is important to realise the fact that many of the effects commonly associated with bilingualism may actually reflect the result of such concomitant biculturalism. This is also one of the aimed objectives of bilingual programmes in many countires as illustrated by Stoller (1977). In an article he discusses an aspect of bilingualism of taking proper account of cultural diversity, languages in the schools, and the need for bilingual-bicultural education. He explains how the United States Office of Bilingual Education, set up in 1974, is operating to achieve positive biculturalism through its language programmes. The distinction between bilingualism with and without cultural duality is also applied to distinguish between compound and co-ordinate bilinguals (Weinreich, 1953). While this distinction has proven to be somewhat slippery, it has generally been taken to reflect the degree of semantic overlap between the two language systems within the individual.

Coordinate bilinguals are considered to have separate (and different) semantic systems, while compound bilinguals are taken to simply have two distinct modes of expression (i.e., the two languages) for a single underlying semantic network (Hornby, 1977). Gekoski (1980) has simplified this distinction as conceptual organisation in bilinguals:

"Compound bilinguals are those who acquire their languages in a joint context and, therefore, are presumed to store linguistic information interdependently. Coordinate bilinguals include those who acquire their languages in separate contexts and therefore are presumed to maintain independent linguistic store".

Although a variety of factors have been related to this distinction, a number of studies (Lambert, Havelka and Crosby, 1958; Kolers, 1963; Ervin-Tripp, 1964; Lambert, 1969; Lambert and Rawlings, 1969) suggest that the question of whether the languages have been learned in two geographically separate cultural contexts may be the variable of prime significance in determining the so-called compound-coordinate distinction. It must be pointed out that this variable is probably confounded with age of acquisition, since individuals acquiring two languages in infancy are more likely to do so in the same cultural context than those individuals acquiring a second language at a later time (De Houwer, 1982). However, the relevance of biculturalism in the consideration of bilingual issues are rather important (Lambert, 1977; Taylor, 1977). Bilingualism in a bicultural setting was also the concern of this study. At the same time such biculturalism does not necessarily mean a total of each significant separation of linguistic systems within individuals.

In relation to compound and coordinate distinctions of bilingualism Fishman (1965) has discussed 'diglossia', another issue of sociolinguistic significance. This term, originally introducuced by Ferguson (1959), is used to refer to those situations in which two or more languages are used differently within a single geographic region. Gumperz (1966) has extended this concept to include variations in dialect, register or variety and thus comes to the inevitable conclusion that almost all societies possess some form of diglossia. One dialect, language or variety will normally be used for some social functions (e.g., education, government and work etc.), while a distinctly different linguistic variety may be employed for the remaining social functions (e.g. family interaction, community and religion etc.). To the extent that these social functions and roles are occupied by distinct social groups, then such diglossic situations are often associated with the existence of separate-language-speaking populations within the same geographic society. Diglossia is a characteristic of societies and social groups whereas bilingualism is a characteristic of individuals though both phenomena are inter-related.

As outlined by Fishman (1967), the theoretically independent relationship between diglossia and bilingualism makes it possible to consider different types of situations with individuals being either bilingual or monolingual in a social context that may either possess or not possess diglossia. Thus, in a diglossic society some of the members may be monolingual in one of the languages, some in the other, while a third group may be bilingual and capable of functioning comfortably in either group or social setting. For instance, in the officially bilingual country of Canada, a demographic study revealed that more than 65 per cent of the population was monolingual in English, about 20 per cent of the population was monolingual in French and only 12 per cent of the population was classified as bilingual (Lieberson, 1970). The relationship between diglossia and bilingualism is quite complex, however, with these dimensions really being only theoretically separable.

As Fishman (1967) points out, societies in which widespread bilingualism exists will tend to move towards diglossia, and in almost all diglossic scoieties there will be some individuals who for economic, political, geographic or other reasons will form a link between the two speech communities and hence will have to be bilingual. This phenomenon is more true in multi-lingual and multi-cultural social development (Fishman, 1980) as is the case with contemporary British society. Martinet (1982) extended the situation even further in a multi-lingual atmosphere. Ferguson (1959) coined the term 'diglossia' for a situation when two varieties of the sáme language are used, each with different social status and function. The term is sometimes useful e.g., for the situation in Greece, Norway and Switzerland, but the distinction between languages and varieties of one language is often unclear. According to Martinet these socio-linguistic criteria limit the use of the term 'bilingualism' to a few individuals and exclude trilingual or pluri-lingual situations. He argues that a term like 'collective bilingualism' would be more useful. Whatever terms are employed, it is the changing nature of a multi-lingual situation in Britain that needs to be stressed in this context.

It shows that the presence of diglossia is also an important contextual factor in considering the implications of bilingualism. Fishman (1972) has pointed out that:

> *"many of the purported 'disadvantages' of bilingualism have been falsely generalised to the phenomenon at large rather than related to the absence or presence of social patterns that reach substantially beyond bilingualism".*

The presence or absence of diglossia is however, only one distinction among a variety of potential social settings in which the bilingual individual may find himself. In fact, Stewart (1968) has developed a typology for describing multi-lingualism that distinguishes ten separate social functions that a second language may serve which range from an official, legally appropriate language for all activities to a language used in connection with the rituals of a particular religion. As bilingualism always occurs within some particular social setting, the potential effect that it will have on the individual may vary widely depending in the particular social significance and function of the two languages. Consideration of this factor is involved in the distinction between 'additive' and 'subtractive' bilingualism introduced by Lambert (1975) and elaborated by Fishman et al (1977) in relation to the existence of English as a second language for a large number of people throughout the world.

The distinction made by Lambert (1975) between 'Additive' and 'Subtractive' bilingualism is helpful in understanding the process between socio-cultural factors and cognitive development. In making this distinction Lambert attaches special importance to one socio-cultural factor, i.e., the prestige or the social relevance of the bilingual's two languages. He notes that in communities where studies have reported positive effects associated with bilingualism, the second language (L2), e.g., a minority language, has been socially relevant language, the learning of which is unlikely to replace the first language (i.e., L1, usually a prestigious or a dominant language). However, for many ethnic minority groups the learning of L2 (usually the majority and more prestigious language) is very likely to lead to a gradual replacement of the L1 (e.g., the mother-tongue). Lambert terms the former type of bilingualism 'additive' in that the learner is adding a new language to his repertory of skills. The latter type of bilingualism is termed 'subtractive' in that a bilingual's competence in his two languages represents a subtaction of L1 and its replacement by the L2. It seems unlikely that, under these circumstances, many bilinguals in 'subtractive' bilingual learning situations may not develop native-like competence in either of the two languages.

The above mentioned phenomena is similar to the 'balance effect' hypothesis of Macnamara (1966) and 'semi-lingualism' notion of Skutnabb-Kangas (1975). In the 'balance effect' situation a bilingual develops skills in one of his two languages and pays for it by a decrease in the competence in the other. The term 'semilingualism' refers to the linguistic competence, or the lack of it, of individuals who have had contact with the two languages since their childhood without adequate linguistic skills, training or stimulation in either. As a result these individuals know both the languages poorly and so do not attain the same levels as native speaker in either of the languages. Therefore, one can assume that stepping up exposure of L2 (second language) may not necessarily solve the problem for the positive results of bilingualism. It actually depends on whether the bilingual learning situation is 'folk' for 'elitist'; 'subtractive' or 'additive'. Cummins (1978) distinguishes those two learning situation into 'Immersion' and 'Submersion' concepts. In the immersion situation learners from a dominant linguistic group are immersed into an L2 learning environment. They have no competence in the school language, but are praised for any attempts they may make to use it. The teachers are familiar with the learner's language and culture. Moreover, the language and culture of the learners are never devalued at schools and in society at large. The target language is introduced in the school after several grades and is taught in the higher grades as its importance is recognised implicitly and/or explicitly.

The situation in the submersion programme is somewhat reversed. The target language is that of the school and the inability of the learners to communicate in the school language is seen as a sign of limited intellectual and academic ability. There may be problems of communication with the teachers because of the lack of the knowledge of the child's home language on the part of the teachers and different culturally determined expectations of appropriate behaviour. The child's language may be seen as a cause of academic deficiency and an impediment to learning the school language. A child's identity which is connected with his language and home culture, is not reinforced in the school environment. In short as Cummins (1978) points out: "In general, what is communicated to children in 'immersion' programme is their success, whereas in 'submersion' programme children are often made to feel acutely aware of their failure". This view was reiterated by Swain (1978), Genesee (1978) and Roy (1980) in their research with 'French Immersion' programmes in Canada.

Clearly then, the academic and cognitive performance of a bilingual child depends on the learning situations in which it takes place. The socio-cultural factors are vital to be taken into consideration in this context. The conflicting findings, in the field of bilingual education research, are the results of these socio-cultural variables. Cummins (1978) has developed the hypothesis of the 'Lower' and the 'Higher' thresholds of bilingual competence in an attempt to identify the links in the casual chain through which the effect of the socio-cultural factors may operate in this process. The threshold hypothesis assume that those aspects of bilingualism which might positively influence cognitive growth are unlikely to come into effect until the child has attained a certain minimum or threshold level of competence in his second language.

However, the concept of threshold levels reconciles the inconsistencies and contradictory findings different researchers have come up with in their study of the relationship between bilingualism and cognition. On this point Cummins states that:

> *"It should be made clear at the outset that the threshold level of bilingual competence is an intervening rather than a basic casual*

variable in accounting for the continued growth of bilinguals . . . The
attainment of threshold is itself determined by more fundamental
social, attitudinal, educational and cognitive (e.g. language learning
aptitudes) factors" (Cummins, 1976, Page 23).

He further elaborates the concept of threshold into a 'lower threshold' of
bilingual competence, the achievements of which would be sufficient to
avoid any negative cognitive effect. On the other hand the attainment of the
'higher threshold' of bilingual competence might be necessary to lead to
accelerated cognitive growth.

Thus, the stage before the lower threshold may be represented as
Lambert's 'subtractive bilingualism' or even as the concept of
'semilingualism' descibed by Skutnabb-Kangas and Toukomaa (1976). The
latter writers point out:

"Although parents, teachers and the children themselves considered
Finnish migrant children's Swedish to be quite fluent, test in Swedish
which required complex cognitive operations to be carried out
showed that this surface fluency was to a certain extent a linguistic
facade".

The situation of the children from the minority linguistic background in
Britain should be seen in this light. Except those children who came to
Britain at a later stage are learning English as a second language in schools,
it would be of great relevance and significance to see what level of
thresholds the others have reached — what is the degree of their
bilingualism and what is the level of their academic performance? If the
children from the ethnic minorities are to be helped and prepared to cope
with and make good use of the facilites offered to them within the British
educational system, the question of the degree and type of bilingualism and
its effect on children's cognitive development are of great pertinence.

Bilingualism, Cognition and Education:

The question of whether the bilingual is cognitively different from the
monolingual has been an issue of long-standing interest in the educational
process. Contradictory evidence in connection with bilingualism and its
effect on cognition and academic development has been produced for the
last two decades. In earlier studies several investigators argued that
bilingualism itself was the cause of 'mental confusion' and 'linguistic
handicap'. Macnamara's (1966) 'balanced effect' hypothesis, which
proposed that a bilingual child paid for his second language (L2) skills by a
decrease in his first language (L1) skills, was representative of this mode of
thinking. The 'linguistic mismatch' hypothesis (UNESCO, 1953) which
stated that the mismatch between the language of the home and the
language of the school led to academic retardation, was another of these
theses. Prior to these studies a systematic investigation of negative and
positive effects of bilingualism were first reported by Ronjat (1913) and

later by Leopold (1969).

The Peal and Lambert Study (1962) represents a watershed in the view that is held in connection with the positive correlation between bilingualism and cognition. They suggested that many earlier studies which compared I.Q. scores of monolingual and bilingual subjects suffered from methodological defects. They failed to control or take into consideration variables such as parents' socio-economic status (SES), sex and the balance of bilingualism in the subjects' knowledge of their two languages. Cummins (1976) gives a comprehensive account of the major studies during the last twenty years which have come up with negative and positive findings in the relationship between bilingualism and cognition.

In a study of the Irish primary school children, Macnamara (1966) reported that those whose home language was English but attended schools where the medium of instruction was Irish, were as much as eleven months behind in problem arithmetic relative to other Irish children taught through the medium of English. However, the problem arithmetic test was expressed in sentences and must have involved mediation of language. No difference was evident between the groups on mechanical arithmetic test expressed in arithmetical symbols. The methodological process of this study was criticised by the following research on the subject (Cummins, 1977b). Tsushima and Hogan (1975) reported that grade four and five Japanese-English bilinguals performed at significantly lower levels than unilingual group on measure of verbal and academic skills. The bilingual and unilingual groups were matched on non-verbal ability as well. However, no details were given of the bilinguals' relative competence in both languages — i.e., their degree of bilingualism and therefore the findings seem to be inconclusive. A study conducted in Singapore (Torrence et al., 1970) reported that the children in grade three, four and five, who were attending bilingual schools, performed at a significantly lower level on Fluency and Flexibility Scale of the Torence Test of Creative Thinking. The direction of the trend was reversed for originality and elaboration, and differences in favour of the bilinguals were very significant. This study cared to take a two-sided approach to bilingualism in education.

The best known of the positive studies in bilingualism is the one conducted by Peal and Lambert (1962) with French-English bilinguals in Montreal. Peal and Lambert used only 'balanced' bilinguals who had achieved a relatively similar degree of competence on both languages. The group of 'balanced' ten year olds bilinguals showed a higher level of non-verbal intelligence and performed at a higher level on the measures of verbal intelligence.

The Peal and Lambert Study was replicated in Western Canada by Cummins and Gulstan (1973) and similar results were reported. In addition, the balanced bilinguals scored higher on the measures of divergent thinking — i.e., the verbal originality. Both these studies clearly show the positive cognitive effects of bilingualism.

In a study conducted by Liedka and Nelson (1968) in Western Canada, children who had become bilinguals before coming to school showed higher level on concept formation than monolinguals. The groups were matched on intelligence, socio-economic status (SES) and sex bases. In Switzerland Balkan (1970) produced evidence to support the hypothesis that the attainment of balanced bilinguals might have a positive effect of cognitive flexibility.

The studies carried out by Ben-Zeev (1972) with Hebrew-English bilinguals in Israel and the United States and by Ianco-Worrall (1972) with Afrikaans-English bilinguals in South Africa supported the hypothesis that bilingualism might positively affect cognitive flexibility. Ben-Zeev reported that her bilingual group had skills in auditory reorganisation of verbal material and were more advanced in concrete operational thinking. Ianco-Worrell's study provided support for Leopold's (1949) hypothesis that simultaneous acquisition of two languages in early childhood accelerates the separation of sounds and meanings or names and objects, a feature of thinking which Vygotsky (1962) believed reflected insight and sophistication of linguistic knowledge.

A study by Sheridan Scott (1973) of French-English bilinguals in Montreal is perhaps the most persuasive because it involved a comparison of young children, some of whom were given the chance to become bilinguals over a period of years and others who were not given the chance. It was decided in advance to start only one experimental class per year (Lambert and Tucker, 1972). Scott was interested in the possible effect that becoming bilingual might have on the cognitive development of children, in particular, what effect it would have on the 'divergent thinking' a special type of cognitive flexibility. Some researchers have considered divergent thinking as an index to creativity (Getzels and Jackson, 1962). Scott found that the youngsters who had become functionally bilingual through 'immersion' schooling were substantially higher scorers for divergent thinking than the monolingual group with whom they had been equated for I.Q. and social class background at the first grade level. Her study gives strong support for the casual link between bilingualism and flexibility, the former apparently enhancing the latter. This study influenced the Canadian programmes for positive bilingualism.

Cummins (1976) argues that:

> "recent studies suggest that becoming bilingual, either as a result of home or school experiences, can positively influence aspects of cognitive functioning. There are indications in these studies that bilingual learning experience in the school setting may be more capable of influencing divergent than convergent thinking skills. However, early or preschool bilingualism does appear to be capable of accelerating the development of convergent thinking" (Cummins,

op. cit., page 10).
Lamy (1976) suggested that adult bilinguals thought that they would not work better or be happier if they only used one of the two languages. These findings confirm the positive aspects of bilingual education.

Lindmann (1977) reported that Swedish-Finnish bilinguals scored higher in Self-rating Tests of Self-esteem and Self-concept compared to the monolinguals in either of these languages. Doyle (1977) discusses some linguistic correlates of early bilingialism which have implications for first cognitions about language. She suggests that bilingual pre-school children may be superior in ideational fluency of first words. During the same year Bruck et al (1977) reported that the achievement, of fifth and sixth grades anglophone children being educated in French were better in cognitive, linguistic and academic skills compared to the students educated in English or French language.

Lambert (1978) reported that the effect of bilingualism on one's sense of personal identity are encouraging in North America. Swain (1978), Genesee (1978) and Cummins (1978a; 1978b) have discussed the positive effects of bilingualism in relation to its introduction at an early age i.e., 'immersion' programmes of bilingual education and attainment of 'threshold' level of bilingualism respectively. Titone (1978) developed the 'glosso-dynamic model' of language learning to explain how the child's cognitive and affective development is enhanced by bilingual stimulation. The core of this model is the emphasis of the integrating, unifying and propulsive power of individual learner's conscious ego. He found that personality of the bilingual child does not suffer from the collision of L1 and L2 . The effect is rather to widen horizons and strenghten the power of adaptation to the world. This research indicates that positive aspects of bilingualism outweigh the negative cliché.

Magiste (1979) conducted a research in a multi-lingual setting in America. The results of his findings support an independent hypothesis of bilingual storage for cognitive development. Genesee et al (1978, 1979) confirmed this in a trilingual English-Hebrew-French programme with grade 3 and 5 children in Montreal. The results of their findings indicate superior profiency in French and Hebrew among the experimental students with no loss to native English language development or to mathematics achievement. Baeten-Beardsmore (1979) conducted two experiments to measure the tolerance level of bilingually marked English in a functional bilinguals' speech and improved graduations were noted in the level of recognition and tolerence level of bilingually marked English. In the same year Prashar (1979) gave account of English bilingualism in India after the independence in 1947. Despite its place as one of the major languages in India, English has not brought down the standard of any of the indigenous languages among students but has a complementary function.

Saunder (1980) produced a report on a longitudinal study of the

acquisition of English-German bilingualism by two Australian born children who, from the onset of speech have always communicated with their father in German and with others including their mother in English. There is no adverse affect on the family and the standard of bilingualism attained by the children is encouraging. Diepietro (1980) makes an evaluation of a language programme for children in grades 1 to 6 at an elementary school in Virginia. The community is a multi-lingual one; the languages chosen are Spanish, Korean and Vietnamese. All children at the school were given the opportunity to study another language regardless of their home language. His findings are constant with those of Lambert and Tucker (1972) who found no harmful effect on the cognitive development of children enrolled in elementary schools where content subject matter is taught via another language. Roy (1980) also hypothesised that strategy may explain in part the evidence in research that immersion language instruction is more effective than traditional first and second language instruction. Finally, he considers in his paper the value of strategy definition for quality control of learning.

Swain (1981) in her continuing research on bilingualism discusses the terminology of CALP (Cognitive Academic Linguistic Proficiency) and reports "the more language instruction in first language (L1) the higher the Second language (L2) proficiency" leading to academic success. Dawson (1982) and Lado (1982) studied the bilingual and bicultural aspects of cognitive development and estab'ished the concept of biliteracy. Lado finds that learning to read developmentally through L1 and L2 turns the reading handicap of Hispanic and other bilingual children into an asset of literacy in two languages and this biliteracy in turn gives them a fuller access to educational opportunities and consequent success. Murtaugh (1982) confirms in his study the linguistic interdependence notion propossed by Cummins (1979) from the discovery that students taught bilingually showed progressively greater success at separating the two languages than their counterparts taught monolingually (i.e., two languages taught as separate entities in the classroom). Cummins and Swain (1983) find the bilinguals also better in CALP (Cognitive Academic Linguistic Proficiency) and BICS (Basic Inter-Communication Skills) tests compared to the monolinguals.

Several factors may be extracted from the various studies which in part account for the contradictory results. For the most part, positive findings are associated with children from majority language groups whereas negative findings are associated with minority-language groups (Lambert, 1977; Burnaby, 1976). One exception to this generalisation which relates to majority group children is Macnamara's (1966) study of English-Irish bilinguals. This study, however, has been criticised on methodological grounds (Cummins, 1977b). Other exceptions, but which relate to minority-language children (e.g., Dube and Herbert, 1975), indicate that the minority group factor can be overcome through the reinforcement and development of high level of L1 proficiency. Another factor, related in part to the first, is the perceived value and prestige of the L1 and L2 in the home and community (Fishman, 1976; Tucker, 1977; Swain, 1980). Positive results tend to be associated with situations where both the L1 and L2 have perceived social and economic value. A third factor, again in part related to the first, is socio-economic status. Higher SES children tend to perform well as explained by Paulston (1975), i.e., the distinction between 'folk' and 'elitist' bilingualism first introduced by Gaarder (1967a). Lower SES bilingual children tend not to perform as well as higher SES children, although they do perform as well or better that unilingual group of a similar SES level (Bruck, Jakimick and Tucker, 1980). Finally, school programme variables play an important role. Positive results tend to be associated with immersion programmes while negative results tend to be associated with submersion programmes (Cohen and Swain, 1976; Burnaby, 1976; Swain, 1980; Genesee, 1978; Cummins 1978).

Research in this area will continue to uncover additional factors and examine the effects of their interaction. Alladina (1979) adapted the Peal and Lambert Study (1962) to Gujrati-English bilinguals in Britain. He made a further distinction to the Peal and Lambert Study by categorising bilinguals to their degree of bilingualism. It was done to test the influence of the degree of bilingualism on cognitive styles as a significant additional factor. However, psychological research into bilingualism cannot be expected to produce completely consistent results in every situation. This is because bilingualism is not one single phenomenon. Neither is there one state of bilingualism which influences the cognitive development of all bilinguals in the same way. There is an enormous variety of bilingual learning situations, in each of which, different combinations of cognitive, attitudinal, social and educational factors are operative. The learning of two languages is likely to affect cognition in different ways depending on the age at which the languages are learned, whether they are learned separately or simultaneously, e.g.,Simultaneous Versus Sequential; early vs late (ref. Cummins, 1979; Murtegh, 1982). It also depends on the context in which the two languages have been learned i.e., compound vs coordinate (See Osgood and Sebeok, 1965); artificial vs natural (Stern, 1973); additive vs subtractive (Lambert, 1977); or the domain in which each language is used (ref; Fishman, 1968; Oksaar, 1971). Other important factors of bilingual education include the opportunities for using both languages in the home, the school and wider environment, the prestige of the two languages, and the functions which the languages serve within wider social contexts.

It has been suggested (Cummins, 1976, 1978c, 1978d, 1980; Toukomaa and Skutnabb-Kangas, 1977) that there may be threshold level of linguistic competence which a bilingual child must attain both in order to avoid cognitive disadvantage and allow the potentially beneficial aspects of becoming bilingual to influence his/her cognitive functioning. One major educational implication of the threshold hypothesis is that if optimal development of minority-language children's academic and cognitive potential is a goal, then the school programme must aim to promote an 'additive' form of bilingualism (Cummins, 1980). Attainments of this goodwill necessarily involve a home-school language switch at some stage in the educational process, but when and how must be determined in relation to the linguistic and socio-economic characteristics of the learner and of the learning environment (Swain, 1980). In the British context where the home language of minority group children is different from the school and the home language tends to be denigrated by others and where the children of minority groups generally come from socio-economically deprived homes, it would appear appropriate to begin initial instruction in the children's mother-tongue and switching at a later stage to instruction in the school language i.e., English.

In the light of the above discussion it can be concluded that the positive effects of bilingualism outweigh the negative findings about this phenomenon. Its advancement for successful minority/majority education depends on what we mean by bilingualsim and how we adopt it for gainful educational process under particular circumstances. At the same time further research is essential to benefit from this phenomenon in contemporary plural societies.

As mentioned before, there has always been interpenetration and co-existence of languages and cultures since the arrival of Nordic, Saxon, Roman, Vikings and Norman newcomers. The entry of the Jewish people and later on of the East European immigrants introduced more languages and cultures into British society. Migrations from Europe into the British Isles, in small and large numbers, have continued up to the present time. A large majority of these immigrants have been assimilated into the host community. The revival and assertion of languages and cultures of these people is a new development and has to be seen in the light of current educational trends. Moreover, this development is also due to the awareness regarding the relevance and valorisation of the Celtic languages and regional dialects other than the standard English in Britain.

The non-European communities from the New Commonwealth and Pakistan established themselves in Britain with their distinct languages. Initially, these communities were expected to assimilate to the dominant society in spite of the hostility and rejection from the mainstream population (Alladina, 1982). This attitude was reflected in education through the total lack of recognition given to languages and cultures other than British. The 'assimilationist model' did not seem to work because of the fact that various communities have attempted to maintain their languages and cultures. Unfortunately their cultures and languages are not accorded the due status and recognition by the dominant society. The community of linguistic scholars has shown very little interest in the new linguistic profile of diversity which has emerged during the last twenty years (Rosen and Burgess, 1980). British scholars seem to know more about linguistic diversity in remote African and Asian communities but they pretend to be unaware of this diversity in their own homeland. The monolingual tradition dies hard and for a long time it made superficial sense to consider Britain as linguistically more homogeneous than any other major industrial country, certainly more than France, Germany, Italy, the United States or Canada as illustrated by Stephens (1976) in his study of 'Linguistic Minorities in Western Europe'. The study of diversity has been concentrated on regional and social dialects (Orton et al., 1974; Trudgill, 1978) and has had a strong historical bias (Lockwood, 1975). Trudgill and his collaborators have used sociolinguistic sophistication to reveal what is alive and changing in current vernacular English regardless of the new linguistic minorities which have grown up in the very recent past (Rosen and Burgess, 1980). It is perhaps through the ideologies of racial and cultural superiority of the indigeneous society (Alladina, 1982).

Britain has now become a 'multi-cultural, multi-lingual society' (DES Green Paper, 1977). This characteristic has been welcomed and accepted by the more forward-thinking people in society. However, we should not lose sight of the fact that, firstly, the multi-culturalism and multi-lingualism got its present shape and form when British society found itself having to co-exist with black cultures and languages in its midst; and secondly, the black communities asserted this need by persistently maintaining their languages and cultures. Multi-culturalism and multi-lingualism mean the existence of many cultures and languages side by side in one society. It does not mean the domination of one on the other. Undoubtedly, language is one of the most important contributors to disadvantage among ethnic minorities (Little, 1978; Parekh, 1978; Swann 1985; Rampton, 1981; Swann 1985). Of all the characteristics of disadvantage, this is one of the most visible and has, therefore, attracted considerable attention. Its perception parallels those of the larger issues of the life-styles and cultures of minority groups; thus, the classic controversy in this area has been the so-called 'difference-deficit' debate. Is it the case that certain languages or varieties of language are inferior in some ways to others, or are they merely different?

The realisation that languages simply differ from one to another, and cannot reasonably be seen as comparatively better or worse, has been current for some time. This is largely due to the work of anthropologists and linguists. No one, for example, would claim that French is better or more logical than English, Chinese or Arabic, and similar sentiments can be expressed for any group or languages. Gleitman and Gleitman (1970) have pointed out that: "No one has succeeded in finding a **primitive** language . . . No one has convincingly demonstrated that there is some thought or idea, expressible in some language that cannot be expressed in another". On the same point, Lenneberg (1967) asks "Could it be that some languages require 'less mature cognition' than others, perhaps because they are still more primitive? In recent years this notion has been thoroughly discredited by virtually all students of language". There may be a language or culture in greater currency, as is the case with English in Britain today, but other languages might supersede English in different social realms for some people. Although English is the predominant language for education, power and status, the community languages have relevance for social vitality and community functions.

In multi-cultural multi-lingual Britain, there are languages and cultures which are diverse (existing side by side and merging at times), collateral (side by side existence but some are subordinate), or parallel (existing side by side but never meeting). Theorists and educationalists need to be clear about what they mean by multi-cultural, multi-lingual Britain. There are a few schools that have included non-European languages in the school curriculum. Most of the mother-tongue teaching goes on after school hours by voluntary efforts of cummunities. We are nowhere near solving the issues of time-tabling community languages, syllabus planning or examination standards for them. The question of giving these languages status or legitimacy has not been considered yet. However, there is ample socio-psychological and academic evidence in favour of maintaining mother-tongues and community languages and giving them status and recognition in schools and society at large (Cummins, 1976; Alladina, 1979).

For many children the school is rather natural continuation and extension of home life. Children from minority groups often experience a sharp discontinuity between home and school. It is important to realise that this is not something which can be easily overcome. The discontinuity will remain so long as there exists a difference between home language and school language and between the playground and the classroom. For some disadvantaged children, particularly those from migrant or ethnic minority backgrounds the discontinuity may constitute a type of 'cultural shock' — the phenomenon one experiences when faced with a foreign and unfamiliar context (Ashworth, 1975; Edwards, 1979). Such children may well by prejudiced against, especially if they are in some way distinguishable either by physical appearance or linguistically from others. Thus, the first day at school for a child may be like going to a new environment in which the inhabitants are not only linguistically strange but perhaps hostile as well. The Bullock Report (1975) 'A language for Life' states:

"No child should be expected to cast off the language and culture of the home as he/she crosses the school threshold, nor to live and act as though school and home represent two totally separate and different cultures which have to be kept apart. The curriculum should reflect many elements of that part of his life which the child lives outside

school." (Committee of Enquiry, Rec. 249, 1975:543)

In contemporary Britain, many languages and cultures exist side by side but the relations of power remain. Of course, English language and culture within British society are dominant but as long as they remain in position of domination without due regard to minority languages and cultures, then multi-cultural, multi-lingual Britain would only go on existing in the minds of a few academics. Educationists and theorists seem to be preoccupied with counting exactly how many languages there are in Britain, how many people speak them and whether they are 'minorities' or 'new minorities' or just an insignificant number. In principle every child's mother-tongue or community language is significant for his or her education. The debate involves suggested change in attitude and practice on the part of the school in order to recognise mother-tongues or community languages of ethnic minority groups. This has led some writers to advocate a more fundamental social change in the process of education of all children.

An awareness of social inequalities, coupled with the realisation that minority populations are more anxious to succeed within the system than to run the risk involved in overturning it, has directed more attention towards broader attacks on the disadvantage position of minorities within society. These often retain a central focus on the school when they see the school in a less isolated and more socially involved role of cultural pluralism. This renewed interest is widely evident in North America where the schools are expected to provide bilingual and bicultural education. The similar trends can, also, be seen in Europe, Australia and recently in Britain.

Initially bilingual education in America was essentially a compensatory measure designed to help minority children of limited English-speaking ability to adjust to and succeed in the mainstream society. In this transitional mode, bilingual education has achieved some success, although proponents of cultural and linguistic pluralism point out that this has actually hastened the assimilation. It is also argued that the proponents of cultural and linguistic pluralism are often ethnic minority group members themselves, but are usually well-assimilated, secure and in a position to reflect at leisure on questions of culture and tradition (Edwards, 1977, 1980a, 1980b; Higham, 1975; Weinreich, 1974). Drake (1979) asserts that the apparent tolerance towards ethnic groups which is found (or at least expressed) today cannot necessarily be equated with favourable disposition towards pluralism. Mercer and Mercer (1979) illustrate this view further in their work on 'Variation in Attitudes to Mother-tongue and Culture'. They quoted Mitchell (1978) distinguishing two basic positions:

> *"Bilingual education . . . . can be either assimilationist or pluralist; it can be used either as a supposedly more efficient tool for the easing-in of minority group children into the majority culture, or for . . . extending the language skills of minority language speakers. Arguments in favour of the use of minority languages as teaching*

media have in fact been advanced from both assimilationist and pluralist positions".

The pluralist position thus sees the introduction of mother-tongue teaching as a means of maintaining and legitimising cultural diversity; teaching in the minority language as part of introducing more minority cultural material into the school curriculum. The assimilationist position, on the other hand, is based on the assumption that the sooner children of minority cultures are instructed to 'normal' school curriculum, the better; if this is done by initially teaching them through the medium of their first language, then this justifies its use in school (Mercer and Mercer, 1979).

Nevertheless, the sentiments from which a philosophy of cultural and linguistic pluralism springs are not ignoble. The difficulty, according to Higham (1975), is to resolve the 'opposition between a strategy of integration and one of pluralism'. He advocates 'pluralistic integration' in which diversity exists within a larger unity in which general interests and specific claims may be attended to. In a way, this is a situation which some ethnic minority groups might like to adopt. Edwards (1977) points out that the forces of assimilation do not entirely nullify ethnicity, and elements of original life-style remain. In our present discussion we are not merely concerned about residue elements but instead the 'core' preservation of cultural and linguistic ethnicity. As cultural pluralists we ought to aim for bilingual education in a 'maintenance' mode rather than in a transitional mode — i.e., a continuing programme which will sustain and encourage a permanent pluralistic society. It is therefore overturning the 'melting pot' as put forward by Fishman (1980) in his study of 'Bilingualism and Biculturalism as Individual and as Societal Phenomena'.

The underlying attitude to bilingualism may emerge as an important factor if present initiatives move into a more concrete, policy-framing stage in Britain. Whenever the attitudes of ethnolinguistic group members are referred to at all in current discussions it seems to be assumed that they universally support the introduction of bilingual education, and that this support is entirely based on a 'pluralist' perspective. For example, in an article on the proposal of mother-tongue teaching with a particular reference to Asian groups, Dorothy Davis (1977), a member of Leicestershire Education Authority, writes:

"There is no doubt that Asian parents are anxious to see their own cultures and religions preserved through their children. They see them exposed to the disturbing influence of modern, rationalistic education, encouraged to challenge authority and to question dogma, and frequently offered the very worst examples of anti-social behaviour by their western peers.

They know that language is the binding string of cultural identity, and . . . they make tremendous effort to hold their children to their own traditions, their own religions and moral values, by preserving their own languages".

This reference is typical in that the views which are usually represented as those of the Asian community are essentially the views of a vocal section of the older first generation of immigrants and it is still relevant in its present situation of bilingual programmes.

The Community Relations Commission itself, while chastising the British government for its failure to canvass community attitudes to the E.E.C. Directive's early draft (circulated in 1975), claims to rectify this by seeking the views of minority group organisations (Education and Community Relations, 1977). The discussion of mother-tongue teaching in Britain, as mentioned before, was stimulated by the E.E.C. Directive of July, 1977. Although this directive was really concerned with the educational needs of migrant workers within the Common Market countries, there has been pressure from bodies like the Commission for Racial Equality and some educationalists to broaden this interpretation to cover the needs of immigrant settlers (e.g., see Education and Community Relations op.cit., and Function, Inner London Education Authority, Autumn, 1977). The declaration was made to extend the application of the Directive to children of all immigrants without regard to the country of origin (Carlyle, 1980). As the term is currently used, mother-tongue or community language teaching is a form of bilingual education, whereby children receive at least some scholastic instruction through their native or first language as opposed to being taught entirely in English, or being taught about their first language as a curriculum subject. The picture is not quite clear. The provision of mother-tongue or bilingual education varies from one local authority to another. A few local education authorities use children's mother-tongue as a medium of instruction while some interpret it as teaching children's first language after school hours or at weekends through voluntary provision.

It is not just a matter of exception that the phenomenon of bilingualism has developed to trilingualism or multi-lingualism with many children in our schools. We ought to be more thoughtful of children's individual language repertoire. Houlton (1983) makes it clear when he quotes the confidence of a ten year old girl who reported: "I speak English at school, Gujrati on my way home with my friends, I learn Urdu at mosque, I read the Koran in Arabic and my mother speaks Marathi". So we have to think about children's linguistic development in these multi-lingual contexts. This notion was established as early as 1944 in the Education Act for England and Wales which requires Local Education Authorities "to contribute towards the spiritual, moral, mental and physical development of the community by securing that efficient education . . . shall be available **to meet the needs of the population** in their area". It further requires the provision of "such variations of instruction and training as may be desirable in view of . . . different ages, **abilities and aptitudes** . . ."

The linguistic aspect of this philosophy was reiterated by the report of the Bullock Committee, set up in 1972. The broad findings and recommendations of this report (1975) 'A Language for Life' have received wide publicity. Chapter 20 of this report entitled 'Children from Families of Overseas Origin' is of special interest for educationalists, administrators, researchers and teachers of modern Britain. At this point it would seem appropriate to reproduce some of its relevant conclusions and recommendations:

Authorities with children from families of overseas origin should carry out regular surveys of their linguistic needs in order to maintain flexibility in the arrangements made to cater for them. (20.2)

In some areas the arrangements do little more than meet the initial language and adjustment needs of new arrivals, whereas these are only the beginning of what for most of the children is a long process. (20.2)

Among families of overseas origin there are considerable differences not only in language and culture but in the stability of their home circumstances and their adaptation to their new country. These differences should be recognised and the stereotypes of the 'immigrant child' should be dismissed. (20.3)

Though there has been little sustained research describing the comparative performance of children of minority groups in Britain, there is enough evidence to show a disturbingly low pattern of attainment . . . well below average. (20.4)

No child should be expected to cast off the language and culture of the home as he/she crosses the school threshold, and the curriculum should reflect those aspects of his life. (20.5)

Teachers in school with children of West Indian origin should have an understanding of Creole dialect and a positive and sympathetic attitude towards it. Work relating both to dialect and to improving the ability to use Standard English should be encouraged on a much larger scale. (20.6)

Specialist teachers of language should work in close liaison with other teachers in the school and should keep in touch with the child's education as a whole. (20.10)

In the secondary school, pupils who are past the initial stage of learning English need help in coping with the linguistic demands made on them by the various specialist areas of the curriculum. To this end there should be close cooperation between subject teachers and language specialists. (20.12)

There should be more initiatives to establish a new role for the language teacher in a multi-racial secondary school, one of consultant and adviser across the curriculum rather than of a teacher confined to a single area. Though staffing difficulties and cost are a problem to authorities with large numbers of second-stage language learners, teachers able to carry out this function should be appointed extra to complement where possible. (20.12)

Authorities with areas of immigrant settlements should appoint advisers with special responsibility for the language development of the children. (20.13)

The provision of nursery classes in the inner city areas has great importance for the early language development of immigrant children. The normal activities of the nursery and infant classroom should be adjusted to suit their individual needs and should be supplemented by specific help with language (20.14).

There should be a more sustained and systematic linking of home and school, with particular emphasis in the case of young children. (20.15-20.16)

In a linguistically conscious nation in the modern world, we should see mother-tongue as an asset, as something to be nutured; and one of the agencies that should nurture it is the school. Certainly, the school should adopt a positive attitude to the pupils' bilingualsim, and whenever possible to help maintain and deepen their knowledge of their mother-tongue. (20.17)

There should be further research into the teaching of their own language to children of immigrant communities and into the various aspects of bilingualism in schools (20.17). Many of these recommendations have not been implemented in all parts of the country.

The message in favour of linguistic diversity, mother-tongue teaching and bilingualism is quite clear in the Bullock Report, and the subsequent evidence and documents which support the case for such an educational practice in our schools. We should now evaluate some further documents and official statements on this subject:

i) The E.E.C. Directive (1977) on the Education of Children of Migrant Workers reiterated two areas of education; the teaching of the official language and languages of the host country and the promotion of the mother-tongue and culture of the country of origin. The Article 3 stipulates:

"Member states shall in accordance with their national circumstances and legal systems, and in cooperation with States of origin, take appropriate measure to promote, in co-ordination with normal education, teaching of the mother-tongue and culture of the country of origin for the children of workers of Member States".

It seems that this directive has few legal powers for its execution. For example, Britain has made little progress in this direction considering the expected enforcement of the directive from 1981 onwards.

ii) The Department of Education and Science Curriculum Advice (1981) along with the recent D.E.S. document 'The School Curriculum' acknowledges the fact that today many pupils have a first language other than English (or Welsh). It states:

"Far more people than in the past have a first language which is not English or Welsh. This constitutes a valuable resource, for them and

the nation. How should mother-tongue teaching for such pupils be accommodated within modern language provisions, so that this resource does not wither away and the pupils may retain contacts with their own communities".

The local education authorities are making painfully slow progress in thi field.

iii)   Both the D.E.S. Linguistic Minorities Project (1979-83) and the Bradford Rising Fives bilingual programme (Panjabi and English 1980-81) along with the E.E.C. Bedford Pilot Project on Mother-Tongue Teaching (Panjabi and Italian languages, 1976-80) demonstrate what the then Secretary of State for the Department of Education and Science (Carlyle, 1980) stated:

"We are in a rather different situation with regard to the E.E.C. Directive on Mother-Tongue Teaching. Because of the general integrationist approach that has been adopted, we have little experience in this field. We therefore need to develop strategies on Mother-tongue teaching and the resources – both human and material – that will enable us to pursue it".

The present inquiry could find very little advancement in these direction outlined by the Secretary of State for the D.E.S.

(iv)   Fifth Report from the Home Affairs Committee (1980-81), Racia Disadvantage: The Home Affairs Select Committee's Report (18) state that:

"The Committee supports fully 'O' and 'A' level examination in mother-tongues recommending that the D.E.S. should actively encourage the incorporation of Asian languages into the modern languages curriculum and that details of such examination be published in the annual statistics of the Department. There has been central initiative from the D.E.S. in the forms of guidelines and financial support".

v)   A national survey of L.E.A.s on Mother-Tongue Teaching (1981) The Commission for Racial Equality conducted the survey which indicate that L.E.A.s have some general awareness of the issue of mother-tongue teaching and bilingualism. It also shows that there is some indication o interest and commitment on the part of some local education authorities ir offering 'O' and 'A' level examinations in Bengali, Panjabi, Gujrati, Urdu Hindi, Polish and Chinese. There are also some initiatives at the Primary school level.

vi)   The D.E.S. Circular 5/81 — The Directive of the Council of the European Community on the Education of Migrant Workers, 31 July, 1981 In this circular the D.E.S. has indicated that it sees its responsibilities under the E.E.C. Directive as follows:

"For its part, the D.E.S. is sponsoring research relating to the provision and educational implications of mother-tongue teaching,

as well as taking a close interest in the E.E.C. sponsored initiatives in this country. Issues arising from the Directive are also within the terms of reference of the Committee of Inquiry into the Education of children from Ethnic Minority Groups in 1979 under the chairmanship of Anthony Rampton and is expected to submit its final report in 1985 under the Chairmanship of Lord Swann. Local education authorities and others may wish to make their views on this subject known to the Committee".

In the same circular, the Department sees it as the responsibility of local education authorities to explore ways in which mother-tongue teaching might be provided, whether during or outside school hours. Local authorities perhaps are expecting for financial support from the central kitty for such provisions as indicated by the L.E.A.s representatives taking part in this research.

vii)   Multi-ethnic Education: The Way Forward, Schools Council, 1981: Little and Willey (1981) report from the School Council's Project: Studies in the Multi-ethnic Curriculum. During this survey 14 local authorities expressed support for teaching minority languages. In Contrast to the current level of actual provision, just over 50 per cent of schools with a concentration of ethnic minority group pupils said that: "they would like to be able to start or extend the teaching of minority languages — the major constraint being the lack of qualified staff and time-tabling difficulties . . .". Six local authorities expressed support for teaching other subjects in the mother-tongues of ethnic minority groups e.g., one Local Authority was quoted saying:

"We think this is important throughout but especially (a) at the start of formal education, (b) in secondary subject areas; this authority would be sympathetic provided that funds were provided for the employment of these teachers, and teachers could be found to cope with fifteen different languages of pupils in the authority's schools".

Very few local authorities seemed to have given any thought for the training and supply of community language teachers so far.

viii)   'In Service Teacher Education in a Multi-racial Society'. The D.E.S. Research Project 1981, University of Keele: In describing the contents of various in-service courses for teachers, Eggleston, Dunn and Purewal note some references to mother-tongues in their report:

"Attention was drawn to the use and maintenance of various languages in amongst ethnic minorities and the extent of linguistic diversity in schools and in British society. Examination of structures of certain languages occurred in several courses and their possible effects on learning English. In the award bearing D.E.S. course consideration was given to policy, theory and practice in teaching mother-tongues in state schools, as a medium of instruction and as a subject for language maintenance or examinations".

This illustrates a step in the right direction in the field of educational research with regard to the considerations of linguistic minorities in Britain.

Considerations were occasionally given to teaching all pupils about the nature of linguistic diversity by different bodies but without much success.

ix)   Linguistic Diversity and Mother-Tongue Teaching: A statement by the National Union of Teachers, February 1982 stresses:

"In publishing this pamphlet on 'mother-tongue teaching' the Union wishes to make a contribution to the climate of welcoming acceptance. We lend our support and add our voice to those who wish to see proper respect given to the variety of home and community languages spoken by the pupils in our schools. The Union would wish to see that the same status is accorded to ethnic minority languages as to other modern European languages, and the teachers and resources made available in schools to ensure that this can be achieved. The pamphlet draws attention to the needs and difficulties inherent in implementing stategies for mother-tongue, and urges those responsible to explore the possibilities and to take positive action so that children can retain pride in their cultural heritage. To value language and culture is to value the child.

For a young child, the language of the home is part and parcel of his or her own cultural and social identity ... From the work that has been done on studying the language and learning patterns of young children in school who do not speak English as a first language, an overwhelming case emerges to show that they are seriously disadvantaged educationally and will be slower to progress with school work if their use of their mother-tongue is not accepted and catered for in school (Brown, 1979). Concept development and language development go hand in hand. Various studies in mother-tongue teaching indicate that children taught basic skills in their mother-tongue in a bilingual education programme (e.g., Panjabi in Bradford) make better progress than children in control groups who are taught only English, and that time spent being taught in their own language does not impair their acquisition of English, and may even assist the process." (Chapman, 1981).

We can say that this was one of the most progressive statements made by any professional body of teachers for minority languages.

x)   Ethnic Minority Community Language: A Statement, Commission for Racial Equality (1982). Commenting on the selection and choice of community language the Commission states:

"These languages may be the mother tongues actually spoken at homes or community languages which are chosen to be studied as literary languages or the medium of instruction. Throughout history groups of people have expressed a desire to learn another language which they see functionally more relevant than theirs. Asian children

who speak Panjabi at home may well want to learn Urdu instead of
Panjabi because this was the traditional language of learning for their
parents. Those from the East Punjab may chose to study Hindi for
religious reasons. A minority of Cantonese-speaking Chinese
children may chose to learn Mandarin which is the national spoken
language of the People's Republic of China and Taiwan. In
responding to the multi-lingual pattern of the community, schools
should develop curricula capable of catering for such preferences".
It goes on to say that:

"A considerable minority of children in our schools are bilingual and
their knowledge of and ability in languages other than English should
be recognised and seen by their schools as a rich linguistic and
intellectual resource that should be encouraged and built on.
Curriculum development that encouraged mother-tongue teaching
would not only contribute to the self-respect of linguistic minorities
but would strengthen school-community links . . . Bilingualism will
not become a reality if learning the minority languages is restricted to
a very small number of classes a week, while every other class is taught
exclusively in English. The challenge to the curriculum is to be able to
accommodate some teaching in both majority and minority
languages."

The Commission emphasises the vitality of mother-tongue teaching and
bilingual education in its usual forceful tone.

xi) Training Teachers of Ethnic Minority Community Languages — Craft
and Atkins, University of Nottingham: A Report for the Swann Committee
(1983). In one of its recommendations on national policy initiatives, this
report stresses that:

"The range of linguistic needs in Britain is varied, and it will require
action by the D.E.S., L.E.A.s, teacher trainers, examining bodies and
community groups if any systematic progress is to be made. The total
programme need not be expensive, but some significant adjustment in
our current approaches need to be made . . . If we are to maintain a
valuable national asset, to avoid educational under-achievement, and
to prevent the alienation of a new generation from their parents,
relatives and a significant element of their bilingual-bicultural
heritage, existing provision should be urgently reviewed.

A clear indication of support for ethnic minority language without any
reservation dominates this report.

xii)   National Congress on Languages in Education (NCLE) 1980-82.
The National Congress on Languages in Education in collaboration with the
Centre for Information in Language Teaching and Research, National
Council for Mother Tongue Teaching and other national bodies set up a
working party on 'The Language of Minority Communitites' in 1980 and
this working party produced its report in 1982. The following comments

made by the NCLE are of some relevance:

"We believe that there are possibilites at various points within the education service for meeting the wishes of many parents and community organisations for some encouragement of people's natural interest in the living languages of their communities. However, we should suggest that where 'the population of their area' includes a significant proportion of speakers of languages other than English, L.E.A.s ought to consider responding more fully than most have so far felt able to support particular linguistic 'abilities and aptitudes' among their populations under the provision of the 1944 Education Act".

The report quoted National Association of Language Advisors (NALA) in these words:

"There is an increasing diversity of languages used as mother-tongue by linguistic minorities in the U.K. Therefore, it is not unreasonable to think that the school curriculum should take account of this picture".

This view was reinforced in Her Majesty Inspectors' View of the Curriculum (D.E.S., 1980):

"There is also a strong case for a modern language in the education of all pupils, and for the establishment of national policy on the place of individual languages in the system. Account has also to be taken of the presence in many schools of British born pupils from ethnic minority groups who are already acquainted with languages other than English, and the children of migrants from the E.E.C. and other European countries, who wish to maintain and develop their mother tongues".

There seems to be an equable support in favour of community languages as an integral part of the school curriculum and the above discussion illustrates the relevance and the need for mother-tongue teaching and bilingual education. We ought to look at the whole rationale of bilingualism in social, ethnic, psychological and educational perspectives. However, for a large majority of people in the world, use of more than one language is a natural way of life. A variety of factors determine as to which language is spoken on any particular occasion (Ervin-Tripp, 1964; Fishman, 1965). Most of the nations of Europe are bilingual or even multi-lingual with two or more ethnic groups speaking different languages. This is also true of the countries of Africa, America and Asia as well as other places throughout the world. It is well illustrated in the national policy of Canada as one of bilingualism with a significant proportion of the population being capable of functioning competently in both languages (Lieberson, 1970).

Until recently in the United States, Britain and Australia, the prevailing 'melting pot' concept as well as a lack of complete understanding of the social significances of languages, has usually led to the assumption that such individuals or ethnic groups will or should eventually give up their native languages and join the 'more natural' monolingual English speaking population. The United States appear to have begun to recognise the value of cultural diversity, as well as its relation to linguistic diversity. Educational programmes that are intended to preserve and nurture what remains of such cultural diversity reflect this new 'enlightened' approach. Because of the close relation which exists between language and culture, this approach must pay particular attention to the question of second-language acquisition and bilingualism. The Bilingual American Education Act 1967 reflects the increasing awareness of the need for programmes that are aimed at the improvement of education through the use of bilingual approaches (John and Horner, 1971).

In the case of Australia, support for ethnic minority languages is ever increasing. Smolicz and Lean (1980) found in their study that one fifth of the Australian population is derived from a variety of non-English speaking backgrounds. The Australian Federal Government Survey of 1975 shows as many as 15 per cent of primary school and 12 per cent of secondary school children had a native tongue other than English. They found that as many as 83 per cent of school children think that minority Australians should keep their own languages. The support for bilingualism within all groups is greater among children than parents. Trainee teachers also supported bilingualism in schools. Rado and Lewis (1980) reported that the Australian official opinion about ethnic language maintenance and the minority communities' view both favour experimentation with community language teaching and bilingual education. They also noted that language maintenance programmes should not be seen as a remedy for the disadvantaged but as an enrichment for the whole school population.

The consideration of the social and psychological implications of bilingualism is a significant issue of national and international importance. Language planning throughout the world is a matter of educational, political and social significance. New language policies are being developed and old policies being revised, and in most instances these include issues of bilingualism and multi-lingualism . Therefore, a constant research in the different aspects of bilingualism and multi-lingualism is crucial in the field of modern education.

Chapter 4

Research Methodology

Human beings continually strive to understand the phenomena they encounter as the basis for dealing more effectively with the problems they present. The means by which they seek answers to these problems can be classified into three broad categories; i.e., experience, reasoning and research. These categories are, of course, complementary to and overlapping with one another. Research is best conceived as a combination of experiences and reasoning (Mouly, 1978). Most of the complex problems facing modern human beings call for the operation of all three categories. The present study had also hoped to use all these broad categories in order to unfold the complexities of mother-tongue teaching and bilingual education in a multi-ethnic society.

Every piece of research is unique in its own right and nature. No two pieces of research are the same in their objectives, contents, direction, methods and the resultant findings. This may explain why there is no universally accepted, inflexible definition of research (Review of Educational Research, 1958). Research is an activity that is both pervasive and diverse (Wise et al., 1967). In one instance it may appear to be childishly simple; in the other, astonishingly complex. Often it is inconclusive or even impractical. It may take place in musty archives or in antiseptic laboratories. It may be the effort of a solitary scholar or a group of researchers funded by an organisation or a department; it may expand the frontiers of human knowledge or merely nudge them a little. But under whatever condition research takes place, it is characteristically and inevitably a systematic inquiry for verified knowledge. In this simple description is implied the whole syntax of research (Verma and Beard, 1981; Wise et al., 1967).

Closely related to personal experience are customs and traditions which provide a large percentage of the answers to everyday human problems. Obviously, experience is a basic part of the foundation on which scientific knowledge must rest. On the other hand experience, as a tool in the

78

discovery of truth, has very definite limitations that must be acknowledged by those who may rely on it. Primary among these limitations is the fact that our experiences are often at the level of those of the blindmen looking at the elephant. A simple hunch or general impression soon becomes an opinion, which in turn, becomes a conviction to which we treat as if it were an established truth. **That is why the present author as a teacher of minority community languages, did not, soley, wish to depend on his personal experience of mother-tongue teaching though it provided useful insight into the area.** It has been the endeavour of the writer to make use of experience, personal or otherwise, with great care and utmost reasoning. Reasoning is another tool for a person's search for truth. Reasoning is further divided into 'deductive' and 'inductive' methods of inquiry. One can think of endless examples of deductive reasoning based on rules of logic. For instance, in this present study the relevance of the experience of 'bilingualism' and 'bilingual education' abroad, i.e., in the U.S.A., Canada, Australia, Asia and Europe, has been examined in relation to the British context.

The next milestone in the progress of scientific knowledge was inductive reasoning as advocated by Francis Bacon (1561-1626). He led a revolution against what he saw as a tendency for philosophers first to come to a conclusion and then to marshall the facts in its support — much as in a debate i.e., presenting a convincing argument in support of a point of view, rather than discovering the truth as a main concern. **For instance, one may conclude that teaching of mother-tongue restores confidence and positive identity among minority group children and then start looking for some examples to support this view before finding the basis for such truth. The author was inclined to make use of this dual approach to compare the situation of bilingualism in Britain with those in various parts of the world.** This dual approach is the essence of the modern scientific method and marks the last stage of human progress towards empirical science, a path that took him/her through folklore and mysticism, dogma and tradition, casual observation and finally to systematic observation.

Verma and Beard (1981) have described the inductive-deductive method under the heading "The modern method of research" which they call as "The scientific method". The reason for using the term 'the modern method of research' is that the scientific method has several meanings and it includes the elements of an inductive-deductive process which are applied to both the natural sciences and the social sciences. This scientific method of research employs hypotheses or questionnaires, data sampling, testing, conclusions, application or some such process. It sometimes refers to the method of controlled experimentation and stresses quantitative and qualitative approaches.

An investigator's concept and ideas might be vague and ill-defined to begin with . He/she has to define the problem in a precise manner eventually. At this point in the research process his/her intuition, speculation, hunch or intelligent guess becomes necessary for the formulation of a clearly defined problem. The problem recognition is perhaps one of the most difficult parts of the investigation process. The hyposthesis or the questionnaire must be stated clearly in order to test its logical or empirical results. The use of a hypothesis or a questionnaire may help to check an investigation from becoming too broad in scope or disorderly in construction but it must be adequate to take into account all the requirements of the research situation (See Appendices 1 and 2).

Van Dalen (1966) writes about the importance of well formulated hypotheses or questionnaires in these words: "No scientific undertaking can proceed effectively without well conceived hypotheses ... Without hypotheses research is unfocused, haphazard and accidental. Tested hypotheses and questionnaires direct the researchers to arrive at objective and valid conclusions." Kerlinger (1973) states that: "The scientist cannot tell positive from negative evidence unless he uses hypotheses". Hypotheses and questionnaires are the backbone of research process and they should be established with logic and objective reasoning. **As the present investigation falls in the purview of qualitative inquiry, it was decided to make use of the questionnaire considering the different demographic, geographical and administrative natures of the local education authorities for an empirical evaluation of language development policy with reference to minority groups in Britain.**

It seems appropriate at this point to look into the different types of research and their application to the present inquiry. Research has been classified in various ways i.e., by method (e.g., historical, descriptive and experimental), by areas of academic discipline (e.g., sociological, psychological, educational etc.), and by purpose. From the various combinations available in the literature, Verma and Beard (1981) identify the four classifications i.e., pure or basic research, applied or field research, action research and evaluation research. These labels do not represent discrete categories. This typology had the advantage of highlighting certain crucial differences between research that is oriented to the development of theory and research designed to solve practical problems.

The present study can be described as 'evaluation survey research' since it aimed to evaluate the implementation and development of mother-tongue (community language) teaching and bilingual education policy with reference to linguistic minorities in Britain following the E.E.C. Directive (1977). If evaluation is carried out at intermediate stages to implement changes in the programme, it is called process or formative evaluation. The evaluation at the completion of the planned programme is known as summative evaluation. The present investigation is a kind of process or formative evaluation research rather than a summative evaluation.

It is perhaps not possible to categorise any piece of research purely in one 'type' or the 'other'. As any research is a complex activity, the variations discussed above overlap with one another in some form or manner. Though the present inquiry may be more inclined to a variety of survey and of 'evaluation research' it surely constitutes elements of applied and action research as well.

The present study has taken advantage of modern educational research from far and wide in the sphere of teaching of minority languages and bilingual education (ref; Chapter 3). As discussed in the previous chapter, the research in multi-lingual and bilingual education has made its headway in the United States, Canada, Australia and Europe. Perhaps this aspect of educational research is still a fledgeling in the British context. The experience and findings of educational researchers abroad with regard to the multi-lingual developments in pluralistic settings cannot be ignored. **The author has tried to support his work in the light of relevant educational research at home and abroad; for instance, the design of questionnaires for the LEAs and schools** (Fishman, 1966, 1968, 1972, 1976; St. Lambert Experiment, 1972).

In educational research there are other issues involved such as ethical considerations which need to be adhered to by professional researchers. These issues were ignored in the past. For example, Dennis (1941) investigated the role of social stimulation on child development by raising a pair of twins in virtual seclusion for a year. The situation is changing fast in modern times and more and more attention is being paid to the ethical consideration of research with human subjects. The research procedures and methods may produce undesirable psychological side effects. In addition to these, human beings have the right to refuse participation in research, the right to remain anonymous and the right to ask the researchers to guarantee confidentiality. Investigators sometimes obtain personal information about the subjects by means of deceptive methods. These practices raise both ethical and legal questions concerning the rights of the research subjects. Verma and Beard (1981) stress that: "The human subjects should not be viewed as an ingredient in the research laboratory". It certainly restricts the scope of educational research in delicate situations. The ethical issues obviously make educational researchers rethink their strategies of research techniques.

A recent trend in educational research has been a greater emphasis on applied rather than basic research. Many researchers believe that it has created a vacuum in the theoretical aspect of education. Whether or not there has been little emphasis on basic research, most consumers of educational research agree that there is a wide gap between research findings and their practical application. This gap can be narrowed if more and more teachers are involved in practical research, and solutions to many of the classroom problems can be sought in the natural setting (Corey,

1953). Bridging the gap between the professional researchers and the classroom teachers, Stenhouse (1975) writes in the chapter on 'The Teacher and Researcher' that:

> "... it is difficult to see how teaching can be improved or how curricular proposals can be evaluated without self-monitoring on the part of teachers. A research tradition which is accessible to teachers and which feeds teaching must be created if education is to be significantly improved".

It is perhaps due to this thinking that currently more and more experienced teachers and educators are encouraged to take up research studies in order to improve the learning and teaching process.

If classified on the basis of the above discussion the present study can fall into various categories. As discussed before, this categorisation of educational research is overlapping and it will be naive to categorise it into any water-tight classification. **So far as its approach is concerned, it can easily be described as a sociological educational research as one of its aims is to evaluate the socio-linguistic aspects of linguistic minorities in Britain and those aspects cannot be divorced from the psycho-linguistic needs of the same groups.** From the data collection point of view the interview procedure has been dominant as a tool to gather the relevant information from different parts of the country. As an educational research, the present study is inclined to be qualitative rather than quantitive in nature. It is a descriptive empirical analysis (i.e., reflective and illuminative) rather than psychometric in techniques. At the same time it can be classified as applied and consumer oriented inquiry in its applicability to curriculum development rather than a 'pure' research. So far as the educational research methods are concerned, this present investigation can be classified as a historical and descriptive piece of research in its nature and contents rather than an experimental inquiry. In spite of all what has been said, it is still an impossible task to classify this work into a neat category or type since these categories overlap with one another. On the other hand it is a kind of case study applying some ingredients of the survey method.

The literature seems to indicate that there is no hard and fast accepted scheme for classifying educational research. At the same time some forms of classification are necessary for evaluating educational research studies when they are related to the specific methodological characteristics of each category. Some sort of classification is advantageous in making the analysis of research process easier to understand and to comprehend since modern educational research constitutes elements of several inter-related disciplines and makes use of different kinds of techniques. As mentioned before historical method, descriptive method and experimental method are the three broad areas of research methodologies. None of these categories is intrinsically superior to the others. All of these make particular contribution to the field of research. **Sometimes a piece of research as the present one may**

fall into more than one of these categories. For instance, after identifying the problem of investigation a research worker may gainfully start with an historical study to determine what has been done in the past, and then to go on to collect data about the present state of affairs regarding the problem, which would constitute a descriptive or experimental study. That is exactly what happened with the present investigation with regard to minority community language teaching and bilingual education development in Britain. Many research programmes in education make use of all three methods. It must be pointed out, however, that the methods, techniques and strategies employed in any research situation are dictated by the nature of the problem and the kind of information required.

Historical method: **This study adopted an historical perspective at the initial stages in order to understand the present British situation of ethnic minority community language teaching in the light of past events and trends in the field of bilingual education programmes in different parts of the world.** In recent times the historical method in educational research has regained the reputation which it had lost during the 1930s because of the misuse of the method by several research projects in the United States (Barnes, 1960). The modern historical research may be described as the application of systematic and rigorous method of enquiry for understanding the past; it is an interpretative synthesis of past events and records. Travers (1978) describes historical research as:

"...*a procedure supplementary to observation, a process by which the historian seeks to test the truthfulness of the report of observation made by others*".

Historical research provides the kind of evidence which may lead to new understanding of the past and its relevance to the present and future. Studies of historical nature in educational research consist of a considerable collection of data. The problems involved in the process of historical research make it a rather difficult task. Barzun and Graff (1970) have produced an interesting work suggesting how to deal with basic problems in treating historical information.

Experimental method of research: The experimental method is often regarded as the scientific approach to research. In the experimental research, through manipulating an experimental variable, attempts are made to determine how and why a particular condition or event occurs. For any experimental study, there has to be an independent variable that is manipulated by the researcher under highly controlled conditions. The experimental method has its roots in the physical sciences and one of the early investigators who extended the use of the experimental inquiry into education was Thorndike (1918). This 'scientific' approach has been extensively adopted in the sphere of educational research in recent times. Admittedly, the control of the independent variable and outside factor is rather difficult, if not impossible, when dealing with human behaviour. That is why the critics of experimental research contend that experimental studies relating to education lack realism, and results obtained have little significance to the teaching-learning situations.

Descriptive method of research: **The present study can be best described in the terms of descriptive method of inquiry.** The descriptive method of research is primarily concerned with portraying the present while the historical method concentrates on the past events. The main difference between various types of descriptive research is in the actual process of description. Descriptive research is not only a structural attempt to obtain facts and opinions about the current conditions of things but it involves elements of comparison, and of relationship of one kind or another. **For example, the present investigation was not only concerned to gather facts and opinions about mother-tongue teaching in Britain but was also expected to compare the language programmes for multi-lingual societies around the world in order to establish the relevance of different strategies and approaches for positive bilingualism (ref: Chapter 3).**

Descriptive research involves a certain amount of interpretation of the meaning or significance of what is described. Therefore, this process is often criticised on the grounds of bias from the investigators' subjective judgements and their superficial impressions of the phenomena. At the same time Verma and Beard (1981) record that: "an examination of the many theses and dissertations submitted in the last two decades indicate that the descriptive method has been widely used". In order to mitigate the validity of the above criticism they put forward an inventory of structural plans for research workers involved with descriptive studies (ref: page 58). There are various means of data collection in descriptive research and it is often suggested that the investigator should be flexible in his/her approach in accordance with the nature of problem, types of techniques, the hypotheses or questions to be tested and resources available for carrying out the research.

Classification of descriptive studies:
There is no generally agreed classification of descriptive studies. For example, an interesting study under the title 'Middleton in Transition' by Lynd and Lynd (1937) has been classified as a survey by Jahoda, Deutsch and Cook (1951) while Young (1966) categorises it as a case study. However, for the sake of convenience Verma and Beard (1981) classify descriptive educational research into four categories: Surveys, case studies, developmental studies and comparative studies. These categories overlap and are complementary. The space in this chapter does not allow a detailed discussion of all these categories. **The author will particularly concentrate on case studies since the present inquiry is predominantly a case study.**

Surveys: It is one of the most commonly used methods of descriptive research in education and other social sciences. This method is frequently used to portray current conditions or particular social trends. Surveys gather data at a particular point of time with the intention of (i) describing existing conditions, (ii) comparing different conditions, and (iii) determining the relationship that exists between specific conditions. Considering all these elements, the present work can be described in the terms of a survey. **For instance, this inquiry aimed at portraying the situation of mother-tongue teaching developments in Britain, and comparing phenomenon of bilingualism in different countries e.g., the U.S.A., Canada and Australia and determining how bilingualism affects minority-majority pupils' education in different environments i.e., in relation to minority/majority social groups within a community (ref: Chapters 3, 6 and 7).**

Case Studies: A case study is a systematic investigation of a specific instance (Nisbet and Watt, 1978). Adelman et al (1977) define case study as: "an umbrella term for a family of research methods having in common the decision to focus an inquiry round an instance". A case study research entails observing characteristics of an individual unit, a pupil, a clique, a class, a school or a community with the intention of exploring attributes of that unit or group so as to establish generalisation about the wider population to which it belongs (Cohen and Manion, 1980). **Similarly, in this particular study a sample from a group of local education authorities in Britain representing the different geographical regions of the country has been drawn to establish the national portrayal of mother-tongue (community language) teaching and bilingual education developments with reference to ethnic minority groups. A case study approach was adopted for this enquiry in order to understand the educational function of bilingualism and mother-tongue teaching** in preference to sociometric and psychometric approaches which have limited scope for generalisation. **A clinical type of case study technique seemed to be more suitable for an in-depth study in the aspects of education of minorities with special reference to bilingual education and mother-tongue teaching developments and policy implementation on a national scale.**

The strengths and weaknesses of the case study method:
The case study looks at a single instance, and aims to identify the unique features of interaction with that instance. Its strengths are that the results are more easily understood by a wide readership beyond the professional research circle; they are immediately intelligible (if the report is well written) and have a three-dimensional reality like a good documentary (Nisbet and Watt, 1978). The case study provides suggestions for intelligent interpretation of other similar cases (ref: Chapters 3 and 5). A particulary important benefit is the possibility of a case study identifying a pattern of influences that is too infrequent to be discernible by the more traditional statistical analyses. It is a style of inquiry which is particulary suited to the

individual researcher, in contrast to other styles which may require a research team.

The case study method is a more unique research tool in that it gives us knowledge about concrete entities (e.g., the British local education authorities in the present study) for general application. Horace and English (1958) echo this view:

"Since case study emphasises the single case or instance, it differs in aim from an experimental and from statistical studies. But the case study often incorporates data from experiments or tests, and a series of case studies may be subjected to statistical study and generalisation.".

Psychologists, sociologists, anthropologists and educationists seem also to utilise the case study method with a view to supplementing the survey method and other research techniques. Young (1966) rightly remarks that, "the most meaningful numerical studies in social sciences are those which are linked with exhaustive case studies describing the inter-relationship of factors and of processes".

The case study as a research method also has a number of weaknesses. For example, the results are not easily generalisable, except by an intuitive judgement that 'this case' is similar to 'that case'. The author had tried to overcome this difficulty through comprehending the demographic patterns of minority group population in different regions of the country. Again, the researcher in a case study has to be selective but his/her selectivity is not normally open to the checks which can be applied in rigorously systematic inquiries such as large-scale surveys — it tends to be personal and subjective. **The author has avoided this pitfall by selecting the local education authorities representing the large number of ethnic minority group settlements in various parts of Britain.** The case study method is, however, flexible, and thus it can pick up unanticipated effects; it can change to take account of a new insight.

Research instruments and techniques:
An important part of the planning and conducting of a research study is the choice of methods by which data or information is to be collected. A research worker, therefore, needs to know about the techniques or tools available to him/her and something of their strengths and weaknesses. There are a number of research instruments available to researchers to collect the required data for final analysis. Most prominent of these instruments are tests, inventories, interviews and questionnaires etc. The interview techniques were the main tools in this research. The interview procedure was made reliable through following two flexible questionnaires. The questionnaires were structured in a way that any possible comparative disadvantage to any interview was minimised by a flexible approach. The interviews were conducted in an informal way to receive valid responses

from the subjects, i.e., the official representatives of the LEAs and the information received was, further, verified by interviewing the teachers in connection with mother-tongue policies and/or bilingual education programmes of the local education authorities. (see Appendices 1 and 2).

Questionnaires: A questionnaire may be regarded as a form of interview on paper. Procedure for the construction of a questionnaire follows a careful selection of questions to collect the relevant data. One cannot ingore Allport's (1942) words in this context: "If we want to know how people feel, what they experience and what they remember, what their emotions and motives are like and the reason for acting as they do — why not ask them." A questionnaire can be sent by post but its response may fall below the required proportion for the validity of final results (i.e., 70 per cent, ref: Nisbet and Entwistle, 1970). **In the present inquiry the role of the questionnaires was supplementary i.e., to standardise the interview schedules** (ref: Appendices 1 and 2). Three sources were brought together to construct the questionnaire i.e., (i) the author's personal experience on the subject as a teacher of community languages, (ii) guidance from the literature in this field (e.g., Fishman, 1968, 1972, 1976), and (iii) the opinions of various colleagues on the subject. The pilot runs for the questionnaires were given to ten different persons of relative experience in each case in order to ascertain the reliability and validity of the questions and to seek their considered opinion, advice, approval and consensus for its use as a research technique.

Interviews: Interviewing is the oldest and yet sometimes the most ill-used research technique in the world (Wragg, 1979). An interview can be either structured or unstructured depending on the design contents and techniques involved to collect the appropriate information. Both these types have their specific purposes and their relative advantages and disadvantages. Structured interviews are based on a carefully worded interview schedule and frequently require short answers or the ticking of a category by the investigator. They are often like a written questionnaire in form, and indeed it is common for a sub-sample of people who have been given a questionnaire to be interviewed, partly to reply and partly to check their written answers. The structured interview is useful when a lot of questions are to be asked which are not particularly contentious or deeply thought provoking. Unstructured interviews are used for in-depth inquiry. These require considerable skill and in areas such as psychotherapy, practitioners receive extensive training in the necessary techniques. Consequently, unstructured interview is not something which can be undertaken lightly or by anyone not well-informed about procedures or hazards. Yet sensitively and skilfully handled, it can produce information which might not emerge otherwise.

There is a third type of interview known as semi-structured. A carefully worded interview schedule is assembled for semi-structured interview, but in this case much more latitude is permitted. Often there is an initial question followed by probes (See Appendices 1 and 2). The schedule may contain spaces for the interviewer to record notes, or a tape-recorder may be used. A semi-structured interview schedule tends to be the one most favoured by educational researchers as it allows respondents to express themselves at some length, but offers enough shape to prevent aimless rambling. **The present author adopted a semi-structured technique of interviewing by using flexible questionnaires.** He was aware of the negative cliches and notion attached to interviews as a research technique. A great care was taken to minimise the personal biases of the interviewees by standardising the interview technique by semi-structured questionnaires. All the interviews were tape-recorded to reduce the chance of memory lapse for afterward recording. Beforehand the pilot runs were tried with two comparative interviewees in each case to establish the validity of the interview schedules and to ascertain the reliability of the procedural techniques.

Sampling: As mentioned before, the present research aimed to portray the development and policy implementation of community language teaching in Britain with a special reference to ethnic minority groups. Probably no concept is as fundamental to the conduct of research and the interpretation of its results as is sampling. Stephan (1948) expresses his views on this: "All empirical knowledge is, in a fundamental sense, derived from incomplete or imperfect observations and is, therefore, a sampling of experience". Research is almost invariably conducted on the basis of a sample from which the investigator derives certain generalisation applicable to the population from which the sample is taken. The 'population' in this present study is represented by the 'local education authorities' in Britain. One can simply define a 'local education authority' as a local government agency responsible for the education of people of all ages within a legally demarcated geographical area. The author has taken a sample from the 'population' of the British local education authorities.

If the sample is to give a true measure of the whole population, it must be a representative sample. One of the common approaches for a sample is that of a random sampling, in which every individual has an equal chance of appearing in the sample. This may be loosely described as a process of 'picking names out of a hat'. In educational research, a random sample is often an inconvenient group (Nisbet and Entwistle, 1970). Therefore, the author had used the 'controlled' sample as an alternative to the random sampling technique. In using a controlled sample, the writer desired to duplicate in his selected examples the same characteristics that existed in the universe or total number of instances. That is, the distribution of a particular characteristic or set of characteristics was deliberately made to conform to a predetermined proportion i.e., the ethnic minorities population in a region. In educational research the controlled sample is extremely useful, because many of our investigations have to do with not one but several pertinent characteristics of 'sub-groups' e.g., the local education authorities in different regions of the country in the present study. Sometimes, when the delineation of 'sub-groups' is clear, the sample is called a 'stratified' or 'representative' sample (Butcher, 1966). The present study can also be described in terms of 'multi-stage sampling' since in this national survey, a sample of regions was selected, within each region a random sample of local education authorities was selected and from these authorities a particular authority or authorities were selected for detailed investigation. It was more of a controlled sample for obvious reasons. Control in sampling is desirable, insofar as the factor controlled is known to be related to the characteristics being studied (Wise and Reitz, 1967).

There were two important facets in relation to collecting a sample for the present investigation. Firstly, the sample should be as varied as possible to represent all different regions of the country for its validity and reliability as a national study. Secondly, it should be taken into consideration that the populations of different minority communities were systematically and proportionately represented in the sample. For this reason an attempt was made to take a sample of more than one local education authority from the regions where there were larger settlements (concentration) of minority groups for different incidental reasons. For example, Southern Region including London and West Midlands Conurbations have high densities of ethnic minorities. These areas were represented by a sample of more than one authority in each case in order to see how the linguistic needs of these sizable minority groups were met in these regions. Scotland was represented by one authority where there was a considerable number of ethnic minority population and a similar sample for study was drawn from one local education authority representing the Welsh Region. The mainland of England was represented by five different regions for this purpose. The division of the local education authorities from the different regions of the country was like this:

Scottish Region	1 Local Education Authority
Welsh Region	1 Local Education Authority
Southern Region and London	3 Local Education Authorities
West Midlands Region	2 Local Education Authorities
East Midlands Region	1 Local Education Authority
North West Region	1 Local Education Authority
Yorkshire and North of England	1 Local Education Authority

The local education authorities were approached by writing to the respective chief education officers. The informal letter with a formal introductory communication from the author's research adviser was sent out to 13 local education authorities in different regions of Britain. Originally it was thought that six local authorities might be enough for a representative sample from the different regions. It all depended on the response from the local education authorities. One local education authority with one of the largest ethnic minority groups in Greater London refused to cooperate in the present study. Two local education authorities, i.e., one in the East Midlands and another in the North of England did not reply. Ten local education authorites representing all the above regions replied in agreement to assist with the research. It shows that 77 per cent of the local education authorities approached wished to take part in the inquiry and 23 per cent of the L.E.A.s were not keen to cooperate. Considering the wide-spread of the minority groups in view of the density of their concentration, it was decided to include all these ten authorities for the investigation.

As discussed in this chapter, interview technique with the help of standardised questionnaires has been used as a research tool to collect the necessary data from the local education authorities in the form of a case study. The interviewees for this purpose vary from the deputy director of an education authority to advisers for multi-cultural education and teachers/coordinators for community languages from the others. The variety of the interviewees helped to know the varied opinion of the different type of representatives of the local education authorities in relation to the teaching of minority community languages in the country. Obviously, none of the representative interviewees could answer all the questions and they had to seek the advice and the cooperation of their relevant colleagues in this connection.

Chapter 5

Case Studies of Local Education Authorities

Analysis of Data:

Having decided on the methods and techniques of collecting data, relevant information was collected from ten local education authorities representing the different regions of the United Kingdom. It was decided to draw the portrayals of these local education authorities highlighting the similarities and differences between the L.E.A.s' policies and practices in relation to the provision of mother-tongue/community language teaching and bilingual education with special reference to ethnic minority groups.

Local Education Authority A:

Local Education Authority A represents the South of England (London) region and it is one of the largest centres of minority group population in the country. The L.E.A.'s 1983 Home Language Survey showed that there were 50,353 pupils attending its schools who used a language other than, or in addition to, English at home. They consisted of 16 per cent of the school population, i.e., roughly 1 pupil in 6. As the Survey also showed, that compared with 14 per cent in 1981, i.e., roughly 1 pupil in 7, by any standards, this is a sizable proportion of pupils and a clear indicator of the need for an effective minority languages policy.

The majority of these pupils of non-English linguistic background were in their early years of schooling. They represented 21 per cent of the five year olds compared to 12 per cent of the fifteen year olds in schools. Thus it is likely that numbers will continue to increase for some time as these pupils move through the school system. Therefore, it would seem imperative that the local authority have a rigorous and comprehensive policy for minority language teaching extending from primary to higher education.

One hundred and forty seven different languages were recorded in the 1983 Language Survey and twelve languages (Bengali, Turkish, Gujrati, Spanish, Greek, Urdu, Panjabi, Chinese, Italian, Arabic, French and Portuguese) accounted for 83 per cent of minority language speakers within the authority's schools. Bengali had more speakers than any other language (apart from English). There were 9,098 Bengali-speaking pupils in 1983, more than twice as many as the next most common minority language, Turkish (with 4,316 pupils). The proportion of Bengali-speaking pupils was substantial in certain schools. For instance, thirty one primary schools had more than 30 per cent Bengali speaking pupils on roll and six of these schools had more than 80 per cent children of Bengali origin. Despite there being large numbers of linguistic minority pupils in many schools, no adequate provision had been made to support mother-tongue teaching and thus to enhance those pupils' educational development (see Chapter 3).

The composition of pupils from the ethnic minorities in the primary and secondary schools of this local authority had changed between 1981 and 1983. There was an increase in speakers of minority languages from the Indian Sub-Continent (particularly Bengali where speakers increased by 65 per cent) and from the Far East. Speakers of most of the European languages had decreased. Only 43 per cent of minority language speaking pupils were rated as fully competent in English by their teachers. Fifteen per cent were assessed as beginners in English, 19 per cent as second stage learners and 22 per cent were rated as third stage learners. It showed that the majority of the pupils from ethnic minorities were not fully conversant with the English language and yet little or nothing was being done to develop children's linguistic repertoire through mother-tongue support and/or bilingual initiatives.

The author interviewed the advisory headteacher for mother-tongue teaching and bilingual education within the L.E.A.'s Multi-ethnic Inspectorate. The relevant information was collected in accordance with the Interview Schedules for Local Education Authorities (For details see Appendices 1 and 2).

The interview revealed that the number of school age children including sixth formers had dropped from a record of 340,000 to 300,000 approximately. It also revealed that one pupil in five (20 per cent) was of minority origin and one pupil in six (about 16 per cent) spoke a language other than, or in addition to, English at home.

Educational use of languages other than English was made in schools. The local authority representative found it difficult to ascertain the scale of their use given the fact that there were 1,300 schools in the local education authority. Ideally, one might consider that the 147 languages recorded in the 1983 language Survey ought to be given equal status in terms of the availability of community langauge teaching, yet most of them were effectively little more than a statistic. It does not mean that the importance of pupil's mother-tongue can be undermined for psychological and social reasons. However, the Advisory Headteacher was able to confirm that the Local Education Authority had made provision to cater for the 12 languages spoken by 83 per cent of the linguistic minority pupils.

He also referred to the Authority's policy document on mother-tongue teaching and bilingual education. That document can be illustrated by the following extracts:

"The document entitled 'Bilingualism in the L.E.A.: the Educational Implications of the 1981 Language Census' considers the educational implications of the 1981 Language Census and makes recommendations for improving provision for the teaching of English as a second language and developing and implementing a policy on pupils' mother-tongue . . . This report considers the educational implications of the census under three headings:

(i)   The L.E.A.'s policy towards bilingualism
(ii) Improving provision for teaching English as a second language.
(iii) Developing and implementing a policy towards pupils' mother-tongues.

The starting point for constructing a sound educational policy towards bilingualism must be neither the importance of English nor the significance of the mother-tongue but the role of the language itself in the educational development of the children. Language is critical in fundamental educational processes like concept acquisition and inquiry, the understanding of cause and effect, interpreting and evaluating evidence. The ability to learn these things is developed in and through all languages. The Bullock Report 'A Language for Life' is a central statement about the role of language in learning in U.K. schools. It discussed bilingualism in this context and concluded (Chapter 20) that:

"in a linguistically conscious nation in the modern world, bilingualism, should be seen as an asset, and mother-tongues as something to be nurtured, and one of the agencies that should nurture (them) is the school".

The report saw the recognition and fostering of mother-tongue as complementing rather than hindering of English as a second language (S.1.C.). 'Confidence and ability in this language (i.e., the mother-tongue) will help the children to the same qualities in English (Op. Cit., Chapter 20).

The L.E.A.'s policy towards bilingual pupils must first be addressed to the learning of English, both in schools and in linguistic minority communities. This is unambiguously recognised as a priority, both in order to control access to the curriculum in schools and in order to equip pupils fully for life and work outside school. For several decades, this Authority has been developing and extending provision for the teaching of English as a Second Language (E.S.L.). There is much evidence of skilled, dedicated and successful practice in this area and an evolving pattern of school response in which all teachers in multi-lingual schools and not just ESL teachers are involved. But there are also clear indications where the Authority's provision needs to be improved and strengthened if the objective of equipping all bilingual children fully for life and work is to be achieved.

. . .The second complementary strand in the Authority's policy towards bilingual pupils concerns the promotion and development of mother-tongue. Although there are a growing number of exceptions, it is true to say that traditionally the U.K. school system has paid little attention to the home languages of bilingual pupils in multi-cultural schools. Great attention has been focused on the teaching of English but pupils' mother-tongues have either been neglected as outside the concern of schools, or in some cases regarded as in competition with English and therefore to be discouraged. Because of these perspectives, it is worth describing some of the main reasons why the Authority is promoting a policy to promote bilingualism and the pupils mother tongues; also to consider the research evidence which bears on the likely effect of such a policy on the English language development of the pupils concerned (S.1.C.).

The LEA's six-point policy:

— It is the right of all bilingual children to know that their mother tongue skills are recognised and valued in schools.

— It is educationally desirable that bilingual children in primary schools should be given the chance to learn to read and write their mother tongue and to extend their oral skills in those languages.

— It is educationally desirable that bilingual children in secondary schools should be given the chance to study the language of their homes in the school curriculum and to gain appropriate examination qualifications.

— The mother tongue skills of bilingual children should be seen as a valuable potential channel for supporting their learning.

— All children should have the opportunity to learn how other languages work and be encouraged to take an interest in and be informed about the languages spoken by their peers and neighbours.

— In developing arrangements for teaching mother tongue and other ways promoting bilingualism, schools should consult with the parents and seek to cooperate with mother tongue classes organised by community groups and other agencies.

First stage implementation of policy:

The Authority seeks immediate action as follows:-

a) The appointment of staff.

b) Increased support (by way of money grants) for mother tongue classes by approved community groups.

c) An allocation of money for building up a collection of existing mother tongue resources and to produce new ones.

d) Money for an in-service training programme for both teachers and other staff.

e) The Inspectorate is to develop local, divisional strategies.

Second stage implementation: bilingual teachers

Urgent consideration will be given to how staff with relevant bilingual skills can be appointed to the areas of the Authority where there are pressing needs of their skills".

"Long Term Goals". In this section of the policy document the L.E.A. goes on to discuss the need for mainstream funding for the language programmes, the development and publication of teaching resources, public examinations and liaison with national educational organisations and other local education authorities.

Such a policy would appear an ambitious one. The document clearly acknowledged the importance of mother-tongue in a child's educational development yet the L.E.A. had made scanty provision for 12 minority languages despite the fact that the language census had recorded 147 minority languages. There was a lack of a uniform approach to support all children's home language and only a limited number of minority languages were included in the school curriculum. As informed by the L.E.A. representative fewer than twelve main languages were given financial support for mother-tongue teaching organised by the voluntary community organisations. Only 50 per cent of the voluntary schools teaching those minority languages received financial grants from the L.E.A. It was apparent from the interview that there was no uniform policy for community language teaching in different divisions of the L.E.A. and that no central records were kept of the numbers of pupils learning each language.

The advisory headteacher representing the L.E.A. confirmed that:

"the first criterion of selecting the community languages for curriculum teaching depended on the goodwill and discretion of the individual school. The second criterion for such selection was based on there being a viable number of pupils wishing to learn their community languages".

Much, it appeared, was left to the discretion of the individual school rather than the linguistic and educational needs of minority pupils being pre-ordinate. The teaching of community languages had been introduced seven years ago and the year 1981 had been considered a turning point. It was then that the teaching of minority languages and bilingual education were officially established on a regular basis. Yet the record showed progress to be haphazard and inadequate as far as the teaching of minority language was concerned. The L.E.A. six-point policy stressed that all children should have the opportunity to learn how other languages work (i.e., the general language awareness of multi-lingual, multi-ethnic society) and that they should be encouraged to study minority languages. Yet apart from Spanish and Italian languages indigenous mainstream pupils were not involved in the learning of ethnic minority languages.

The L.E.A. had made provision of forty five teachers to teach community languages and most of these had qualified status. Given the number of linguistic minority children in primary and secondary schools the number of community language teachers could only be considered inadequate to support the mother-tongue teaching programme. As highlighted in the first stage implementation of the policy no special provision had been made for the initial and in-service teacher training of community languages although this aspect of the policy was said to be under constant review by the local education authority. It was also revealed that the Authority had realised that some thought should have been given to the teachers' training for community languages and bilingual education.

The L.E.A. did not seem to have any system of selecting pupils for community language teaching in schools. One would deem it necessary in view of the excessive demand for minority language teaching compared to the scarce teaching resources to meet such demand. The position of schools with regard to such selection was not consistent. It was entirely left to the discretion of the head-teachers and teachers. The local education authority did not decide specifically the criteria of inclusion of schools or colleges for mother-tongue community language teaching. All schools and colleges were asked to consider such proposals. In other words the schools and colleges had to make their case for teachers and resources to support a minority language teaching programme and then the authority would provide the facilities. This statement by the advisory headteacher showed that the decision for such a crucial educational issue was left to the discretion of schools regardless of the linguistic needs of minority group pupils.

There were about 200 voluntary supplementary language schools run by various community organisations to teach minority languages in the evenings or at the week-ends. The L.E.A. representative informed the author that the Authority had some liaison with these voluntary schools and could only afford to give support to half of them in the form of grant-in-aid, free accomodation, and other lending resources and materials. One might raise the question whether it was justified and satisfactory not to support the other half of the voluntary language schools whose provisions and educational importance might seem equally valid. This discriminatory policy with regard to financial and professional support to voluntary schools was contrary to the essence of the six-point policy outlined earlier. There was also some provision for adults from the minority and indigenous communities to learn ethnic minority languages through evening classes at the local schools, colleges and community centres. The Authority's spokesman, responsible for mother-tongue teaching and bilingual education, emphasised that teaching of mother-tongue was important to help pupils develop their abilities and potential while supporting their cultural and ethnic identity in a plural society.

The ethnic minority community language programme was extensively financed through the funding under section 11 of the Local Government Act 1966 with some additional Urban Aid. It seemed that no specific money was set aside within the general education budget for this aspect of curriculum development. No specific method of evaluation except public examination had been adopted by the L.E.A. to check the pupils' progress in this respect. A very small proportion of minority language learners took G.C.E. 'O' and 'A' level examinations. Ironically, no figures of such entrants were available at the time of the interviews as no such record was kept by the Authority. No provision for the C.S.E. examination in community languages had been developed by the L.E.A. It should be remembered that with the introduction of the 16 plus (G.C.S.E.) Examination in 1988, all local authorities have to develop new syllabuses for all subjects (Joseph, 1984). The L.E.A. claimed to be in the process of developing its own graded objective tests in minority languages such as were already available in German, Urdu and Italian languages.

It was pointed out by the L.E.A.'s representative that:

"racism in British society was one of the main problems encountered in operating these policies and the community language teachers felt isolated as if they were working in a vacuum i.e., the teaching of minority languages was not considered as an integral part of the school curriculum. The opposition to these policies by the teaching profession was enormous. Eighty per cent of the mainstream teachers were opposed to minority language teaching".

Commenting on the attitude of the general public the L.E.A. spokesman asserted that "nine out of ten members of the host community were against these policies". He also stated that:

"50 per cent of the ethnic minority parents were in favour of mother-tongue teaching and the other 50 per cent were uncommitted. The local media displayed mixed reactions to the whole programme of minority community language teaching."

What has been reported above gives a clear indication of the difficulties the Authority is fighting to surmount in order to implement its mother-tongue and bilingual education policies. It may also suggest that anti-racist education may be a pre-requisite to a good multi-ethnic educational practice.

The L.E.A representative expressed his opinion by saying that:

"Mother-tongue teaching and bilingual education will develop for some time to come and perhaps its strength will water-down as we go along in history. It is a transitional phase to some extent rather than a permanent feature of the educational system."

Howsoever valid this opinion may prove to be in the long term, one might feel entitled to question whether the existence of such preconceptions among the pioneers in this venture might reflect a lack of enthusiasm and resolution on their part to carry through such an important educational programme.

The author of this work also visited a primary school and interviewed a bilingual teacher of Bengali/English children. This teacher was not aware of the school's policy for bilingual education and mother-tongue teaching. The Bengali and Urdu languages were used as media of instruction in addition to English for most of the time in her school. All children from minority backgrounds understood their mother-tongue (See Appendix 2 — Interview Schedule for Schools and Teachers). There were some voluntary supplementary schools in the neighbourhood of this primary school but no liaison had been established with them. This suggested that the teacher concerned had not been aware of the importance of such relationships despite the fact that many of her school's pupils attended these supplementary schools in the evenings and at the week-ends.

The teacher was of the opinion that the majority of the parents fully supported the community language teaching programme and were very cooperative and helpful in the school activities. The Authority's representative had put the figure of parental support at 50 per cent. An up-to-date record of each child's linguistic progress was kept with the help of graded objective tests devised by the teacher. She also confirmed that mainstrean teachers in the school were very enthusiastic about bilingual education as they appreciated the importance of mother-tongue and children's bilingualism in everyday classroom work. On the other hand the advisory headteacher for the authority had suggested that there was 80 per cent opposition to such policies from the teaching profession.

The teacher interviewed explained that her headteacher was a keen supporter of minority children's mother-tongue and thought that there were good chances of its development in the future because of the E.E.C. support for such programmes. Answering the questions about ethnic minority parents' attitude she predicted that Sylhetti people (i.e., the speakers of a Bengali dialect Sylhetti) would like to maintain their community language while the middle-class educated minority parents might not favour their mother-tongue . She put forward the notion of class structure in relation to the maintenence of ethnic values, cultures, languages and traditions. Undoubtedly, the interviews with the authority's representative and the teacher provided enough ammunition for further discussion of the issues.

Local Education Authority B:
This is one of the London Borough Education Authorities with a substantial multi-ethnic community. The local authority's representative put ethnic minorities at 40 per cent of the borough's population and the Times Educational Supplement (17 February, 1983) reported this number as 50 per cent. This particular authority is considered to be one of the fore-runners for its multi-cultural and anti-racist initiatives. A

borough-wide school survey was conducted between May, 1982 and April, 1983 to obtain statistics of linguistic minority pupils. Details of the survey conducted in 103 out of 104 borough schools are given below. It is worth noting here that of the 35,051 pupils surveyed out of 37,482 (2,431 being absent), 12,362 spoke languages other than English, i.e., about 35.3 per cent of the school population. Gujrati and Urdu were the two topmost minority languages within the L.E.A. The top twenty minority languages spoken by the pupils were as follows:

1. Gujrati	5,180 pupils	11. Portuguese	179 pupils
2. Urdu	1,025 pupils	12. Cantonese	165 pupils
3. Jamaican Creole	609 pupils	13. Bengali	137 pupils
4. Panjabi	603 pupils	14. French	134 pupils
			(+10 French based Creole).
5. Greek	561 pupils	15. German.	120 pupils
6. Hindi	407 pupils	16. Japanese	120 pupils
7. Italian	336 pupils	17. Farsi (Persian)	103 pupils
8. Spanish	314 pupils	18. Gaelic	95 pupils
9. Hebrew	226 pupils	19. Polish	92 pupils
10. Arabic	184 pupils	20. Turkish	74 pupils

Of the 12,362 pupils who spoke languages other than English 6,084 were boys and 6,278 girls.

The above table showed that the authority might have considered giving support to these 20 minority languages rather than supporting the home languages of all children. These top twenty languages represented 10,662 (about 86 per cent of the total linguistic minority pupils); the remaining minority home languages spoken by 1,700 (about 14 per cent) of the linguistic minority pupils seemed to have been ignored.

Of the 12,362 pupils who indicated skills in other languages only 7 were reported as able to understand but unable to speak any language other than English. Details of the other pupils' oral abilites/literacy in the minority languages were given as follows:

One spoken language	11,291 pupils
Two spoken languages	960 pupils
Three spoken languages	104 pupils
One spoken languages but no literacy	6,894 pupils
Two spoken languages but no literacy	367 pupils
Three spoken languages but no literacy	44 pupils
One spoken language and literacy in one	4,261 pupils
Two spoken languages and literacy in one	435 pupils
Three spoken languages and literacy in one	48 pupils
One spoken language and literacy in two	128 pupils
Two spoken languages and literacy in two	155 pupils
Three spoken languages and literacy in two	10 pupils
One spoken language and literacy in three	8 pupils
Two spoken languages and literacy in three	3 pupils

The two tables above show the rich linguistic repertoire of a considerable number of pupils. This would point to the desirability of the Authority having a strong multi-lingual policy to support mother-tongue teaching.

An interview was conducted with the Local Education Authority's representative, an Assistant Education Officer (Schools) with a special interest in multi-cultural development.

He put the number of school-age children at approximately 38,000 of which the ethnic minority pupils made up some 40 per cent. In reply to the questions regarding the medium of instruction he admitted that only English was used for this purpose but provisions were being made to introduce other languages. This would suggest that ethnic minority pupils entering school with no background of English might well suffer disadvantage because of the absence of mother-tongue support in their schooling.

The 1982-83 Language Survey showed that more than twenty languages in addition to English were spoken by different minority group children, but the authority chose to concentrate its support in ten of these languages (i.e., Gujrati, Urdu, Panjabi, Greek, Hindi, Italian, Chinese, Bengali, Arabic and Turkish). It had no comprehensive policy to support home languages of all children and thus may have deprived many ethnic minority pupils of the opportunity to maintain or learn their mother-tongue.

The Authority had some guide-line policies on bilingualism and mother-tongue teaching in schools and these were produced in the form of reports by the Director of Education. Their contents can be gauged from the following extracts:

"Bilingualism in Schools:

This paper is intended to initiate discussion and debate in an area about which teachers in the L.E.A. are concerned, i.e., the education of their bilingual pupils. Bilingualism has traditionally meant that offering of two or more languages as the official means of communication and instruction, e.g., French and English in Canada. The situation within Britain, let alone this local authority, is more complex than this. A wide variety of second languages are present, e.g., Spanish, Chinese, Gujrati, Urdu, Bengali etc. There is no such thing as a homogenous bilingual community. Hence we need to take a new look at the concept of bilingualism which would include creating a positive attitude towards the use of other languages in schools and in society . . . The suggestions made in this paper are intended to lend support to work being done by individual teachers and schools and to encourage schools to discuss and work out the formulation of a positive policy towards bilingualism."

"Report on Bilingualism: .
The last decade has seen a vast increase in the number of pupils in the

Borough whose native tongue is not English.

The phrase 'bilingual education' itself covers a range of possibilities. At the one extreme is the possibility of teaching subjects through the medium of the mother-tongue, and teaching English as a second language. (In the centre is the possibility of teaching the main curriculum in English, and maintaining the mother tongue in special classes.) At the other end of the spectrum is the possibility of the casual use of the mother tongue in informal encounters between teachers and students and the use of English for all other purposes.

...Indeed to implement a broad bilingual education policy without due thought could do more harm than good to the cause it seeks to serve. Before bilingual education can be introduced to any considerable scale, there needs to be in our schools a thorough acceptence of multi-cultural education ... There is a need for in-service education in this area and this could be provided through day time courses at the Teachers' Centres and there should be school-based courses to encourage a flow of ideas and information between teachers in the same school ... Involvements of parents, of the P.T.A's is of great importance.

...As far as bilingualism is concerned, the present policy of the schools is to teach the children English through giving them extra tuition, and to sometimes ignore their mother-tongue ... Many parents are concerned for their children to continue to learn their mother-tongue and send them to Saturday schools for this purpose ... This need to foster the mother-tongue is not at present being met by all schools, which must in future play a fuller role.

...There are at present considerable numbers of children coming to nurseries and reception classes who speak only their mother-tongue. This situation is likely to continue so long as marriages continue to take place with partners from other parts of the world and so long as the minority communities choose to foster their mother-tongue rather than English .... Primary schools can do a great deal to raise the esteem of other languages by encouraging their use between staff and children, parents and staff, and between children, when appropriate ... The secondary school is better adapted to introduce mother-tongue teaching. Mother tongue should be offered as a modern language option, possibly as early as the first year and should lead to public examinations in this subject ... The policies outlined in this paper are essential for educating our pupils to form, and live in, a harmonious multi-cultural society".

This latter Document was referred to the Governing Bodies of schools so that a survey could be conducted among them to establish the extent of the problem in schools. It was pointed out in another report that the Governing Bodies were divided over the advantages and disadvantages of mother-tongue teaching. Before making an appraisal of the document, it would be appropriate to look at these extracts from the L.E.A.'s latest statement on mother-tongue teaching. (i.e., the Report of the Director of Education, July, 1983):

"Policy Statement on Mother Tongue Teaching:

It is crucial that the Authority has a policy statement on the subject of bilingualism if it is to be treated in a serious manner. I would suggest the following:

This local authority is committed to a policy of encouraging a positive attitude among those involved in the education of its children to the languages that the pupils bring into our schools. As this borough has increasingly become a multi-cultural society and the Authority is committed to a policy of multi-cultural education, the prevailing notion of a monolingual society is anachronistic.

The Authority intends to help bilingual children develop systematically their full educational and cultural potential by supporting home and community languages. There are good educational reasons for encouraging children, whose first language is other than English, to become bilingual.

There is a wealth of teaching experiences in languages other than English and it is the intention of the Authority to exploit this to the advantage of all its children. The Authority is also committed to encouraging with help, all voluntary groups who intend to run after-school language classes on school premises.

Recommendations:

The Committee is asked to agree to the policy statement on mother-tongue teaching as framed above. The Education Committee is asked to decide on whether it wishes to pursue any, some or all three options that are outlined below:

1. A team of teachers of Gujrati (and maybe Urdu) to work within the classrooms at infant level, working in tandem with the English teachers to support lessons through mother-tongue.
2. That all secondary schools, as part of their modern language options offer appropriate Asian languages such as Gujrati, Urdu, Hindi, Panjabi and Bengali.
3. Free school premises after school hours be made available to community groups who run voluntary language classes. After the team of teachers has been selected, training courses should be arranged with the School of Oriental and African Studies and the Institute of Education, University of London. Opportunities for training should be extended to teachers who run voluntary after-school classes. Every school should be encouraged to develop its own language policy with a view to utilising fully the resources the pupils bring into the school. Every secondary school must include some language/languages of non-European countries in its option system. Responsibility for

organising the training of teachers and monitoring the work in the schools and after-school voluntary classes should lie with the Modern Languages Adviser working under the Principal Adviser and Education Officer for Schools, but in close co-operation with the Multi-cultural Adviser".

Both the documents on 'Bilingualism in Schools' and 'Mother Tongue Teaching' have their merits as well as shortcomings. It should be acknowledged that the Authority took the initiative of embarking on a policy of bilingualism and mother-tongue teaching despite the fact that some other neighbouring local education authorities had apparently given no thought to these issues. The Local Authority seemed to be open-minded in its approach to the phenomenon of bilingualism in Britain. It should also be pointed out that the document assumed that bilingualism would be a transitional phase i.e., it would exist as long as marriages continued to take place with partners from other parts of the world. It means that the basis of bilingualism was not established on the principles of genuine deversity of ethnic and linguistic groups of the population. Moreover, the document was more like a discussion paper rather than being a concrete proposal for action; that could perhaps have been the reason for its rejection by some governing bodies.

The second report "Policy Statement on Mother Tongue Teaching" was a carefully drawn comprehensive document on a wider basis of multi-cultural philosophy. It was not specific in its recommendations to the Education Committee as it appeared to offer three vague options as regards its implementation. There was the possibility that the whole issue might descend into debate over how best to proceed with these options rather than firm decisions being taken to act. Other recommendations seemed to be pre-empted and imaginative except that there ought to be a clear distinction between comprehensive mother-tongue teaching and modern languages option at the secondary level. In other words community languages ought not to be treated as modern languages and, therefore, there should be a separate department for community languages within the L.E.A. working in close liaison with the other language departments.

The interview with the Local Authority's representative revealed that 200 children were involved in learning community languages (i.e., mainly Gujrati and Urdu) — 100 each at primary and secondary levels. This number seemed to be a very small proportion of the borough's linguistic minorities. No provision seemed to have been made within mainstream education for minority languages other than Urdu and Gujrati. Only six teachers were engaged to teach mother-tongue although the L.E.A. language Survey showed that 22 teachers were available within the Authority, capable of teaching different community languages. The L.E.A. appeared to be progressive in making arrangements with the Institute of Education, University of London for the in-service training of teachers for this purpose. The teaching of community languages had been introduced in 3 secondary and 8 primary schools. This amounted to little more than a pilot scheme, despite there being a need for its scope to be extended, and the programme to be put on a more permanent footing. There were 18 after school classes in minority languages run by voluntary organisations (i.e., seven in Gujrati, four in Urdu and one each in Chinese, Greek, Indonesian, Polish, Spanish and Portuguese). There seemed to be no established practice to encourage liaison between the L.E.A. and these voluntary language classes although some financial help was being given from the Urban Aid Grant.

The L.E.A. representative disclosed that there was no provision for adults from both minority and mainstream communities to learn minority languages. According to him the Authority would like to investigate the need and demand in this respect. As regards the planning and co-ordination of mother-tongue teaching and bilingual education programmes he went on to explain that:

"Mother-tongue teaching is necessary to make the indigenous population realise that everyone is equally important. This is a subtle way to make minority languages prestigious. This development is not a black problem but a white problem and the L.E.A. wants an enthusiastic co-ordinator for this aspect of the curriculum development. We are pressing on regardless of Section 11 financial provision. The Modern Languages Department is closely involved in the evaluation of these initiatives".

The interview also revealed that an unspecified but small proportion of pupils take 'O' and 'A' levels examinations in minority languages and there was no provision for C.S.E. examinations. Because no examination result figures were available one might feel entitled to question whether the Authority was effectively monitoring examination courses available. The L.E.A representative commented:

"We are thinking to consult parents for their opinion for mother-tongue/community language teaching programmes and their subsequent evaluatation in terms of academic standards and examinations etc."

While the desire to take parents into full confidence as regards their children's education could be considered commendable, it could be argued that the Authority had a responsibility to give a professional lead in its approach to mother-tongue/community language teaching.

The recruitment of teachers for this programme was regarded as the main problem the Authority faced. Analysis of the report on 'Bilingualism in Schools' and the interview suggested that the Local Authority was not making the proper use of the teachers available to offer community language teaching in schools. Commenting on the further questions the L.E.A. representative mentioned that the response of headteachers and teachers to the mother-tongue teaching policy was rather mixed, whilst the local teachers' unions and other professional bodies were very supportive of such programmes. Ethnic minority parents were very much in favour of the Authority's initiatives on bilingualism in schools. The attitude of the general public was reported as being against such policies at the initial stages but it had changed recently. In response to the question about media reaction he commented that the local media was "hysterical at first" but its attitude in relation to language policies had been levelling recently. It seemed that there was a need to convince the mainstream population of the benefits of such policies.

The L.E.A. representative predicted:

"Mother-tongue teaching and bilingual education will expand. It is something permanant not transitional. I do not think it will phase out. Diversity should flourish. There are not enough white people who could ignore it. It is a challenge to racism."

Such views indicated the will and the enthusiasm for such programmes. Progress, however, seemed to be painfully slow although there was a goodwill on the part of the local education authority. The Education Officer ended by saying, "We have some problems but we should, hopefully, succeed if we play our cards right under the changing circumstances".

The author also interviewed a teacher of Gujrati language working at the Authority's Curriculum Support Centre. She was responsible for Asian Languages development. She confirmed that English was the only language used as the medium of instruction in school even though 40 to 50 per cent of school children came from non-English backgrounds. She explained that there had been no development of independent community language policy by schools with the exception of one secondary school in the Borough. Gujrati was considered to be the main language to be introduced in the Authority's schools. As mentioned earlier the L.E.A. was not making comprehensive provision even for its top twenty minority languages reported in the borough-wide survey. It had only been able to introduce two community languages (Gujrati and Urdu) and those only in three secondary schools. Only one hour a week was devoted to the teaching of these languages. These languages were included in the school curriculum but there was a lack of specialist teachers for this programme.

The advisory teacher for Asian languages said that only pupils who could speak their mother-tongue were selected for community language courses. The L.E.A representative had reported that there was no procedure for such selection and all pupils were given equal opportunity to learn their mother-tongue. Such a view seemed to lack plausibility as there were only six mother-tongue teachers in three schools compared to a substantial number of linguistic minority pupils as shown by the L.E.A. Language Survey. The advisory teacher mentioned that more than half the pupils could understand their mother-tongue. It seemed that the Authority laid stress only on the written aspects of language learning and that no comprehensive provision existed that would facilitate the development of proficiency in either or both spoken and written skills in those languages. The teacher also pointed out that the parents were not offering satisfactory cooperation with the mother-tongue teaching policy although the L.E.A. Education Officer had suggested that there was full parental support for these programmes.

The interviews reported above reveal conflicting views on the issues of mother-tongue teaching and community languages. Commenting on the attitudes of various people towards the Authority's policies, the advisory teacher expressed the view that:

"Some headteachers are sympathetic and others, perhaps, are not. Ethnic minority languages are not given a proper status in the modern languages set-up. The ethnic minorities have to fight hard for the survival of their languages and cultures. The ethnic minority parents have to be articulate enough to see the community languages as part of the school curriculum. We hope that minority languages would develop and it would be a shame if the richness of linguistic diversity disappears."

An uncertainty about the future of minority community languages was apparent in her concluding remarks. It might be due to the lack of expected progress, the absence of clear-cut policies and their execution within the Authority.

Local Education Authority C:

This Local Education Authority is a county council education committee representing the South of England region and is one of the largest local authorites in the country. It has sizeable pockets of ethnic minority population in many of its industrial towns. The Local Community Relations Council, in its survey of July, 1983, found that the County had 33,695 persons in households where the head of family was born in the New Commonwealth and Pakistan (NCWP), representing 2.37 per cent of a total population of 1,423,143 at that time. The distribution of the minority group population in fourteen main areas of the County was recorded as follows:

District 1	1,424	(4.2 per cent of NCWP population)
District 2	1,598	(4.7 per cent of NCWP population)
District 3	2,696	(8.0 per cent of NCWP population)
District 4	1.003	(2.9 per cent of NCWP population)
District 5	3,897	(11.6 per cent of NCWP population)
District 6	6,479	(19.2 per cent of NCWP population)
District 7	2,208	(6.6 per cent of NCWP population)
District 8	5,703	(16.9 per cent of NCWP population)
District 9	1,758	(5.2 per cent of NCWP population)
District 10	1,210	(3.6 per cent of NCWP population)

District 11 1,253   (3.7 per cent of NCWP population)
District 12 1,607   (4,8 per cent of NCWP population)
District 13 1,282   (3.8 per cent of NCWP population)
District 14 1.555   (4.7 per cent of NCWP population)

Well over half of the County's NCWP population was contained in four districts, i.e., 18,776 (55.8 per cent). One area (District 6) had the highest minority population in the County, nearly one fifth of the total NCWP population.

According to the 1981 Census Small Area Statistics, not a single ward in the county was without a NCWP household. One hundred of the County's 379 wards had 2 per cent or more NCWP residents.

Future projections for school rolls were being based on figures provided by the OPCS monitor FM1 81/4 in 1980: Thirteen per cent of live births in District 6 were to mothers born in NCWP (the county average was 4 per cent compared to 8 per cent for England and Wales). This figure did not take into account the increasing number of women in younger childbearing ages who were of NCWP ethnic origin but were born in the United Kingdom.

The above figures would appear, broadly speaking at least, to lend support to the opinion, expressed in November 1983 by the Authority's Assistant Inspector for Multicultural Education, namely that there were considerable numbers of minority group settlers throughout the county, seeking to preserve their linguistic, religious and cultural heritages, through voluntary efforts, if no other means were available. The Local Community Relations Council under the enlightened guidance of its Community Relations Officer appeared to be an active pressure group to bring about some practical changes through multi-ethnic, multi-linguistic initiatives.

The author interviewed the County Assistant Inspector for Multi-cultural Education to collect information bearing on mother-tongue teaching and bilingual education programmes within the L.E.A. The information was collected in accordance with the Interview Schedule for Local Education Authorities (Appendix 1). The local authority's representative (as mentioned above) revealed that there were 4,297 pupils from linguistic minorities out of a total of 144,246 pupils in the County's schools (about 3 per cent of the school population). Although it appeared to be a comparatively small percentage, it was noted that in certain areas of the county the children from ethnic minority groups made up more than 50 per cent of the population in some primary schools. English was the only language used as the medium of instruction at all levels but it was reported that consideration was being given to the possible introduction of other languages for this purpose. Panjabi, Hindi, Urdu, Bengali and Chinese (Cantonese) were some of the home languages of linguistic minorities within the County and none of these languages was included in any capacity in the L.E.A.'s school curriculum.

The Authority did not have any official policy for community language teaching but the County Assistant Inspector who was also responsible for multi-cultural education development within the County had produced, in November, 1983, the following statement in this respect:

"Mother tongue teaching in (Local Education Authority C):

In this County, as throughout Britain, there is no evidence of a diminution of the desire of ethnic minority parents for their children's instruction in their mother-tongue. While there is universal recognition that English is the language of school and career, mother tongue maintenance is required for preserving links with the older generation in this country and the country of origin, for understandable reasons of heritage preservation, and perhaps most importantly for access to religious traditions.

So we see literally hundreds of primary age children in different towns attending Panjabi classes at the Sikh Temples and the Community Centres; Urdu and Arabic classes for Moslem youngsters, as widespread as (from one end to the other end of the county); and the establishment of supplementary Sunday or 'Twilight' classes for Chinese and Bangladeshi pupils.

Some of these continue to study up to public examination standard; in particular, at the link course held at a college, where the pass rate at 'O' level this summer was 100 per cent ... Pupils are generally satisfied with the arrangement of studying outside school. 97 per cent of pupils interviewed would not wish Panjabi as a curriculum option if it meant dropping another subject.

It is not to the benefit of the Authority, the Communities or the individual child that a separate educational system exists totally divorced from mainstream schools, with inferior facilities, outdated methods and often untrained staff. The solution of bringing these languages into the mainstream curriculum is at the moment not desirable on educational grounds (being divisive, lacking qualified staff, and being unwanted by pupils themselves) and is obviously impossible on financial grounds.

But there are relatively inexpensive strategies that we can adopt, to ensure greater co-ordination, direction and harmony of approach between the two systems. One of the tasks of the team of the Multi-cultural Education Resources Centre, starting in January 1984, will be to foster this coming-together, an approach which is supported by community leaders and the mother-tongue teachers themselves, who recognise the educational drawbacks of the present arrangements and the 'ghetto' status that their languages sadly hold.

The approach includes:

1. maintaining a survey of the communities and language teaching provision, drawing up a 'language map' of the County;
2. bringing together, from time to time, mother tongue teachers for training sessions and seminars, to share the concept of good educational

and language teaching practice;
3. establishing a resource bank of materials from other LEAs and supplementary Centres around the country, so that we all have access to the best current developments;
4. liaising with the Schools Council Mother Tongue Project, the London University Institute of Education 'Linguistic Minorities Project' and the National Council for Mother Tongue Teaching;
5. visiting the twilight teaching groups, to support and advise on techniques and assist liaison with schools over premises and other facilities.

A first step has been taken by the Education Committee's decision in June to foster a 'Pre-school Partnership Programme' to enable the five year old children to settle more rapidly into school by forging links with the community for pre-school experience, and providing an element of mother tongue availability in schools during the settling-in period. A Support Service Teacher will be largely concerned with this school/community liaison.

It is anticipated that the Centre will gradually become a focus for mother-tongue coordination throughout the County. It is possible that the case might have to be considered later for the establishment of a full-time Mother Tongue Teaching Co-ordinator within the County, a post which would be eligible for 75 per cent support from the Home Office under Section 11 of the Local Government Act 1966."

To judge from the above statement and the interview conducted with the L.E.A. representative it would appear that the Authority had not made much of a positive response to its obligation towards the cultural and linguistic minorities in the light of the E.E.C. 1977 Directive 77/486 and the subsequent D.E.S. (1981) Circular 5/81 in connection with the Education of Children of Migrant Workers. The Mother-tongue Teaching Statement appeared to support the maintenance of mother-tongue merely for social reasons rather than for any educational benefits (as discussed in Chapter 3). There was an apparent contradiction in the Mother-tongue Teaching Statement. Although opposition was expressed to the idea of ethnic minority children being taught under "a separate educational system totally divorced from mainstream schools" (and by implication this included the teaching of minority languages), the statement equally rejected, on educational grounds, the inclusion of those languages in mainstream schools.

The suggestion that minority pupils were reluctant to study community languages in mainstream schools because they "clashed" on the time-table with other important subjects was unsubstantiated. Even if there were strong evidence to support it, might there not be a case for a closer appraisal of schools' option systems to see whether better arrangements could be made? Also unanswered was the issue of parental reaction to that 'reluctance'. No evidence was offered of parental consultation on this important curricular matter.

To build an argument, using in part financial constraints, against the introduction of mother-tongue teaching in mainstream schools would seem faint-hearted. Such considerations appeared to overlook the fact that such provision could be eligible for Home Office support; under Section II of the Local Government Act 1966; 75 per cent of the costs incurred, if approved, would be met from national government funds. It seemed there was a lack of coherent policy and goodwill on the part of the L.E.A. to embark on the development of minority language teaching and bilingual education except for the peripheral gesture of 'Pre-school Partnership Programme'.

As there was no policy for minority community language teaching, the L.E.A. representative expressed the view that, 'such policy would be a desirable thing but because of the ignorance about the whole issue it would be difficult to have any such policy'. He tried to circumvent the issue by saying that, 'there were very few L.E.A.'s policies in other areas of the curriculum'. None of the ethnic minority languages was taught in the mainstream schools. The L.E.A. representative mentioned that attempts had been made but that these had proved unsuccessful. He could not account for this failure. He also emphasised the necessity to take the white and black communities with them if there was to be a successful outcome. He cited the white population's hostile reaction in another Authority to such a policy development. One might wonder whether such an example constituted a valid reason for maintaining the status quo.

Asked to comment on the support expressed for mother-tongue teaching by the then Secretary of State for Education at the E.E.C. Bedford Project Colloquium (24 March 1980), the L.E.A. representative retorted: "Mark Carlyle can say this but the D.E.S. does not give any financial support for these developments. To me this is an irrelevant muddle". Perhaps his comment was not entirely invalid, given the lack of real initiatives in that direction from the central government.

He admired the local Community Relations Officer's resourcefulness in this direction through introducing a 'Panjabi Language Link Course' up to G.C.E. 'O' level studies at a local college. It was apparent that there were no specific teachers for teaching community languages in the mainstream schools with an exception of one teacher appointed for nursery education liaison in one of the County's towns with a substantial ethnic minority population. The Authority was on the process of establishing close links with voluntary supplementary language schools since it was looking at these schools as the only source to develop community language teaching within the County. The L.E.A. had not provided any kind of assistance to these supplementary language schools run by the various voluntary community organisations. It was apparent that the Authority had given no consideration to initial or in-service teachers' training for teaching ethnic minority community languages.

The author, realising that the momentum of the interview needed to be maintained despite a succession of negative answers to his questions, persisted nonetheless.

Commenting on the Authority's planning and co-ordination with regard to mother-tongue teaching and bilingual education the Assistant Inspector expressed the view that 'recognition of children's linguistic need was their prime goal but they had no special provision or strategy for the development of minority community languages at that time'. At the same time he stressed that he was personally committed to the philosophy of mother-tongue teaching. His own report, quoted earlier, and much of what he said in the interview tended to give a different impression altogether.

When the author inquired about the response and reaction of headteachers, professional bodies representing teachers and the general public towards the teaching of minority community langauges within the county, he was informed that, 'the majority of headteachers maintained that there was no persistent demand by the parents for such programme'. As mentioned by the Authority's bilingual teacher at a later stage of the interview, it might be due to the factor that the linguistic minorities could not organise themselves as an effective pressure group to make a demand for mother-tongue teaching in the mainstream schools. It was also revealed that, 'the reaction of the general public to these issues was rather mixed. There was a good support on the whole from the teachers' unions and the local politicians when it was put to them in a proper context'. One might be tempted to interpret the version of 'proper context' as the mother-tongue/community language teaching being confined to out-of-school voluntary efforts.

Asked about the future of minority community language teaching in the British Education System, the L.E.A. representative was philosophical saying that "bilingualism is to be appreciated and developed. Mother-tongue teaching is the best means of building self-confidence and positive identity among minority pupils in order to combat racism". One could not help but wonder why the Authority acknowledging the benefits to the individual in terms of educational and social development, had failed to take any positive steps to promote the teaching of mother-tongue in its schools.

The author was told that 20 assistants were employed, under a Manpower Services Commission scheme, in nursery and infant schools. Their role was to facilitate etnic minority home/school liaison, not one involving teaching mother-tongue. It seemed to be a step in the right direction for mutual understanding.

The author also interviewed a Punjabi/English bilingual teacher who worked in four primary schools facilitating communication and acting as an interpretor for home/school liaison. She confirmed that minority community languages were learnt in after-school voluntary supplementary classes and the Authority had taken no initiative to introduce these languages in the mainstream schools; there was no effective liaison between the L.E.A. and the supplementary schools organised by minority community groups'. She expanded on this statement by saying that: "people are not aware of the educational needs of linguistic minorities and nothing has happened in real practice to recognise minority languages and their teaching in schools. The minority communities have to organise themselves to press their case for mother-tongue teaching". Asked about the teaching profession's response and reaction to such development she stressed that teachers needed educating about these issues along with the general public. She fore-saw the importance of mother-tongue learning in these words:

"Mother-tongue teaching will give children the basic confidence and self-discipline. When one is master of one language, it is much easier to learn other languages. Lack of mother-tongue knowledge can lead to frustration and failure in secondary and further education. The communities are not organised as pressure groups to demand such policies. It will take a long time for these policies to happen. If there is an opportunity more and more pupils will come forward to learn their mother-tongue up to academic standards. Religious education should be part of mother-tongue teaching. Community languages ought to be more important than the European languages in the curriculum".

This view was clearly at divergence with that of the Local Authority. The L.E.A. representative claimed in his report that 97 per cent of minority pupils did not wish to study their mother-tongue as a curriculum option if it meant dropping another subject and the teacher argued that "if there is an opportunity (i.e., under the right conditions) more and more minority pupils would like to study their mother tongue."

The author also met the local community officer to find out his views about the mother-tongue teaching initiatives at the local level. He summarised his feelings by saying that, "Politicians are a problem. They do not understand the multi-cultural education philosophy". He had imaginatively devised a 'Panjabi Language Link Course' (the language spoken by 90 per cent of local minority groups) at the local college for young people and adults and this course provided opportunities to study the Panjabi language successfully up to G.C.E. 'O' and 'A' levels standards. The ideas behind this link course were being extended to other minority languages.

Local Education Authority D:
The Local Education Authority D is a metropolitan city education authority. It represents the conurbation of West Midlands and is one of the largest education authorities in the region. Being in the industrial heartland of Britain, it also contains within its boundries a large variety of ethnic

minority groups that have settled there since the post war economic boom. The co-ordinator and leader of the community language teaching team was delegated to take part in the present investigation on behalf of the local authority. He puts the total number of school-age children including sixth formers at 184,000 approximately. Pupils of ethnic minority origin constituted about 30 per cent i.e, nearly 55,000 of the Authority's school population. The Asians and the West Indians, perhaps, were the two largest ethnic groups in the metropolitan district. English was the only language used as the medium of instruction and the interviewee thought that it would be ideal if the children were taught through their mother-tongue, at least, during the early years of their schooling.

The author was also informed that Panjabi, Urdu, Creole, Hindi, Gujrati, Bengali and Chinese were the main ethnic minority languages in the area. Arabic, Greek, Turkish, Polish and Ukranian were the home languages of other smaller minority groups in the district. The L.E.A. had some guidelines for the teaching of minority community languages as a part of the multi-cultural education development policy within the City. Some relevant abstracts from this document (dated 14th February, 1984) are quoted below:

"Education (Schools and Special Education Sub-) Committee — Report of the Chief Education Officer.

Education for a Multicultural Society — Report on the Responses from Schools:

A number of responses lay great emphasis upon the linguistic needs of pupils from various Asian backgrounds both in terms of their acquiring standard English and of retaining their mother tongue/community language. Many schools itemize and praise the work of their English as a Second Language teachers whilst at the same time express concern that they are unable to provide effective second stage E2L work because of the constraints of pupil numbers and time (SIC).

Many responses express concern that the performance of non-English speaking children at nursery and infant level is being impaired because the Authority has few bilingual teachers or classroom assistants. As one Head puts it:

"When children start school and find themselves with adults who do not speak their language, it can be quite terrifying, and it is extremely important that the transition period from home to school is as easy as possible."

This recognition of the importance of mother-tongue is not restricted to the infant level. Requests are made for the initiation of, or support for, such teaching throughout the Primary sector. It is argued that evidence suggests that, 'Performance in a second language is parallel to improved fluency in the mother tongue'. A number of Heads argue that far from impairing the acquisition of English, mother tongue teaching could actually enhance it.

The obvious connection between language and culture is emphasised in several responses.

The following issues are highlighted from the responses of Primary Schools:

(a) the need for continued support for schools in curriculum development and in-service training given the evidence of the low level of awareness of the multi-cultural perspective in many schools;

(b) the desirability of ensuring that as many staff as possible within a school take part in discussions relating to education for a muilti-cultural society leading to a clearly developed policy in all schools;

(c) the need for more statistical educational data related to the performance of ethnic minority children;

(d) the request for community language/mother tongue teaching at primary level;

(e) the need for effective liaison between home and school;

(f) the desirability of additional E2L support and more bilingual teachers and classroom assistants.

A number of schools with large concentrations of one particular ethnic minority/linguistic group report their attempts at mother-tongue teaching both in mainstream and supplementary provision. Some responses include requests for financial and teaching help either to begin or continue mother-tongue/community language teaching.... The need for communication with ethnic minority parents is raised by a number of schools. Differences in languages are being overcome in some instances by the use of translators and the sending out of official letters in a number of languages.

Key issues then, raised by the secondary schools' responses include:

(a) the need for additional E2L support;

(b) the paucity of educational data related to the performance of ethnic minority pupils;

(c) the requests for (i) to help to bridge the home communities and the school, (ii) for guidance in meeting special needs of ethnic minority pupils and (iii) further help for community language/mother tongue teaching initiatives.

Conclusion and Possible Courses of Action:

It is recommended that the position of community language/mother tongue teaching be kept under close review and that every effort be made to develop initiatives which will establish close links between children's home, local community interests, and schools".

While this report was arguably a step in the right direction, it seemed nonetheless to offer more in the way of tentative suggestions than it did in terms of pressing for firm action. It must be acknowledged that it stressed the overall importance of the role of community languages within a pluralistic development; yet there remained the very real danger that the value of community languages in the educational and social development of ethnic minority pupils might be obscured, even lost in the middle of an ill-defined multi-cultural education. The extracts from the report on multi-cultural education emphasised the inadequacies of the provision for mother-tongue/community language teaching and bilingual education but the L.E.A. had not come out with any proposed policy programmes of a definite nature to overcome the present inadequacies and to cater for the special needs of linguistic minorities in the district. The positive attitude of headteachers and teachers, highlighted in the report, towards mother-tongue teaching and bilingual approaches was a healthy sign for desirable future developments in this respect.

In addition to the above report the co-ordinator for mother-tongue teaching also out-lined a brief description of the progress of community languages:

"In (the L.E.A.), the Community Languages Unit, consisting of eight teachers has been set up to offer Urdu, Panjabi and Gujrati as modern languages in secondary schools. A teacher of Bengali will be appointed in the very near future. These teachers are working on a peripatetic basis and each is covering from two to three schools.

It is envisaged that community languages teachers will work closely with modern language teachers to share materials and expertise and to participate in the running of 'Language Awareness Courses' which among other things aim to giving all pupils an understanding and sympathy for linguistic diversity.

The Community Languages Unit will also liaise with mother-tongue teachers engaged in the voluntary sector and monolingual teachers who are using a wide variety of strategies to help ethnic minority children to maintain and develop their mother tongues on the lines suggested by the Schools Council Mother Tongue Project Team".

One might wonder whether an *eight*-member community languages teaching team could be considered adequate to meet the linguistic needs of 55,000 minority group pupils — quite apart from the fact that the team only offered four of the many minority languages. Equally open to question was the use of a peripatetic system of teaching with the consequential loss of opportunity to develop the more widely based teacher-pupils rapport that comes from a teacher working full time in one school. The equating of mother tongue teaching with the modern languages teaching semed to be far from convincing as the former is classified as L1 (first language) and the latter are L2 (second languages). The role of both types of these languages (i.e., L1 and L2) with regard to children's perceptive, conceptual and cognitive development is quite different (Merril Swain, 1981); although both types are complementary to each other in this respect. Mother-tongue develops with the child right from his/her birth, whereas 'modern languages' are introduced at a later stage. There should be mutual co-operation between the modern languages and community languages departments in the L.E.A. to take advantage of each others expertise but their approaches to teaching should be relatively independent.

The plan for Language Awareness Courses proposed by the Authority for all pupils to understand and to appreciate the linguistic diversity around them was imaginative and praiseworthy. The Community Language Unit's endeavour to liaise with the voluntary mother-tongue institutions and interested monolingual teachers ought to bear fruit in achieving desirable linguistic goals for all pupils in a multi-lingual plural society. One might have hoped that the L.E.A. representative's stance had been more in keeping with the approaches suggested by the School's Council Mother Tongue Teaching Project Team with regard to the maintenance and development of minority children's mother tongue.

Asked about the criteria for selecting community languages for curricular teaching the L.E.A.'s representative replied that: "It mainly depends on the demand and viability of groups for teaching such languages". It was apparent from the Community Languages Unit's document that priority was given to Panjabi, Urdu, Gujrati and Bengali languages. Moreover, it appeared to be a Herculean task for a small team of eight community language teachers to provide facilites for nearly 55,000 linguistic minority pupils to learn their mother-tongue in mainstream schools. There was certainly a need for a considerable extension of the community language teaching programme to provide equal opportunities to children from all minority groups to learn their mother-tongue.

The interviewee also said that the selection of pupils to be taught community languages was done by the schools. There was an understanding that no child was forced to learn community languages nor were these languages offered to pupils rejected from other options. Community languages ought to be offered to all pupils who wished to learn them and there should be no hard and fast selection criteria. There were some examples of white pupils learning ethnic minority languages in the L.E.A's. schools. The teaching of community languages was introduced in the schools which showed interest in this development and where the headteachers were considerate and sympathetic towards the mother-tongue teaching philosophy. The interview revealed that this programme was in operation in 3 secondary schools as an integral part of the curriculum and three other schools offered mother-tongue teaching classes immediately after school hours. The pupils involved in learning these languages in the state schools were as follows:

1. Panjabi 300 approximately
2. Urdu 300 approximately
3. Gujrati 80-90 approximately
4. Bengali 30-40 approximately

These figures constituted a tiny proportion of the total population of approximately 55,000 school age pupils of ethnic minority origin.

The author was also informed that records showed there to be about 25 voluntary supplementary language schools for teaching Panjabi, Urdu, Gujrati and Bengali. Over 5,000 minority children attended these supplementary schools. It should be pointed out that the Authority seemed to concentrate on the four minority community languages referred to above and there were substantial gaps as provision for the other minority languages were concerned. The L.E.A. had a long-term in-service training programme for the mother-tongue teachers working in the voluntary sector. Some financial and personnel help was given to voluntary language schools through the Urban Aid and the Manpower Services Commission programmes. Teaching resources and books were also provided to supplementary language classes by the L.E.A. It appeared that the Authority had adopted a very liberal and co-operative policy to support the supplementary language schools run by the minority community organisations. Evening classes for adults to learn minority languages were also taking place dependent on the demand from different groups.

When asked about the provision of in-service training for mainstream teachers and initial supply of teachers for this programme the L.E.A. representative replied that, "There is no specific in-service training for mainstream teachers to support mother-tongue teaching and it will, perhaps, take place in the future. Hopefully, young candidates will train for community language teaching but the L.E.A. has no provision for that aspect at this time". One might wonder how an L.E.A. of that size could afford to ignore the aspect of teacher supply if it was, sincerely, committed to community language teaching as a permanent feature of its schools' curriculum development.

Commenting on the aspects of planning, co-ordination and evaluation strategies of mother-tongue teaching he went on to say that 'Mother tongue teaching will facilitate learning for those children whose home language is not English. We are seeking sympathy of the headteachers and all concerned as a special strategy and also to support community language teachers with all resources built up at the Multi-cultural Support Centre. This programme is, extensively, being funded through Section 11 and Urban Aid Programmes. We will be developing our own techniques for the evaluation of mother-tongue and bilingual education. A small number of pupils took public examinations up to G.C.E. 'O' and 'A' levels. The Authority was thinking of introducing C.S.E. examination in community languages but the D.E.S. latest decision of 16+ (G.C.S.E.) examination should persuade all L.E.A.s to centralise their efforts to develop community language syllabuses for the new examinations to come into operation in 1988. The L.E.A. Community Languages Unit was proposing to introduce an evaluation programme to monitor this work. Pupils' progress would be regularly assessed and these assessments used to prepare annual profiles for each pupil.

As regards the future of mother-tongue teaching and bilingual education, the L.E.A.'s representative went on to say:

"We would like to see more provision for bilingual education. There is a strong current among parents and teaching profession in its favour and it will gather momentum. Unless these languages are accepted by the dominant society, they have no future. The Multicultural Support Service should seek feed-back from all headteachers in order to respond accordingly".

The author also interviewed a peripatetic teacher of Panjabi with a major responsibility in one secondary school. He was in the process of developing his own mother-tongue teaching policy at the school level independent of the L.E.A.'s statement. Perhaps the example set of good practice in individual schools might be one way in which Authority policy could be influenced. Commenting on the selection of pupils by the schools for community language teaching, he was concerned that only remedial type children (i.e., under-achievers) were given the community language option against the choice of modern languages such as French. This showed the low status attached to non-European community languages in the school curriculum. This particular teacher had taken his own initiative in establishing close liaison with four supplementary language classes in the neighbourhood of the schools in which he worked. He also informed the author that the increase in fees had discouraged adults from attending classes to learn ethnic minority languages.

Asked about the reactions of the teaching profession and other bodies toward mother-tongue teaching the teacher explained:

"The reaction of fellow teachers is rather mixed when the headmasters are supportive of these programmes. The media at the local level is against such policies of the L.E.A.".

This seemed to contradict somewhat the opinion expressed by the Authority's representative. The community language teacher predicted that these policies would gain in strength in the future. He also stressed the need for ethnic minority teachers to organise themselves and the minority groups in order to achieve the required goals of developing community languages as an integral part of the school curricula. He also emphasised the need for minority languages and cultures to receive the due recognition and a rightful place in Britain's plural society. It showed the determination and hopes of some teachers committed to multi-cultural, multi-lingual education developments.

Local Education Authority E:

Local Authority E is another metropolitan local authority representing the large conurbation of the West Midlands region. It is a newly developed City Local Authority that has arisen out of the ravages of the World War II. This City became a dynamic centre of commercial and industrial enterprise and, thus, attracted a large variety of immigrant groups seeking a prosperous and better future in post-war Britain. The author had the opportunity to interview a general adviser with special responsibility for multicultural education as the L.E.A.'s representative. The Authority, at the time of interview, had approximately 56,700 pupils including sixth formers in its care and 9,905 came from different ethnic minority backgrounds i.e., about 17.5 per cent of the total school population. A more detailed breakdown into the different minority groups was not available at that time.

In 1982-83 the L.E.A. produced a document entitled 'Language Diversity in **(The City)'**. It would, perhaps, be appropriate to draw some facts and figures from this document before discussing the contents of the interviews held with the L.E.A. adviser and the Mother Tongue Co-ordinator. Some of the relevant extracts from that document are as follows:

" . . .In this booklet, we examine just one aspect of multi-cultural education, that of making provision for a multi-lingual community.

In the school system 'English for immigrant was identified as the key issue during the first stage of settlement in the inner city. In **(this city)** as in most other metropolitan L.E.A.s, specialist staff were appointed to teach English as a Second Language (E2L). The funding of this operation was, and still is, supported by Section 11 of the 1966 Local Government Act. E2L teaching continues to be important for many **(city)** schools though it is no longer seen to be the only response schools can make to a multi-cultural society.

This initial emphasis on pupils learning English and being 'absorbed' into British society meant that very little attention was given to the diversity of languages represented in the classroom. **Two Secondary Schools** took the initiative in promoting Asian languages but it was only recently that some schools had begun to recognise Mother Tongue as a positive feature, to be fostered rather than ignored.

In Spring, 1981 the Linguistic Minority Project (D.E.S., 1981-83) in collaboration with the L.E.A., carried out a detailed 'Schools Language Survey.' . . . The results of this survey give an accurate and informative picture of language diversity in the **(City)** Schools. Out of a total of 49,000 pupils 7,183 were identified as speaking a language other than English, i.e., 14.4 per cent of the total . . . The detail of the Schools Language Survey 1981: Number of pupils surveyed — 49,990. The main languages (other than English) spoken by 7,183 pupils were as below:

Panjabi	59 per cent	Gujrati	15.8 per cent
Urdu	6.7 per cent	Hindi	2.7 per cent
Italian	2 per cent	Bengalid	1.9 per cent
Polish	1.9 per cent	Creole	1.3 per cent
Chinese	1.2 per cent	Others	7.5 per cent

Community Provision: The rich pattern of language diversity identified in the City Schools by the L.M.P. is reflected in the voluntary Community-based classes which thrived within the City. Many of these, as indicated previously, are attached to places of worship and the languages taught often had both a social and a religious affiliation. A number of secular and religious bodies have made representation to the L.E.A. and are consequently allowed free use of certain school premises. Such arrangements tied in with the community policies adopted by the L.E.A. and helped to establish the character of schools and their relationship with the local community.

Community based classes operate successfully mainly through the enthusiasm, energies and goodwill of their participants. They face a number of drawbacks, however, and there are frequent problems with lack of funds, inadequate teaching materials and sometimes inexperienced tuition. These difficulties have not blunted the initiatives of community groups and classes fill a real need as expressed here by a participant:

"Mother tongue classes maintain communication between generations and throughout the extended family at home and abroad. They reinforce a sense of cultural identity and help to preserve religious and socio-cultural values".

... Mother Tongue in Schools:

This short section cannot explore in any detail the number of ways in which mother tongue can feature in schools. At present mother tongue work ranges from a bilingual approach with nursery children (rhymes, songs and stories etc.) to G.C.E. courses to 'O' and 'A' levels in several secondary schools. In this latter form mother-tongue should be seen within the field of the modern languages department.

The appointment (in 1979) of a mother tongue co-ordinator to the Minority Group Support Service has helped to develop some of this work, but resources of staff and teaching materials are inadequate to meet the demands made by schools. Nevertheless, progress is being made and even monolingual teachers have found ways of supporting bilingualism, through tapes, charts and books in different languages.

A number of English teachers have become actively involved in learning Panjabi as a voluntary activity. Many schools have involved parents in the process of bringing community languages on to the time-tables and invaluable help has been received in this way for story-telling, conversation, drama work etc. The appointment of language aides in certain primary schools has reinforced the expertise in these areas.

The Schools Council Mother Tongue Project has been instrumental in building up information and suggestion for supporting teachers in the multilingual classroom and the **(City)** teachers have benefitted from liaison with the Project.

Conclusion:
Whilst the emphasis in this booklet has been on supporting those pupils who speak a language other than English, the existence of a variety of languages in schools represents an advantage to those children who speak only English. Through an approach that recognises language diversity, all pupils can be given fresh insights into language and come to see world micro-cosm reflected in their classrooms. This may be a starting point from which to study other modern languages but more importantly it is a basis for a multi-cultural approach to learning".

Some brave words and ambitious thoughts find expression in this document. It should be pointed out that this booklet merely offered an explanation of the situation and the latest position with regard to the linguistic minorites in the City. It did not seem, in any way, to be the L.E.A.'s policy statement or a report proposing course of action. Nevertheless it could be said that it had drawn the map of linguistic diversity in the city. Certainly, it was the first document of its kind to provide comprehensive information about the variety and the size of linguistic minority groups within the borders of the L.E.A. Although the Authority had taken some positive steps to include minority languages in some of its mainstream schools, it was apparent from the above document that voluntary organisations through supplementary schools, were in the fore-front of the mother-tongue/community language teaching. This situation was substantiated through further information from the L.E.A. representatives taking part in this research exercise. (see below).

The L.E.A.'s 'Language Diversity' booklet noted the drawbacks and shortcomings of the voluntary sector operation i.e., lack of funds, inadequate teaching materials and inexperienced tuition etc. Yet the Authority had failed to put forward its own plans and proposals to tackle the problems and eradicate these drawbacks either through providing financial and professional assistance to voluntary language classes or through making a whole sale provision of mother-tongue teaching and bilingual education in the mainstream schools. The inadequacy of the L.E.A.'s provision for mother tongue teaching was confirmed through the latest information supplied in writing by the Mother Tongue Co-ordinator:

Mother Tongue teaching in **(the City)** is as follows:
Maintained schools: (the figures refer to the number of pupils (students):

Primary -	Panjabi 208	Urdu 2	
	Gujrati 5	Bengali 2	Total 217
Secondary -	Panjabi 202	Urdu 69	
	Gujrati 1	Hindi 9	Total 281

Evening classes at community Primary schools and colleges (6-18 age range):

	Panjabi 40	Urdu 30	
Panjabi as second lang.	50	Hindi 22	Total 142

Grand Total 640

Voluntary Sector (6-18 age range):

Panjabi 520	Urdu 170
Gujrati 270	Bengali 100
Polish 75	Ukranian 35
Chinese 20	Tamil 16

Quranic Studies (Urdu) 60
Quranic Studies (Gujrati) 80

Grand Total 1,346

As mentioned earlier the Voluntary Sector had made provision to cater for teaching community languages to more than twice as many pupils as the L.E.A. It should be pointed out that these figures were compiled by the Authority and some margin of error (intentional or unintentional) should be allowed for in such statistical calculation. It was quite clear from the above information that the local authority was more inclined to collect statistics about minority languages than to expand its own programme to take a major role in the field of mother-tongue teaching and bilingual education (See Alladina, 1982).

The author also interviewed the Authority's representative (an adviser for education), in order to supplement and up-date the information provided above.

Asked about the use of languages as the medium of instruction in the L.E.A.'s schools he replied that,"it is a difficult question to answer as some schools might make use of six languages and the others will use, only, one i.e., English". He was not specific at all as to which additional languages were used as the medium of instruction if any, in what circumstances and at what level etc. The sole evidence of the use of languages other than English was that contained in the 'Language Diversity' document which stated that children's home languages were supported through story-telling, rhymes and drama work during the settling in period in nursery and infant schools and not for the teaching of other content matter in the curriculum.

The L.E.A. representative went on further to say that: "There is no official policy for teaching community languages in the mainstream schools but there is a substantial practice. I am suspicious about the status of such a policy . . . The modern languages adviser and myself have appointed right type of language teachers and developing a policy for mother-tongue teaching".

There was a degree of apparent inconsistency in this statement. The Authority had, it was stated, no official policy as regards community languages. This might suggest that it attached little or no importance to them; as yet it allowed community languages to be taught in its schools. True, there was only the equivalent of 4.8 teachers in the L.E.A.'s schools and no specific provision had been made for the in-service training of community language teachers; but, as the author was informed, mother-tongue teachers were encouraged to participate in modern languages in-service training.

Asked to comment on how pupils were selected for community languages teaching, the adviser suggested that selection was not a problem: "the problem is really the other way round, that is, there are fewer pupils that we can cater for". This was a surprising answer. From the Authority's own figures, there were 7,183 linguistic minority pupils and yet there was only an equivalent of 4.8 community language teachers. This should surely have meant that high degree of selectivity had to be exercised. As regards the suggestion that there was a lack of demand, this was inconsistent with the number of pupils attending voluntary mother-tongue classes, because the Authority was unable to make adequate provision within mainstream schools.

There was a provision for teachers to learn Panjabi (P2L — Panjabi as a second language) which was the dominant minority language in the city. Asked about the L.E.A.'s long-term planning in relation to the initial training for the supply of community language teachers the author was told: "We are a very small authority for such a planning and provision but we can approach the local university to assist us for teachers training". The Authority had given no consideration to this important aspect of initial teachers training in terms of meeting future educational needs in this respect. Commenting on the evaluation aspect of mother-tongue teaching the L.E.A.'s representative said:

"Public examination in the form of G.C.E. 'O' and 'A' levels is the only means of evaluation so far. We are thinking to introduce C.S.E. examinations. Individual, teachers may have their own way to assess the pupils' progress in community languages but the Authority has no system of its own for this purpose".

No local authority can afford to neglect this vital aspect of self-evaluation of its educational programmes.

When asked about the aims and objectives (rationale) behind the community language teaching programme he said:

"We pursue this programme to recognise that other languages are valuable in addition to English. The minority community language teaching is necessary to develop the plural aspect of our society".

As regards the problems in executing the mother-tongue teaching programme, reference was made to the three main difficulties i.e., the lack of financial sources, the unavailability of teachers with the right training and qualifications, and the inability of the parents, in the past, to value their own languages. The existence and progress of voluntary language schools in the City shows that the parents must be enthusiatic and very much in favour to value their mother-tongue for all kinds of reasons.

Commenting on the attitudes, responses and reactions towards the minority community language teaching i.e., with regard to head teachers, teachers, professional teaching bodies, general public and the local media, the adviser for multi-cultural education (the L.E.A.s representative) stated:

"We have seen a substantial shift in favour of this programme from the head-teachers. Teachers, as a whole, are supportive and enthusiastic. Traditionally, the teachers unions have not shown the slightest interest but lately, they seem to be interested. The general public is totally unaware of it, and it simply does not touch the indigenous parents. The ethnic minority parents are favourably mixed while the media at the local level is neutral with no reaction".

This statement suggested that the climate of opinion was not encouraging as far as the development of community languages programmes in schools was concerned. If it really wanted to, the Authority ought to be able to make progress in this programme.

Asked how he saw the possible development of mother-tongue teaching and bilingual education as part of school curriculum, the interviewee said:

"It depends how successful we are in building a multi-ethnic society and the ethnic minority languages will flourisch accordingly. The number of community language teachers are declining and the fresh supply of teachers is very important".

As mentioned earlier the Authority had not taken any decisive action towards the training and supply of teachers for this purpose.

The author also had the opportunity to interview the Authority's Mother Tongue Teaching Co-ordinator who was involved in peripatetic teaching at seven different schools in addition to his administrative duties. He confirmed that English language, in the main, was used as the medium of instruction though there were twenty minority languages aides at nursery and infant schools to support Panjabi, Gujarti, Urdu, Hindi and Bengali languages. It meant the other minority languages mentioned in the Authority's '1981 Schools Language Survey' were not offered the equal support to their speakers during the early years of their schooling. The languages introduced for mother-tongue teaching were reported to be Panjabi, Gujrati, Urdu, Bengali and Italian. Only two of the secondary schools had developed their independent policies since 1974 to teach mother tongue/community languages. In these two schools some pupils, predominantly Asians were studying for G.C.E. 'O' and 'A' levels examinations in Panjabi, Urdu and Gujrati languages.

Contrary to the view expressed by the L.E.A. representative the Mother Tongue Co-ordinator admitted that the teaching force of about five mother tongue teachers was far from sufficient and the schools had to select viable groups for teaching home languages in the time-table. The interview with the co-ordinating teacher revealed that there was a demand for the non-speakers i.e., the mainstream pupils to learn minority languages, but it was not large enough to warrant a teacher for this purpose. All the teachers involved in teaching community languages had qualified status but they were not, solely, occupied for language teaching in all instances. It was interesting to learn that 95 per cent of pupils from ethnic minority backgrounds could speak and understand their languages and the other 5 per cent were shy of speaking in their mother tongue. The teacher interviewed thought that it was due to the internationalisation of negative and inferior perception of minority languages depicted by the dominant group of society. He also admitted that he could not find enough time to establish close liaison with the minority supplementary language schools which was rather essential.

Commenting on the attitudes of ethnic minority parents towards mother tongue teaching, the co-ordinator felt that some parents were in need of 'education' on the issue, that is, they needed to be encouraged to develop a more positive attitude towards their languages and cultures. Talking about the evaluation aspect of the mother-tongue teaching programme he confirmed that there was an access to G.C.E. 'O' and 'A' levels examinations for some pupils. He did not see this as being an adequate means of evaluation and yet no other method was being applied to assess the progress of the majority of pupils learning community languages. The Mother Tongue Co-ordinator felt that there was a need for some other locally devised tests to check the progress of all pupils learning their home languages. While speaking about the main problems encountered in operating this programme he said:

> *"The minority communities are not ready for it yet. They want schools to concentrate on other academic subjects such as mathematics and science. Pupils are allowed to learn these languages as a last option or in other words minority languages are given as a last choice to pupils".*

It did not seem to be a satisfactory arrangement for teaching community languages in mainstream schools.

When the author asked about the responses, reactions and attitudes of teaching profession, majority and minority parents, governing bodies of schools and the local media towards community language teaching, he was told that:

> *"Some teachers seem to be very supportive but on the whole teachers feel threatened by such developments. It is not very easy to guage the position of mainstream teachers. Headteachers are willing to listen but slow to react. I have no dealing with school governing bodies and would not know about their standpoint. There is no opposition from white parents and minority parents are all for it. So far as the media is concerned, I have not found any opposition from it towards ethnic minority community language teaching".*

The situation, on the whole, seemed favourable for such policies.

While answering questions on the future of community languages in the school curriculum and the education system, he commented, "I think it would develop but it will take some time yet. It will come when the people know the advantages of bilingualism. It will, hopefully, develop for some time and after that it depends on the minorities' insistence". It shows the uncertain future of minority languages' progress as foreseen by the interviewee. He also stressed that there was a need for teachers' training institutions to train teachers in community languages to a suitable level and standard. He also stressed the need for further research in this aspect of education from a variety of angles.

Local Education Authority F:
The East Midlands Region of the country was represented by the Local Education Authority F. It is a county local authority covering the County City, some small towns and the rural areas within its borders. The County City, as mentioned in one of the B.B.C. television programmes, is one of the richest metropolitan districts in western Europe and certainly, it is a thriving centre for business, commerce and industry of various kinds. Thus it is an attractive area for immigrant settlers seeking a better life in a new country. The towns adjoining the County City have a sizeable number of people from the ethnic minorities among their inhabitants. According to the written information supplied by the L.E.A., the total number of pupils (full-time only) in the Authority's maintained schools in June, 1984 were 142,360 (i.e., 68,341 in primary, 72,631 in secondary and 1,388 in special education). With regard to the number of pupils from ethnic minority groups, the situation was as follows:

	Primary including Nursery	Secondary
African	122	172
Afro-Caribbean	520	590
Asian	8,735	6,339
Far Eastern	199	165
Middle Eastern	69	34
European	462	565
Mixed	943	469
Others	16	19
Total =	11,066	8,353

Grand Total = 19,419

The number of pupils from minority groups constituted about 13.6 per cent of the whole school population of the Authority; this would suggest a large enough base to warrant a policy to support the home languages of minority children. It must be remembered that in nursery schools there were 1,585 children of ethnic minority origin out of 5,008 children on roll i.e., 32 per cent of the nursery population.

In his official letter, the adviser for multi-cultural education wrote: "On the question of the major languages spoken in our schools, our figures for the secondary sector are not very reliable but for primary and nursery schools they are as follows:

African Languages	30 pupils
Afro Caribbean Languages/Dialects	164 pupils
Gujrati	5,117 pupils
Panjabi	1,145 pupils
Bengali	313 pupils
Hindi	224 pupils
Kutchi	376 pupils
Urdu	184 pupils
Other Asian Languages	284 pupils
European	499 pupils
Far Eastern	188 pupils
Middle Eastern	57 pupils
	Total = 9,469 pupils ".

Such a figure represents just over 85 per cent of the ethnic minority pupils in the primary sector (9469/11066). If one used that proportion as the basis for estimating the numbers of linguistic minority pupils in the secondary sector, one would obtain a figure of 7,100 (85% of 8353). (Such an estimate might even be on the conservative side, since one might expect the younger age range to have a greater proportion of second generation ethnic minority youngsters than the older end). Such a calculation would give an estimated school population of over 16,500 linguistic minority pupils (9469 + 7100). Even arrived at in this way, such an estimate would appear to offer ample justification of the need for the Authority to give serious consideration to the provision of minority language support and teaching in mainstream schools.   The City Council (i.e., the County Town) and the Local Council for Community Relations (C.R.E.) carried out a detailed survey in November 1981 and published their report entitled 'Ethnic Minority Languages in the Classroom: A survey of Asian Parents in the City'. It will be relevant to look at the following brief summary of this report's findings and some conclusions:

"Summary of the Findings:
  — Parents in the sample were shown to be multi-lingual.
  — All of them still speak their first language.
  — Most of them can read and write in their first language.
  — **The first language is the main language used in the home and with the children.**
  — **The first language is also used extensively outside the home.**
  — A high proportion of the sample can speak and understand English.
  — However a quarter of the sample experience communication problems outside the home, due to a lack of English.

— There is a recognition of the importance of English. **Nearly all of the respondents' children learn an Asian language as their first language.**
— **Most of their children can still speak their first language but very few can read and write it.**
— Nearly all the children can speak, read and write English.
— **The respondents think it is important for their children to be able to speak and also read and write in their first language.**
— They also recognise the need for their children to be fully conversant with English.
— **Although few parents have actually sent their children to classes to learn their first language, the majority of parents expressed a wish to send their children to classes if the facilities were available.**
— **The majority of parents would like their children to learn an Asian language at school and take a public examination in it.**

... Conclusions:

The survey findings indicate that the language base of the Asian community is multi-lingual rather than monolingual. Any discussion of the issue of teaching Asian languages should be based on an appreciation of this fact. The majority of parents have taught their children Gujrati, Panjabi or Kutchi as their first language and this language dominates the linguistic environment of the house. Thus the children's early language development takes place in a language other than English.

The finding of the survey clearly indicate that there is a parental support for the maintenance of the first language and that there is a parental demand for facilities for teaching it. The survey findings also indicate that people's first language is still a living language and there is likely to be a continuing role for it. This has implications for service providers and others.

The challenge of the multi-cultural and multi-lingual society cannot be ignored. It should be positively recognised so that opportunities can be created for the development of mutual respect between individuals and the enrichment of society as a whole".

This research survey document, certainly, had its implications for the Authority's education service. The Authority set up a Working Party on Multi-cultural Education. This Working Party produced its interim report for the Local Education Authority in September 1983. It is an extensive outline report on multi-cultural education. The reader's attention is drawn to these extracts from that report which deal with the minority community language/mother tongue teaching provision within the L.E.A.:

"Report from the Chairman of Schools Committee Working Party on Multicultural Education:

Education should prepare people for life in the wider community and must help all people to develop attitudes and ways of behaving which are appropriate to living in a society which wishes to eradicate racial prejudice and the social scars it produces. We, therefore, recognising that this County is a pluralistic society and part of a country of many culture, and believing that all pupils and students across the county should be given an appropriate knowledge and awareness of the variety of cultures which make up our society, identify the major objectives of developing the education service in a multi-cultural society as:-

(a) to prepare all pupils and students to live and work harmoniously and with equality of opportunity in that society;
(b) to build upon the strengths of cultural diversity in that society;
(c) to define and combat racism and any discriminatory practices within the education service to which it gives rise;
(d) to meet appropriately the particular educational needs of all people, having regard to their ethnic, cultural, linguistic or historical attachments.

Repeatedly the attention of the working party has been drawn to the sentence in the Bullock Report 1975 (A Language for Life) which reads, "No child should be expected to cast off the language and culture of the home as it crosses the school threshold". In this context it is clearly most important that schools should take advantage, whenever possible, of the contribution that bilingual parents can make. Equally, school should not discourage pupils from using their mother tongue within the school context, and in the case of Afro-Caribbean children there are strong reasons for encouraging them to make full use of their linguistic repertoire in creative work in English, drama and general discussion.

The representative of the ethnic minorities have left no doubt in the minds of the Working Party of their strong desire for mother tongue teaching in the classroom . . . bilingual teachers to assist children in the early years of primary education . . . Equally, it will be appropriate to make further studies of existing projects concerning the teaching of the mother tongue, as opposed to teaching in the mother tongue, and the provision of examination courses upon the mother tongue.

The Working Party recommends that the L.E.A. reviews its policy regarding support to and co-operation with the supplementary schools which provide mother tongue teaching for many ethnic minority pupils outside school hours. In particular, financial support towards the hiring of rooms and purchase of books and material is recommended.

The Working Party recommends the regular collection of appropriate statistical information upon ethnic minority students in the Authority's schools to facilitate the identification of areas of need, to add weight to claims made under Section 11 of the Local Government Act of 1966 and to enable the L.E.A.'s provision to be kept under review ... The Working Party intends to see other representatives from ethnic minorities and to continue the process of identifying and clarifying needs. It will wish to pay particular attention to the question of mother tongue teaching in secondary schools...".

It should be pointed out that the interim report, from which the above extracts are taken, was more of a discussion paper in term of multi cultural and multi-lingual education rather than being a policy statement intended to give the lead to multi-cultural, multi-lingual initiatives in the Authority's schools. There is no doubt that this document set the scene for a multi-ethnic philosophy of education while valuing the importance of ethnic minority languages in the school curriculum. Although five new posts of bilingual teachers were mentioned in the report, the Working Party did not however, appear to be in favour of teaching in the mother tongue. It seemed to be more concerned with the teaching of the mother tongue to pupils. But these aspects of bilingual education and mother tongue teaching cannot be separated; and they are complementary in terms of children's linguistic development. The Authority's intention to support and to cooperate with the supplementary language schools confirmed the importance of voluntary sector in the teaching of minority community languages in a plural society.

The Authority's Adviser for Multi-Cultural Education who was the L.E.A.'s representative in this investigation, had also put before the Working Party on Multi-cultural Education a paper (Nov. 1983), concerning the 'Teaching of Mother Tongue and Community Languages in Schools'. In his letter to the author he confirmed that this paper had been adopted by the Working Party and that the recommendations within it would be incorporated within the Working Party's Report to the Authority's Schools Sub-committee. In the light of this relevant development a brief digest of this paper 'for further discussion' is given below:

"Teaching Mother Tongue and Community Languages in Schools:

1. **Demand**

   The Working Party has received a number of submissions (from the City Council for Community Relations, the Local Branch of the National Anti-racist Movement in Education (N.A.M.E.) and the Indian Workers' Association) which call on the Authority to make provision for mother tongue teaching in the schools. It has also considered the report of a survey carried out by the Local Council for Community Relations and published jointly with the City Council in 1981. In this report 90 per cent of a sample of over 300 Asian parents expressed interest in their children learning an Asian language at school and 60 per cent would like their children to take public examinations in their chosen Asian language. Organisers of Asian supplementary schools in the City and another town, in recent discussions with the Adviser for Multi-cultural Education, unanimously requested that Asian languages be taught in both primary and secondary schools and similar views were widely expressed at the Conference held in Oct. 1983.

2. **Present Local Authority Provision**
   Little Formal mother tongue teaching takes place at present in the Authority's schools. The bilingual Teaching Project currently operating in 10 infant or primary schools is not concerned with formal language teaching and does not cover literacy skills . . . . other cognitive and linguistic skills cannot be used if mother tongue is disregarded . . . . Only one primary school provides teaching of Bengali, Gujrati, Hindi, Panjabi, and Urdu. At secondary level, one Community College is the only institution providing teaching of an Asian language as part of the normal curriculum.

3. **Voluntary Provision**
   A large number of voluntary organisations provide tuition in a range of Asian and European languages to children from the various communities in the County . . . Facilities are often inadequate, with overcrowded teaching spaces, unsuitable books and very limited space . . . with generally unpaid teachers with little or no training in language teaching.

4. **Why teach mother-tongue or community languages in schools?**
   Until recently many educationalists saw bilingualism as an educational problem and considered bilingual children to have an educational handicap, believing that bilinguals were unable to use either their first or second language with total fluency or accuracy . . . Within the last twenty years a number of studies in Britain and abroad have pointed to positive results from bilingualism and from mother tongue teaching. Recognising children's bilingualism indicates that their home language and, by extension, their culture, are valued by the school.

5. **Organisation of mother tongue teaching in schools**
   Opponents of mother tongue teaching often say that it would be impossible to offer it in schools, yet up and down the country there are many examples of successful practice . . . However, difficulties in making formal arrangements for mother-tongue teaching need not preclude any teaching centring around pupils' mother-tongues.

6. **Which languages do we teach?**
   The choice of language(s) to be taught in school will depend on a number of factors. First, which is the language, other than English, most commonly spoken at home? . . . Secondly, is this language the one which parents would prefer to see taught in school, or is the demand stronger for the teaching of a community language instead (e.g., Panjabi or Urdu in the case of Pakistani ethnic groups)? . . . Thirdly, what languages are staff able and willing to teach to an acceptable

standard?

7. **Where are the teachers?**
   Few Asian teachers in British schools have had specific training to teach Asian languages, either as mother tongues or as foreign languages. However, they are the main existing resource on which the development of mother-tongue teaching depends ... There are many former teachers in Britain who were trained in Asia, East Africa and elsewhere, whose qualifications are not recognised by the D.E.S. Attention must be given to the means whereby the experience and knowledge of these teachers could be used in schools.

8. **Teaching materials**
   There are very few teaching materials designed for the teaching of ethnic minority mother tongues in the British school setting.

9. **Funding the operation**
   The team of bilingual teachers set up in 1982 will, it is hoped, be funded under Section 11 of the 1966 Local Government Act. When approval of the Authority's application is received, the 75 per cent grant will enable us to quadruple the posts in the team. The Authority may wish to consider making regular grants to the voluntary language schools ... say £500 a year per organisation plus free accommodation if required ...

10. **Supporting the teachers**
    The development of mother-tongue teaching in the Authority, if it is to be successful, must be based on sound professional advice. The early appointment of an advisory teacher for this area of work will be a priority if the authority decides to expand provision. Such a person would assist with the development of materials, organise in-service courses, assess applicants for teaching posts and evalute teachers' work".

This document, perhaps, was the most appropriate to set the priorities and thinking with regard to the scope of mother tongue/community language teaching within the L.E.A. It seemed that the Authority was more inclined to support minority childrens' bilingualism during their early years than provide proposals for a comprehensive mother-tongue teaching policy. There was a big gap between mother-tongue support at the primary level and its development at secondary level. Although the above document was concerned about the availability of the right type of teachers for ethnic minority languages, it failed to prompt any initiative by the L.E.A. to meet present or future needs. It appeared that like all other local authorites this particular Authority was counting heavily on Section 11 of the 1966 Local Government Act for funding the mother tongue teaching or bilingual education programme. One might wonder what would have happened to ethnic minority language maintenance and development if this special assistance had not been available from central government funding.

The interview with the L.E.A. representative revealed the Authority's emphasis with regard to ethnic minority mother tongue support was on Asian languages (i.e., Gujrati, Panjabi, Hindi, Urdu, and Bengali) rather than providing facilities for mother tongue teaching for all linguistic minorities. Although the Authority's philosophical approach to this aspect was praiseworthy, it had no formal policy for teaching minority languages. The Authority had not introduced any mother tongue teaching in its mainstream schools except one primary and one secondary school, though the L.E.A. had appointed six teachers to support minority pupils' bilingualism at 9 primary schools and 1 secondary school. Six teachers were hardly adequate to support a bilingual programme for the L.E.A.'s over nineteen thousands ethnic minority pupils.

Commenting on the future of mother tongue teaching and bilingual education in British schools, the L.E.A.'s Adviser for Multicultural Education said, "It seems that bilingual education is a permanent feature for some time. It may dilute after the year 2000 and perhaps it will be regrettable". One would hope that this short-term vision would not affect the long term planning for ethnic minority mother tongue teaching policy programmes.

The author also interviewed a teacher with a special responsibility for mother-tongue teaching in a primary school. More than 160 pupils (80 per cent of the school population) were involved in learning four different ethnic minority languages (i.e., Panjabi, Gujrati, Hindi and Bengali) but English was the only language used as the medium of instruction. The teacher responsible for minority languages had intended to develop an independent policy for mother-tongue teaching by April 1984 but it had not materialised by the July of that year. He also expressed the view that one hour per week for mother-tongue teaching was not enough for satisfactory results. Surprisingly, quite a high proportion of pupils could understand their mother-tongue. In the case of Gujati 100 per cent of his children could speak it. There were very few children who did not understand their mother-tongue. The teachers agreed that mother-tongue learning had improved minority children's self-identity.

Speaking about the main problems in this respect, the interviewee revealed that:

> "The Authority does not give encouragement for mother-tongue teaching. The community language teachers are not accorded due regard and comparative status for their special efforts. We are not treated fairly within the education service. The mainstream teachers are not very supportive for this programme. Indigenous parents are totally opposed to mother-tongue teaching in schools when minority parents are delighted with this provision. The local media support these programmes."

It seemed mother tongue teaching still lacked the support it deserved from all sections of the population.

Asked about the future of community languages in mainstream schools, he was uncertain, saying, "So long as the present headteacher is here we can see it growing. What happens after we do not know. If these policies are in right hands, they will survive". He also stressed, "Teaching of community languages deserves more support from the public, politicians and mainstream teachers. The teachers of community languages should be rewarded properly. Ethnic minorities as well as the indigenous population will benefit from minority language teaching programmes".

Local Education Authority G:
This Local Education Committee is a metropolitan city authority representing the North West England i.e., Merseyside Region of the country. It is also one of the largest education committees in the region catering for the education of a variety of ethnic minority groups within its boundaries. As in many other cities, the minority groups had arrived in this area since the industrial expansion of the post World War II era. It is also one of the oldest centres with pockets of immigrant settlements within its borders. The Head of the Multi-cultural Development Service took part in the present research on behalf of the local education authority.

This particular local authority was among the pioneers in its attempts to develop multi-cultural education. In the development of multi-cultural educational initiatives it is appropriate to begin by looking at some of the reports, statements and other documents put forward by the Authority of its intention in respect of multi-ethnic development in education with special reference to multi-lingualism.

The history of such development within the Authority goes back as early as April 1975, when the Policy and Estimates Sub-Committee received a detailed report from the Chief Education Officer about the provision then made for ethnic minority pupils. The emphasis of this report centred on the provision of English as a Second Language. No need was then foreseen for any educational provision for the home languages of ethnic minority pupils. There have been many developments in the field of inter-cultural education since that report was compiled, not least changes in emphasis.

It was followed by another report by the Chief Education Officer to the Policy and Estimates Sub-Committee in April 1978, entitled 'Multi-cultural Education in Schools'. Under its introductory caption 'An ideal policy' it reads:

"In an ideal system a local education authority with a significant number of pupils from ethnic minorities in its schools should aim to develop a strategy based on these main features:

(i)   The development of teaching programmes on race issues that reach pupils in all schools to increase understanding and reduce feeling of

fear, prejudice and hostility.
(ii)   Early identification of the educational needs of children of ethnic
         minorities and provision of special additional resources including
         courses for teachers to meet those needs.
(iii)   Recognition that while literacy through special arrangement for
         teaching **English as a foreign language** must have priority; it can be
         misleading to believe that once language needs have been met there is
         a little more to be done.
(iv)   Systematic monitoring of the effectiveness of the educational system
         in providing for pupils from ethnic minorities to detect
         under-performance and seek to rectify it promptly.
(v)   Recognition that while membership of an ethnic minority is often
         found in company with social disadvantage it adds an extra dimension
         to the latter".

This report was compiled months after the 1977 E.E.C. Directive about
the education of children of migrant workers which gave special emphasis to
mother-tongue teaching and cultural maintenance. The Authority's report
showed little imagination, failing to recognise the importance of the
contribution of home languages to the acquisition of English. Moreover, its
classification of English as a foreign language showed confusion; for the
great majority of its ethnic minority pupils, born in Britain, English was a
second language, not a foreign language. TESL and TEFL are separate
issues and should not be confused. The Authority also seemed to have
undermined the concept of bilingualism and language repertoire.

At least the Authority took pains to gather information about the number
of pupils from minority backgrounds. The statistics available at that time
suggested that there were about 8,000 pupils from ethnic minorities in the
Authority's schools, equivalent to about 9 per cent of the school population.

It was followed by another similar report in June 1980. This concentrated
on statistical information about the ethnic minority community . It
highlighted that:

> *"According to the 1971 census data, the ethnic minorities in 1971
> formed 3 per cent of the total population of the city. The survey
> information for 1978 showed these figures to have risen to 10.5 per
> cent. The statistics of the school age population reflected a different
> percentage. The number of ethnic minority pupils rose from 6.4 per
> cent in 1971 to 10.9 per cent in 1978 of the total school population".*

This showed a steady increase over the years in the proportion of pupils
from ethnic minority backgrounds. These trends would suggest that there
was a need for a concerted effort from the L.E.A. if it was to meet the
linguistic needs of an increasing proportion of ethnic minority children in
the school population.

The same report made a note, for the first time, about 'Mother Tongue
Tuition'. It says:

"In February, 1978, the committee set aside a total of six teaching posts for Mother Tongue work. To date 11 teachers (the equivalent of 4.5 full time teachers) have been appointed and a number of languages including Panjabi, Gujrati, Bengali, Hindi, and Polish are taught. This provision was made in three primary schools, seven secondary schools and two community centres, by teachers who are employed on peripatetic basis. A major difficulty has been in finding appropriately qualified staff, and it may be that further expansion in this area could best be carried out by the use of volunteers. With the approval of parents and teachers, most of this instruction is provided outside the normal school curriculum".

It was questionable whether the appointment of the equivalent of 4.5 full-time teachers was in any way sufficient to meet the linguistic needs of nearly 10,000 pupils of ethnic minority origin. Moreover, only a few minority languages had been selected to be taught in a few schools of the Local Authority. The Authority did not have any comprehensive plan to train teachers for community languages and it seemed educationally unsatisfactory to depend on unqualified volunteers for teaching ethnic minority languages in schools. At the same time the Authority seemed to be ducking its own responsibilities by leaving the major provision of mother-tongue teaching to voluntary organisations outside the normal school curriculum.

In 1981 the Rampton Interim Report was published. This Committee of Inquiry established in March 1979 under the Chairmanship of Anthony Rampton had terms of reference which required it to examine the needs of children from ethnic minority groups in our schools, and to do so "recognising the contribution of schools in preparing all pupils for life in a society which is both multiracial and culturally diverse". The interim report found evidence of under-achievement among the ethnic minority pupils in relation to their peers. It was also established in this report that lack of proper linguistic development of the ethnic minority children was one of the major contributory factors to their educational under-achievement. The Authority responded to the Rampton Report through one of its own report in October 1981:

'Multi-cultural Education: A report of the Chief Education Officer to the School's Sub-Committee'. Among its main recommendations the following were relevant to the present study:

" . . .Increased provision to assess and meet the particular needs of children from minority ethnic groups.

Development and resourcing of ways on encouraging home/school links among minority ethnic groups.

Positive consideration of ways of encouraging the recruitment and promotion of teachers from minority ethnic groups and development of a framework to encourage greater involvement of minority ethnic groups in the education service as parents and governors and through contacts with the minority ethnic group communities.

Initiation of work to assess the benefits and practical difficulties involved in providing (i) teaching minority ethnic groups' languages in schools, (ii) teaching other subjects in minority ethnic groups' mother-tongues, (iii) support for language teaching organised by the minority ethnic group communities".

The above recommendations in the Authority's report suggested that ethnic minority community languages were of vital importance for the development of multi-ethnic initiatives in the different spheres of the education service. Ironically, the Authority's Mother Tongue Scheme only provided for the equivalent of six full-time teachers and they provided community language instruction based at a number of schools outside the normal time-table. The languages currently supported included: Urdu, Bengali, Gujrati, Cantonese, Panjabi, Hindi and Polish. The Authority did not have any precise records of the ethnic minority languages spoken by different ethnic groups. It was surprising that an Authority with a sizeable ethnic minority population had not carried out a detailed language survey to ascertain the scale and diversity of minority languages spoken by its ethnic minority population. Since a step would seem a logical prelude to the making of appropriate educational provision to meet those needs.

The same report under its heading 'Language Policy' added:

"Institutions and areas should examine the language requirements of all courses and if necessary make special provision for students from ethnic minority groups. Subject staff who are not language specialists should have training in language teaching to sensitise them to the language needs of ethnic groups. Mother tongue teaching should be available where possible to enable students from ethnic groups to study their language as a modern language and, if possible, take appropriate examinations. At a minimum the institution, department, or centre should make contact with local voluntary groups involved in mother tongue teaching and offer every assistance".

Undoubtedly, the Authority was engaged in a watered-down approach to ethnic minority mother-tongue teaching rather than adopting an educational philosophy for such developments as discussed in the third chapter of this study. These reports seemed more like discussion papers than whole hearted attempts to develop policies designed to make real progress in multi-cultural and multi-lingual education.

A number of recent reports have informed the committee for action in the multi-cultural field though insufficient and unsatisfactory as it seemed. In addition two reports in 1982 have described action taken and proposed within the Continuing Education Field. One of these two reports entitles 'Report of the Chief Education Officer to the School Sub-Committee:

Multi cultural Development Service' was issued in October 1982. Obviously, this document touched on the development of mother tongue teaching in the purview of the local education authority. The following excerpts from that report should be considered to guage the extent of any subsequent developments in that field:

"Since the committee made provision for an establishment of the equivalent of six full-time teachers of mother tongue, there has been a steady development of this important area ... Because the great majority of children in our schools who speak a language other than English at home, are Muslims from the Punjab, whose community language is Urdu, this is the language which has been concentrated on. There are five teachers teaching this language in six high schools, two sixth form colleges and four primary schools. Support is also provided to community based week-end classes in the city's other principal minority languages: Hindi, Polish, Bengali, Panjabi and Chinese. Although this support is welcomed by each of the communities involved, it must be acknowledged that it is only a limited support."

These excerpts from the statement would suggest that little or no real progress had been made beyond the February 1978 provision of the equivalent of six full-time teachers. The teaching strength had remained the same through to 1982 and beyond despite the fact that statistical data had shown that there had been a steady increase in the numbers of ethnic minority pupils in the L.E.A.. Moreover, with the exception of Urdu, all community languages had still been ignored by the Authority in terms of school based support. As mentioned earlier the Authority was inclined to leave the responsibility for most mother-tongue teaching to voluntary organisations rather than make it an integral part of mainstream provision.

The report goes on to say:

"An objective survey of the languages spoken at home – the Linguistic Minorities Survey – was begun in February 1982. It is hoped that it will be possible to complete it this year and that it will serve as a basis on which to estimate the extent of need for both minority language teaching and English as a second language. It seems very likely that considerably more resources ought to be developed in this area and a report of this survey and its implications will be made in due course".

That survey had still not been completed when the L.E.A. representative was interviewed in January 1984, almost two years after work on the survey had begun. Such slow progress would suggest a lack of expediency on the part of the Authority. it might also be seen as calling into question the whole resolve of the Authority to act on the linguistic needs of its ethnic minority pupils.

The report referred to above was supplemented by an appendix in the beginning of 1984. This confirmed that no detailed information was available on the number of languages spoken within the L.E.A'.s boundries, nor on the number of speakers of each language. It was known, at least, that a considerable linguistic diversity characterised a number of the Authority's schools. For example, one high school had children with 34 different home languages. Most of these languages were however represented only by one or two speakers, and the major languages spoken were Bengali, Cantonese, Gujrati, Hindi, Italian, Panjabi, Urdu, German and French. Urdu was the only minority language being taught in some of the Authority's schools and colleges and none of the other ethnic minority languages was catered for in any of the local authority schools. So there was not equality of opportunity for all ethnic minority group pupils to learn their mother-tongue in schools. Moreover, such provision as was available in mainstream schools was not equally available to all.

Urdu classes in the Authority's schools:

The following table shows the number of pupils being taught and times of classes:

Schools	Class no's 1983/84	Time of Classes
1. High School (Upper)	38 pupils	TT, LT
2. High School (Lower)	42 pupils	AS,
3. High School (Lower)	10 pupils	AS, LT
4. High School	6 pupils	AS,
5. Sixth Form College	17 pupils	AS
6. High School (Lower)	34 pupils	LT
7. High School (Upper)	10 pupils	TT, LT
8. High School (Upper)	45 pupils	TT, LT
9. Sixth Form College	20 pupils	TT
10. Primary School	37 pupils	TT
11. Primary School	22 pupils	AS
12. Primary School	32 pupils	TT
13. Primary School	80 pupils	TT, LT
Total =	393 pupils	

Key:
TT = Time-tabled
LT = Lunch time
AS = After school

These classes are taught by three full time and three part time Urdu teachers.

Community Language Classes taught on community premises:

There is a considerable range of community language classes arranged by community associations . . . It has not been possible within the resources available to support all of these and indeed where support has been possible it has had to be on a small scale. Those community language classes which the Education Department supports are: Polish, Bengali, Chinese, Hindi, and Panjabi. The number of teaching hours paid for by the Committee is as follows:

Language	Teaching hours
Polish	16
Bengali	2
Chinese	2
Hindi	3
Panjabi	2

Total = 25 hours

The scale of mainstream school community language provision i.e., the teaching (not entirely within the normal school timetable) of **one** language to 393 pupils — could not be described as more than a token gesture, given nearly 10,000 ethnic minority pupils. Equally, tokenry was the financial assistance given to support 25 hours a week of teaching, spread over five languages, through voluntary organisations.

The same appendix to the previous report noted an interesting development in bilingual education in the Authority's schools. It says:

"The programme of teaching community languages goes alongside and is complementary to, the programme of bilingual infant teaching recently agreed by the Committee. The one teaches the languages directly as subjects while the bilingual programme uses the language of the home to support early learning. It is hoped that, in supporting early learning through the use of the mother-tongue, wherever possible, a firmer foundation will be laid for future development of the community languages. Four appointments have been made to this programme but it has been found difficult to recruit sufficient qualified staff for these posts. The prime reason for this difficulty is quite simply a shortage of teachers so qualified and a large growth in authorities demand for such staff".

The recognition given to the principles of community language teaching and of bilingualsim could not be faulted, although existing provision clearly fell some way below the ideal level. What was lacking in the report was any intimation as to how (or whether) the L.E.A. proposed to overcome the problem of recruiting suitable staff.

If such recruitment was to be actively pursued, the L.E.A. ought to have posed itself a number of questions, These would include: Did the Authority offer attractive career prospects to those ready to undertake such teaching? Had it canvassed ethnic minority bi-linguals already on its payroll? Did it have plans to develop its own in-service training programmes to offer re-training in the appropriate teaching skill to such teachers engaged in teaching in other areas of the curriculum? As things stood, it appeared that answers to questions of that sort would all have been in the negative.

In addition to obtaining the documentary information referred to above, the author interviewed the Authority's Head of the Multi-cultural

Development Service. He confirmed the L.E.A.'s plans to conduct a language survey but admitted that it had been subject to a number of delays as regards the L.E.A.'s estimates of the size of the ethnic minority school population. He suggested that the latest one was in order of the 12,000 pupils. He also admitted that the policy for mother-tongue/community language teaching was not yet as clear-cut as it could be. He confirmed that six teachers had been appointed to teach community languages which, as has already been pointed out, represented a very small teaching force, when set against the estimated size of the ethnic minority school population.

When asked about the provision of teacher training for the programme, the head of the multi-cultural development service replied that, "there was a provision for Royal Society of Art Qualifications for teachers in ethnic minority languages at the local college". There were many voluntary supplementary schools for mother-tongue teaching but there was no formal liaison between the Authority and the voluntary language schools. The local authority did not seem to be very liberal or generous in its assistance to these supplementary schools through financial help, free accommodation or teaching materials. Asked how he foresaw the bilingual education and mother-tongue teaching development in the whole curriculum, the local authority's representative said that, "it is very difficult to gaze into a crystal ball. There will be development in this city for these languages in the modern languages curriculum. It would be immensely sad if ethnic minority languages phase out altogether. I hope they won't." The Authority, certainly, did not seem to have shown much enthusiasm for the development of ethnic minority community language teaching programmes over the last ten years.

The author also interviewed a teacher engaged to teach Urdu as a community language on peripatetic basis. She confirmed that she had been involved in mother-tongue teaching for the last five years and also in bilingual education work. Both these projects were run on an experimental basis. Because of the scarcity of places to learn community languages, pupils were selected for this programme. In an ideal situation one would envisage mother-tongue teaching being available on educational and social grounds to all ethnic minority pupils. However, as has already been made evident, here the situation was far from ideal, hence the need for selection.

The teacher representative confirmed that there was little liaison between the schools and the voluntary supplementary language classes taking place in the neighbourhood. She stressed that the teaching of mother-tongue was essential to boost the child's image of himself/herself and acquaintance with his/her community and culture. Thirty per cent of the children learning community languages took public examinations in these languages. When asked about the main problems in operating this programme, she went on to say:

"The community language teachers do not have the due status within

the teaching profession. Times of teaching these languages are not convenient, for instance, at lunch time or late after school hours. Sometimes their fellow teachers are not sufficiently interested in these programmes. Moreover, peripatetic teaching is a physical drain on teachers".

She also commented that:

"Mother tongue teaching is very demanding when you have to travel to different places within a day. Teaching conditions for these languages are not desirable. Community language teachers felt left out from the general school life. There are very little career prospects as a majority of the mother-tongue teachers are on the bottom of the teaching ladder i.e., main-scale teachers.

Such an opinion would suggest that much has still to be done, if mother-tongue teaching is to be successfully conducted in schools — as far as both pupils and teachers are concerned.

Local Education Authority H:

The Local Education Authority H represented the Yorkshire and North of England region of Britain. This again is one of the largest metropolitan authorities in the region with a considerable ethnic minority population. In the heyday of the post-war industrial boom, this City Metropolitan District held a magnetic attraction for unskilled and semi-skilled workforce of immigrant settlers. It should be pointed out that the ravages of the recent economic recession have taken a heavy toll of this region with the running down of the local textile industry, and the immigrants, perhaps, were the most affected group by the consequent unemployment and deprivation.

The Authority had recently gathered data on the ethnicity and home languages of its minority pupils. The ethnic origins of the schools' population, at March 1984, were given as follows:

	First Schools	Middle Schools	Upper Schools	Nursery Schools	Language Centres	Special Education	Total =
Afro Caribbean	278	253	396	10	2	21	960
	0.8%	1%	1.6%	1.7%	0.1%	1.3%	1.1%
Asian	7,594	5,138	4,128	231	1,324	392	18,807
	22.6%	20.8%	16.9%	39.9%	99.4%	24.5%	21.8%
UK & Eire	25,413	19,115	19,186	331	1	1,167	65,213
	75.7%	77.3%	78.3%	57.2%	0.1%	73%	75.6%
European	133	155	292	2	3	18	603
	0.4%	0.6%	1.2%	0.3%	0.2%	1.1%	0.7%
Others	131	75	145	5	3	2	361
	0.4%	0.3%	0.6%	0.9%	0.2%	0.1%	0.4%
Unspecified	4	1	335	0	0	0	340
	0.1%	0%	1.4%	0%	0%	0%	0.4%
Total =	33,553	24,737	24,482	579	1,333	1,600	86,284

The opposite figures showed that more than 23 per cent of the school population consisted of pupils of non-white background. This was a proportion significant enough to warrant provision for any special educational needs. Moreover, a considerable number of pupils came from minority groups whose home language was other than English. The L.E.A.'s Schools Language Survey carried out in March 1983 showed that about 20 per cent of the children in the District's Schools used a language other than English at home. Out of a total of 87,266 children on roll, 17,571 pupils used one or more languages other than or in addition to English. Ten major spoken languages were listed separately. Panjabi, Urdu and Gujrati were reported as the languages spoken at home by 85 per cent of the children in addition to English.

The following table summarises the finding from the Authority's School Language Survey:

Language Spoken	Number of children who speak each language	Percentage of the total number of Second Language speakers speaking each language
Panjabi	9,542	54%
Urdu	2,657	15%
Gujurati	1,422	8%
Panjabi (Gurmukhi)	1,370	8%
Bengali	795	5%
Pushto	551	3%
Italian	268	1.5%
Polish	164	1%
Cantonese	143	1%
Creole	99	0.5%
Other languages	579	3%
Total =	17,571	100%

It should be noted that the individual totals for each language add up to more than the final total because some children were recorded as speaking more than one language. At the same time it should serve to justify a multi-lingual policy for community language teaching within the L.E.A. The supplementary language schools run by immigrant voluntary organisations were the only means of learning ethnic minority mother tongues until 1982 when the Directorate of Educational Services made recommendations for introduction of Mother-Tongue And/Or Community Language Teaching in their report entitled 'Race Relations: A Position Statement'. This was the first document to give any consideration to bilingualism and community language teaching within the mainstream education service. Before considering a separate report on Community Language Teaching (CLT) produced in the same year, it would be appropriate to record the main points of the former in order to discuss the development in progression:

"Mother Tongue and/or Community Language Teaching:

... The Bilingual Child:

i)   there is a growing amount of research, in this and other countries, which suggests that support for a child's first language facilitates, rather than hinders, the learning of a Second. It would seem to be complementary to and supportive of the learning of English (Ref: MOTET, 1981-2).

ii)   CLT provides an important link between school and home, and school and community.

iii)   by raising the esteem and status of the child's first language, it helps to develop confidence and self-esteem in his/her identity.

iv)   it allows the child to use what he/she has already learned and supports further learning.

v)   it is an additional resource which extends the individuals' vocational and life options, and which should not be allowed to wither away.

vi)   literacy in the community language allows the bilingual pupil to maintain contact with wider family and community groups, in this and other countries; it also gives him/her access to a range of cultural and literary tradtions.

Multi-Cultural Education:

i)   CLT is one way of responding positively to the needs of a multi-cultural society.

ii)   CLT demonstrates that the languages used by local communities have value and status in mainstream education;

iii)   it increases all pupil's awareness of language, and of linguistic and cultural diversity.

The Progress Report:

i)   In March, 1981, the Linguistic Minorities Project carried out a survey of bilingualism in the City schools. Approximately 15,000 pupils were, to some extent, bilingual, and spoke between them approximately 63 different languages. Panjabi, Urdu and Gujrati were used by 11,000/12,000 pupils (these figures had been revised by the latest survey reports).

ii)   Last year, 4 additional posts were created for the teaching of Urdu and Panjabi. Next year there will be 10, including a mother-tongue co-ordinator's post. It is later hoped to increase the number of Asian languages offered.

iii)   At present most of the support for and teaching of community languages takes place in voluntary community/religious schools, attended by large numbers of children.

iv)   In first schools and nurseries where there are bilingual teachers and nursery nurses, there have been considerable changes in attitude and approach. Whereas it was once considered wrong to encourage the child's use of any language other than English, most schools now make use of their teacher's/nursery nurse's bilingualism, in, for example, Panjabi story-time and explanation about work, as well as discussions with parents. In some schools, parents participate in story-telling sessions. Many schools have advertised posts in the hope of recruiting bilingual members of staff, but, as indicated elsewhere, the lack of applicants is a major obstacle to the development of bilingual policies".

The report went on to make use of the Schools Council's Mother Tongue Project teaching material and guidelines to suggest to the LEA ways of supporting mother-tongue/community language teaching in schools. As was found when reviewing the current state of practice in other LEAs studied, here too was another report of the discussion types document, interspersed only here and there with concrete suggestions for mounting the operation in schools. The report could not be faulted in general terms for the way in which it presented the case for mother-tongue teaching in a multi-cultural society — what it had to offer in terms of increasing, among all pupils, awareness of linguistic and cultural diversity and in terms of reinforcing a positive self-identity among ethnic minority children, and so on. What was disappointing about the report was the lack of evidence of positive action being taken to develop work in the classrooms. What had been done in practical evaluative terms? Was the creation of four or even ten additional teaching posts for this purpose adequate to meet the linguistic needs of over 17,000 pupils for ethnic minority groups? Had the Authority set any target for its schools for such a policy programme with a follow-up evaluation across the Authority? It was quite clear that nothing on these lines had happened.

It appeared that the Authority had been pre-occupied with writing report after report. For example, two specific documents were produced by the Metropolitan L.E.A. In 1982 and 1983, both entitled 'Community Language Teaching'. It is proposed to draw on the main points of both these to see whether any new intiatives were discernible as far as community languages policy was concerned:

"Mother Tongue Teaching or Community Language Teaching (CLT) in the City Schools:
Introduction:
The 1980 'District Trends' stated explicitly that the City faced the special challenge of accepting that it is now a multi-racial, multi-cultural society. 'District Trends' 1981 stated that a third of the City's school children will be of 'Asian descent and that the cultural values and traditions — in terms of

language and religion are likely to remain distinctive'. It also recognises the need to move from concentraing on E2L teaching to other more complex issues in the schools, 'Which will involve the whole range of the curriculum and the education of all children in all parts of the district'. One of the main issues concerning the educational needs of ethnic minority children is the role of the education system in relation to the maintenance and support of the Community Languages (mother tongue).

. . .**The Council's Policy:**

The City Metropolital Council's Equal Opportunity Policy (Nov., 1981), states that every section of the community has an equal right to maintain its own identity, culture, **language**, religion and customs.

. . .**Priorities:**

1. CLT in the initial school reception of young children speaking such a language before school entry: A transitional period of CLT as part of bilingual education for a continuation of concept development in the language of the home at Nursery and First school stage would facilitate a much smoother and a more positive introduction to education for such children.

2. Development for such potentially bilingual children of literacy in the Community Language as well as in English during their first school and middle school years: Where possible this stage of development ought to take into account the voluntary provision of CLT through supplementary schools, thus establishing a much desired link between the community and the schools.

3. Continue to expand the CLT programme in our Upper Schools on the same optional basis as other modern languages.

The Directorate's Policy

Objectives: (in brief)

To maintain and develop knowledge of that language which the child uses in his/her daily environment.

To successfully develop a bilingualism which will make it possible for the child to feel at home in the home and the school (different cultural environments).

To extend the range of languages offered in our schools."

The reports went on to cover the following: the diversity of languages spoken within the Authority's area; how the L.E.A. could support local voluntary supplementary language schools, e.g., through liaison work; and an up-dated progress statement as far as school-based community languages provision was concerned. The last of these reports noted that 1982/83 will be remembered as the most important time for the establishment of Community Languages in the City's schools.

One thing that emerged very clearly from these reports was that the LEA had woken to the reality of accepting the linguistic diversity among pupils in its schools and had showed such goodwill in its recognition of the multi-lingual needs of the area as a whole. How successful the Authority could be said to be in its provision for community languages in schools was another matter. That could be better adjudged by reference to this information provided by the Community Languages Team Leader:

"The number of pupils taking Community Languages in 7 Upper Schools:

3rd Forms	459 pupils
4th Forms	492 pupils
5th Forms	268 pupils
6th Forms	68 pupils
Total =	1,287 pupils

Break-down of languages taught:

Urdu	1,192 pupils
Panjabi	69 pupils
Gujrati	24 pupils
Hindi	2 pupils
Total =	1,287 pupils

The number of pupils for 1984/85 is likely to increase. There are two first schools and a middle school who teach Urdu, Panjabi and Gujrati on an extended day basis. The total number of pupils involved in learning these languages is roughly two hundred".

The above information showed that the L.E.A.'s emphasis, with regard to community language teaching, was on pupils in secondary schools and that there was a wide gap during the first and middle school phase of their education during which the majority of ethnic minority pupils were without due support for their mother-tongue in the mainstream schools.

The author also had the opportunity to interview the LEAs representative who was an Adviser/Inspector for Multi-cultural Education throughout the whole Authority. The interview with the Authority's spokesman revealed that English was the only language used as the medium of instruction in schools but the L.E.A. had a policy of ad-hoc provision to support bilingual education. A diversity of 63 home languages among the pupils in the L.E.A.'s schools was noted and Panjabi, Urdu, Gujrati, Bengali, Chinese and Polish were the main ethnic minority languages. The Authority offered Urdu, Panjabi and Gujrati (and nominally, Hindi), mainly in its Upper Schools — and only in some of them. Provision was only considered where the numbers of pupils wishing to learn a minority language and the level of demand from the schools themselves and parents warranted it.

The L.E.A.'s representative also stated that 10 qualified teachers and 3 unqualified instructors were involved in teaching minority community languages. It seemed a slim teaching force to cater for a potential market of more than 17,000 pupils from the linguistic minorities. The Authority had a special provision for the community language teachers' in-service training at a local university. Credit must be due to the Authority for its close liaison with more than 50 supplementary voluntary language classes. The L.E.A. had one supplementary provision co-ordinator for thi purpose and regular training for voluntary community language teachers was organised by the Authority. The L.E.A. in conjunction with the Urban Aid Programme had made a grant of £100,000 in 1984, to 17 voluntary schools in support of languages, religions and cultures.

It seemed a generous financial aid to a small number of voluntary schools particularly when the Authority appeared to have ignored the rest of the supplementary language classes in terms of any financial assistance.

The L.E.A.'s adviser for multi-cultural education also told the author that the Authority was running regular courses for mainstream teachers in Hindustani and there was a provision for white adults to learn ethnic minority languages. Asked about provision for the further supply of community language teachers, he said:

"There is no room for complacency. We should take all the initiatives to train new teachers. At the moment we have appointed instructors for mother-tongue teaching and they will be sent for full-time teacher training at the Authority's expense".

Commenting on the planning and co-ordination of community language teaching and bilingual education programmes, the LEA's spokesman stated:

"We are looking for a comprehensive provision to meet the educational demands of multicultural, multilingual society. The usual procedure is sometimes forsaken for expediency. On the whole, it is better to create a good healthy atmosphere in the education system for such developments rather than pressing for special treatment. The Section 11 of the 1966 Local Government Act is the only source for financing these policies. The evaluation is the responsibility of the community language co-ordinator".

There was a lot to digest in this statement. One could not deny the apparent reasonableness of the approach towards a comprehensive community languages teaching policy. Yet, in practical terms, current mainstream provision only amounted to a few minority languages and these available almost exclusively to a small proportion of the older ethnic minority pupils.

When asked about the attitudes and the responses of a variety of parties to mother tongue/community language teaching policies, the L.E.A.'s representative answered:

"All head teachers are in favour of these policies. The heads of modern languages departments are also supportive and there is a goodwill, among most of the teachers. The local teachers' unions have the most damaging effect at the Council level. The NUT and NAS/UWT representatives are so naive and ignorant of the whole

issue of mother-tongue teaching. The general public have very little understanding. Ethnic minority parents are extremely keen but the media is never our friend. Out of 116 articles in the local press, only two can be classified as positive."

The general atmosphere did not appear particularly favourable to community language teaching though the LEA's spokesman was very optimistic about the whole issue and expressed his feeling in these words:

"It is the most exciting development in Britain today. The indigeneous population would regard this as one of the tremendous assets the minority groups brought to the islands. I believe every person in these islands will be appreciative of this asset".

This statement reflected the importance of interdependence of different national, cultural and linguistic groups in the modern world with its pluralistic permeation.

The author also met the Community Languages Team Leader to find out his view about the mother-tongue teaching situation within the L.E.A. In addition to the administrative and co-ordinating responsibilities of his post, the team leader for community languages was mainly involved in teaching mother-tongue at one of the L.E.A.'s upper schools. This particular school had 176 ethnic minority pupils out of a total of 650 on roll i.e., about 27 per cent of the school population. Yet English was the only language used as the medium of instruction. The school had no policy of its own with regard to ethnic minority community language teaching though it offered Urdu and Bengali languages with the help of peripatetic teachers. These languages were given one hour per week in the school time-table and the community language teachers admitted that this offered inadequate time to prepare pupils thoroughly to meet the standards of public examinations.

Pupils were 'selected' for community language teaching on the basis of options choice. While they were free to study a community language if they wished, there was always the problem of priority; opting for a community language usually meant 'dropping' a 'traditional' subject on the school curriculum. As has been referred to earlier (see Case Study L.E.A. **C,**), some option schemes leave ethnic minority pupils with invidious choices to make.

The teacher interviewed said that more than 90 per cent of pupils of ethnic minority origin could understand their home language and it could be a useful basis for extending development through school-based instruction overall. The school did not have any liaison with any supplementary language classes held in the neighbourhood.

When asked about the evaluation procedure for community languages, the co-ordinating teacher expressed his intention to use graded tests in the near future to record pupils' individual progress. The public examinations at the C.S.E. and G.C.E. 'O' and 'A' level were the only means currently available of assessing pupils success in learning their mother-tongue.

Commenting on a problem of a different but related nature, the community languages co-ordinator emphasised that the lack of suitable teaching materials was one of the main difficulties in this area of the school curriculum. He outlined the future in these terms:

"There is a great future ahead for community languages and there has been a lot of development in this area of the curriculum. We need more support from the central government and the local authorities. I cannot predict the distant future but for the near future I can see a great development taking place with regard to community language teaching".

Local Education Authority J:
This is one of the Scottish Regional Authorities of Education. This regional education authority is considered to be the largest in the Western Europe, because of its geographical size. It consists of six large divisions for administrative convenience. One of these six divisions caters for the education service of a large city with a considerable multi-ethnic community. At the same time the immigrant population is also scattered in the other divisions throughout the length and breadth of the Authority. The Regional Council Department of Education compiled in September 1983 an 'Annual Data Review: Education of Children whose First Language is not English'. The details of this data review are as follows:

Country of Origin	*Numbers of Pupils in Schools*
Division 1:	
India	8
Pakistan	—
West Indies	—
Hong Kong	—
EEC	1
Europe Non-EEC	5
Asia	9
Africa	—
South America	—
Others	4
	Total = 27
Division 2	
India	36
Pakistan	12
West Indies	—
Hong Kong	98
EEC	16
Europe Non-EEC	13
Asia	12

Africa	3
South America	1
Other	8
	Total = 199

Division 3

India	89
Pakistan	98
West Indies	3
Hong Kong	73
EEC	12
Europe Non-EEC	7
Asia	19
Africa	14
South America	28
Other	34
	Total = 377

Division 4

India	845
Pakistan	2310
West Indies	3
Hong Kong	376
EEC	47
Europe Non-EEC	15
Asia	115
Africa	106
South America	9
Other	—
	Total = 3826

Division 5

India	35
Pakistan	156
West Indies	1
Hong Kong	85
EEC	13
Europe Non-EEC	—
Asia	71
Africa	11
South America	—
Other	29
	Total = 401

Division 6

India	9
Pakistan	16
West Indies	—
Hong Kong	32
EEC	1
Europe Non-EEC	1
Asia	5
Africa	1
South America	—
Other	6
	Total = 71

The above data gave a grand total of 4,901 pupils from ethnic minority backgrounds within the Authority. It should be pointed out that the documents referred to above emphasised the national or continental backgrounds of minority group children rather than documenting their home languages. The number of linguistic minority pupils had been increasing steadily i.e., from 3,595 in November 1977, to 4,901 in September 1983. The next survey of this nature on the similar ethnicity basis took place in March 1984. In summary, the statistics from this survey were as follows:

Children whose first language is not English (Primary Schools)	3,258
Children shose first language is not English (Secondary Schools)	1,611
Children whose first language is not English (Special Schools)	106
	TOTAL = 4,975

This latest survey of the Authority showed an approximate increase of 1.5 per cent on the previous data of pupils from the linguistic minority backgrounds over a period of six months i.e., an annual increase of 3 per cent approximately. Although the Regional Education Authority was aware of its obligation to make provision for mother-tongue/community language teaching for pupils from minority groups under the terms of the 1977 EEC Directive, very little had been done to introduce ethnic minority languages within the school system.

In addition to the above documentary information the investigator also interviewed the Depute Director of the Regional Council Department of Education for further information on the subject of mother-tongue teaching and bilingual education within the region. He confirmed that English was the only language used as the medium of instruction in schools. When asked about the detail of ethnic minority pupils' home languages, he said that Panjabi, Urdu, Chinese, Hindi and Polish were the main ethnic minority languages. He had no breakdown of the numbers speaking particular minority languages, nor precise information on the languages spoken; the Authority's reviews had not sought that degree of detail either. The aim of those exercises had merely been to record, division by division, the numbers of children whose first language was 'other than English'.

The Regional Authority had no official policy for teaching mother-tongue/community languages. The local Authority's representative mentioned that:

"There was, perhaps, a mention in one of the minutes of the education committee meetings to set up a working party to produce a policy document for minority language teaching. An interim paper for such development is still at a discussion stage".

The depute director of the LEA added that teaching of Panjabi, Urdu and Chinese languages was being introduced in some schools from September 1984. When asked about the number of pupils wishing to learn these languages he said that "it has not been ascertained yet". This seemed a rather haphazard approach to such an innovation.

The Authority did not have any record of teachers from ethnic minority groups who could be deployed for teaching mother-tongue or community languages as necessary. There were no pre-supposed criteria for the selection of community languages for curricular teaching. Urdu had been taught in one secondary school for the previous two years in addition to modern languages. As mentioned above, the Regional Authority had decided to introduce Panjabi, Urdu and Chinese within the time-table of some secondary schools but there was no provision for the teaching of these languages in the primary sector; such provision would have facilitiated a structured progression in the languages throughout the whole school system. When asked if this ad-hoc provision of teaching some community languages in a few schools was to be put on to a permanent footing or whether it was merely experimental, the Authority's representative replied that no decision on this had yet been taken. This would suggest that the whole issue of mother-tongue teaching provision was undecided and haphazard at all elvels and much uncertainty remained.

Three qualified teachers had been appointed to teach Panjabi, Urdu and Chinese languages. The Authority's own statistics showed that this was a token gesture far from sufficient to cater for the linguistic needs of all the pupils from ethnic minority groups in the region. The Authority did not have any special provision for teacher training for this purpose.The local Authority's representative agreed that there was a need for such arrangement and they would approach the local teachers' training colleges for the supply and training of teachers for ethnic minority community languages. It seemed that the Authority had not given any thought in advance about this essential aspect of supply and training of suitable teachers if the teaching of community languages was to be put on to a permanent and wider footing.

Asked about the criteria for selection of schools to introduce the above three community languages, he answered:

> *"Three schools have been selected i.e., one school for each language. It has been resolved by tripartite consultation i.e., the head-teachers of schools, the local Community Relations Council and the minority community organisations".*

Credit should be given to the Authority for involving the interested parties in the decision-making process.

There were quite a few voluntary supplementary schools engaged in teaching ethnic minority languages in the evenings and during the weekends. The Local Authority was unable to supply exact information about the number of such schools, languages taught in these schools and the number of pupils attending voluntary languages classes. There was no formal liaison between the Authority and supplementary language schools for mother-tongue teaching. The Local Authority's Depute Director indicated that 'The Authority had tried to meet the organisers of voluntary supplementary language schools once a year and it would like to approach them on more regular intervals'.

In his correspondence with the author, the Local Authority's representative commented:

> *"Within the region a small sum of money, £20,000 is made available to the various ethnic minority groups to enable them to teach language, culture and religion in the evenings and at weekends and outwith the school system. The procedure was instituted as a small token reaction to the E.E.C. Directive on mother-tongue teaching. In addition the various ethnic minority groups are offered the services of our language adviser and the use of audio-visual equipment to enable them to teach the languages better to children and young persons".*

Undoubtedly, this was a helpful gesture on the part of the Authority towards the ethnic minority groups engaged in providing voluntary classes for learning community languages but the financial assistance earmarked for this purpose was certainly insufficient considering the total number of pupils from different linguistic minorities.

The Regional Education Authority did not make any provision for adult classes for the teaching of ethnic community languages. However, the Authority had undertaken to subsidise such language classes for adults at the Local University Extramural Department. Because of the initial difficulties in embarking on day-time teaching of ethnic minority languages, no in-service programme for teachers to learn these languages had emerged. The Authority's representative confirmed that, 'they would seek the co-operation of the local university for the training of teachers for minority languages'. It was ironic that the Authority seemed to be leaving everything to take place or emerge in the future rather than attempting any serious planning for gradual development in this sphere.

When questioned on the ethos and philosphy for multi-ethnic, multi-lingual educational development he said assuringly:

"It displays other cultures' benefits to the nation in an atmosphere of pluralistic development. It is also an effective means to combat racism and provides a humane approach for mutual understanding among different groups of our society".

Commenting on the lack of earlier progress in this field he said:

"Because of some initial difficulties with the registration of teachers in ethnic minority languages, development of the teaching of mother-tongue in the day school has been rather slow to develop".

This suggest that the DES and the Scottish Education Department should take special steps to recognise the qualifications of teachers from overseas who are suitable to teach ethnic minority languages.

There is also another anomaly; Section 11 of the Local Government Act 1966 which includes special financial assistance for language programmes was not applicable in Scotland. One might wonder that why this anomaly was not rectified long before. The Local Authority representative stressed that 'there was no special financial arrangement for funding mother-tongue/community language teaching programmes except Urban Renewal Grants'. It is desirable that the Local Authorities have additional financial assistance from the central government for such developments but the terms of the 1977 E.E.C. Directive make it obligatory for the L.E.A.s to make provision for mother-tongue teaching in schools through their general budgets.

When asked about the development of academic studies for examination purposes, the Depute Director of Education added that 'The Scottish Examination Board has given assurance to develop 'Ordinary' and 'Higher' grades examination in minority languages'. As has already been mentioned elsewhere, progress towards the establishment of a structured system of academic standards for community languages has been painfully slow. Commenting on the other methods to be applied by the LEA to assess the progress in mother-tongue/community language teaching and learning process he said:

"Scottish Education Departments are quite keen to give a lead in the aspect of evaluation. We would develop all the appropriate channels for the assessment of progress in ethnic minority languages".

It should be pointed out that the Scottish Education Department following the Directive of the Council of the European Community on the education of migrant workers issued Circular 1071 (1981) with reference to possible ways of supporting the mother-tongues of minority communities. So far the Regional Authority seemed to have ignored the spirit of this Circular.

It was encouraging to hear from the Local Authority's representative that the local university was thinking of establishing a chair for South Asian languages in Scotland. It might take some time under the present circumstances for such a development to materialise. Commenting on the problems encountered in operating mother-tongue teaching policies he pointed out that the politicians needed to be made aware of the necessity for such developments.

Asked about the responses and reactions of the teaching profession as a whole to these policies, the Depute Director of Education replied:

"There is no adverse reaction or resistance from the headteachers towards ethnic minority language progrmmes. I can't speak with truth for the rank and file teachers. Perhaps, they are neutral. The General Teaching Council for Scotland is supportive for these initiatives. The Educational Institute of Scotland (Teacher's Professional Body) has accepted it in principle. The Chairman of the LEA is very much in favour of such developments".

In spite of the expression of goodwill on the part of all involved, it was difficult to convince oneself that the issues concerning minority languages had been tackled with the speed and effectiveness they required. No further development had taken place for some time and the situation within the Regional Education Authority mainstream provision for ethnic minority community language teaching remained at status quo (ante) till the beginning of 1987.

Local Education Authority K:
This Local Education Authority represents the south of Wales region and possesses one of the oldest immigrant communities of the United Kingdom. It is a County Authority covering a large city within its boundaries. Sailors and seamen of different nationalities, languages and cultures have been settling in this area over the centuries. In spite of being one of the oldest centres of immigrant settlement, no exact record of pupils from ethnic minority backgrounds was available at the time of the interview. The Authority seemed to have taken no initiatives to meet the linguistic and cultural needs of ethnic minority pupils in its schools. This particular Local Authority had no policy nor guidelines for multi-cultural developments in the school curriculum. Another adjoining Local Education Authority in Wales summed up the situation in its Chief Education Officer's letter to the author:

"I regret that I am unable to assist you in your research on 'The Mother-tongue of Linguistic Minorities in Multi-cultural Britain' as there are insufficient numbers in the ethnic minority groups in the Authority to justify a teaching policy for the development and implementation of the mother-tongues".

Perhaps this was a reflection of the attitude of the whole region towards the minority groups.

The Adviser in Special Education took part in this research on behalf of the Local Education Authority as there was no L.E.A. official with the sole responsibility for multi-ethnic education. The Authority catered for an approximate total of 70,000 pupils in its schools. When asked about the number of children in schools from ethnic minority groups, the Local Authority's representative answered, 'No such record of ethnic origin is kept. One time we used to count heads but it is very difficult to keep track of children's movements'. He put an estimate of 2,000 pupils from ethnic minority groups in the Authority's schools. This would represent approximately 3 per cent of the total school population. It ought perhaps to be incumbent on every LEA to keep proper records as to the size of its ethnic minority school population. Only in this way could an LEA begin to gauge the likely scale of potential demand for special linguistic and other educational needs and then take steps to develop programmes to meet them.

English and Welsh were the only languages used as the medium of instruction. No language other than English and Welsh was supported at school despite the fact that the Secondary School Survey suggested that 24 different languages were spoken at home by the pupils from ethnic minority backgrounds. No mother-tongue or community language was taught at any level within the school timetable. The Authority had no policy for teaching minority languages. The Authority's representative replied to the questions on mother-tongue teaching by saying:

"There is no policy of mother-tongue/community language teaching, but I am very optimistic about this aspect of education. A working party has been established to produce some document on multi-cultural education, and mother-tongue teaching is hoped to be covered in that statement".

No such document or statements had materialised by the end of 1984. Progress seemed to be painfully slow in this area of curriculum development.

When asked about the existence of voluntary schools for teaching ethnic minority languages, the LEA Adviser said, 'There are some supplementary schools which teach mother tongue and community languages but not to the extent one would expect'. There was no formal liaison between the Local Education Authority and these voluntary language schools. The Local Authority representative went on to say that some financial aid was given to some of these voluntary supplementary schools organised by ethnic minority organisations. He was unable to give any precise details of such financial support. Free accommodation was provided to these schools only if asked for. There was no formalised pattern, nor procedure, for providing financial support to the voluntary schools. It was rather a haphazard approach to the whole issue of mother-tongue and community language teaching.

The Local Authority made no provision for adult classes to learn ethnic minority languages except Arabic and apparently there was no in-service programme for teachers to learn these languages. The Local Authority's spokesman expressed his interest in such development. He constantly used the catch phrase of 'sensitivity' to the whole issue of ethnic minority languages but his interview suggested rather that the L.E.A. was 'insensitive' to the needs of linguistic minority pupils. Answering the questions about the planning and co-ordination of community language teaching and bilingual education programmes, he said:

"Such development is necessary for the respectability of children's cultural and linguistic background and it provides facilities for the children who wish to learn their mother-tongue".

When asked about the response of the teaching profession towards such policies the LEA Adviser commented:

"The teachers' attitude is rather mixed but some heads are supportive. Dogmatism is teachers' problem in this matter while the teachers' unions are in favour of such programmes".

Commenting on the media coverage of the issue he said, 'The local press is rather weak for a balanced portrayal of the whole issue of mother-tongue teaching'. He foresaw very sensitive development in relation to ethnic minorities and welcomed the Council leader's enthusiasm for such developments.

In addition to the interview with the L.E.A. representative the author also interviewed the County Community Tutor with a responsibility for minority groups from non-English or non-Welsh backgrounds. He was also involved in running a community centre for adult education. When asked about the community languages of the pupils in schools, the County Community Tutor mentioned Greek, Spanish, Italian, Bengali, Gujrati, Panjabi, Urdu, Pushto, Chinese, Japanese, Vietnamese, Arabic, French and German as the home languages of pupils from minority groups. He confirmed that there was no provision to teach any of these languages in the Authority's schools. It seemed that the Local Authority was pre-occupied with making provision for the Welsh language in schools at the expense of ethnic minority languages. The County Community Tutor vouched for this trend in the whole region.

There were about a dozen teachers of ethnic minority origin employed by the Authority and none of them was utilised for teaching community languages. Asked about the importance of minority languages, the County Community Tutor said:

"The minority community languages should be the integral part of the school curriculum. It is essential to give these languages due status up to university level".

The Authority had ignored the whole issue at all levels. The teacher representative said that there had been difficulties with the implementation of Welsh language programmes in school; these had now been overcome. He predicted that there was a chance for the introduction of minority languages in schools next. One might have thought that the issue of Welsh language in the region would not have been a hindrance to the introduction of a mother-tongue teaching policy for all ethnic groups on equal terms.

Commenting on the attitude of the teaching profession towards ethnic minority languages the Community Tutor added:

"Some teachers will support such developments. The teaching profession has changed slightly in favour of community languages but not to a desirable extent".

He also made an economic point by saying:

"The economic recession affects headteachers' interest for the development of minority languages. Teachers as a whole are indifferent to this challenge. If the case is presented clearly, there should be no difficulty then".

He was not specific as to whose role it was to present this case. One might have felt that it was one of his responsibilities as a County Community Tutor to encourage the Local Authority to develop some sort of policy for mother-tongue and/or community language teaching within the school system.

In spite of the lack of any positive initiative on the part of the Local Education Authority,the mother-tongue and community language teaching was provided by ethnic minority voluntary organisations. The figures, according to the County Community Tutor for children learning ethnic minority languages in the evening and/or at weekend voluntary classes, were as follows:

Arabic	300 pupils
Bengali	120 pupils
Greek	40 pupils
Spanish	60 pupils
Urdu	80 pupils
Total =	600 pupils

The Local Authority's teacher representative pointed out that he was only aware of the above voluntary classes taking place out of school hours and there might be more of which he was not aware. It showed that the Authority had not attempted to establish any systematic formal liaison wih voluntary schools involved in teaching ethnic minority community languages. The lack of such liaison meant that the Authority had no policy to support voluntary ethnic minority languages in schools on a regular and/or planned basis, i.e., either through financial aid or free accommodation. There was some provision for learning ethnic minority languages in voluntary supplementary schools for only 600 pupils out of the approximate total of 2,000 school-age children of ethnic minority origin. This figure represents 30 per cent of the total number of pupils from ethnic minority groups. It showed that the remaining 70 per cent of children from minority backgrounds were apparently deprived of any opportunity to learn their mother-tongue or community languages.

Asked about the future of mother-tongue teaching and bi-lingual education within the Local Education Authority, the County Community Tutor saw some grounds for optimism saying:

"We should have enough provision and supply of teachers to justify the teaching of minority community languages. My experience and knowledge of ethnic minority groups warrant that mother-tongue teaching should be pursued with enthusiasm. A lot depends on diplomatic pressure for such developments".

Commenting on the strategy for teaching ethnic minority languages he went on to say:

"The strategy of take it or leave it in this connection is not good enough. The case of bi-lingualism should be put strongly. Directions should come from the top i.e., the central government. There should be a cabinet minister for ethnic minority developments i.e., a Minister of the Crown. Minority languages and cultures are very important in the way of overseas trade and commerce".

The County Community Tutor had a great vision and strong words for the development of ethnic minority languages and culture. He had been unsuccessful in his attempts to influence the Authority to embark on any policy for the implementation of mother-tongue teaching within the Authority's schools or to support community languages through voluntary efforts. The Welsh Language Society had gone through an arduous struggle to obtain status for Welsh Language on a par with English language in its schools. One might hope that the Welsh Language Society would be magnanimous enough to accept the need to develop other ethnic minority languages on equal terms. The study of the L.E.A. suggested that the Welsh region had not responded positively to the linguistic needs of its ethnic minority groups.

Chapter 6

Research Findings and Conclusions

The analysis of the relevant data in the form of L.E.A.s' portrayals with regard to the provision of ethnic minority mother-tongue/community language teaching reflected some interesting differences and similarities in educational practice in this context in different parts of the country.

The role of the decision makers e.g., at political and executive levels is important in the formulation and implementation of any educational policy. The author would have liked to interview the locally elected members (councillors) of the education committees and the linguistic minority organisations and the ethnic minority parents in order to find their views on the teaching of minority languages in their areas. It was not possible to carry out such a task in view of the limited time available for this study.

As discussed in the first three chapters of this study, it is abundantly clear that the teaching of mother-tongue and the development of bilingualism/multi-lingualism are vital for the harmonious progress of a multi-ethnic, multi-lingual society. These are equally important for the educational and cognitive development of pupils from ethnic minority groups. The inter-cultural and intra-cultural permeation of social developments should be reflected in all aspects of the school curriculum. Lynch (1983) commenting on 'a polyethnic survival curriculum' and 'education courses for a multi-cultural society' refers to Smolicz within an Australian context of school courses which will help to provide conditions of pluralism and social cohesion. The latter advocates six kinds of courses: "multi-cultural education, ethnic education concerned with ethnic studies, ethnic education concerned with **community languages.**, **bilingual education.**, English as a second language; and **education for bilingual/bicultural teachers and other educators**". (Stresses by the author). In 'a set of paradigm multicultural aims', Lynch (1983) goes on to say:
"In practice and in content this implies excellence in the lingua franca and development, not just maintenance, of mothertongue competence, ... which will enable the individual to develop effective interchange

relationship within and across groups as well as between individuals". (Stresses, the author's).

The previous chapter was devoted to the study of the multi-cultural, multi-lingual developments with special references to the provision of ethnic minority language teaching in Britain. This exercise was undertaken at the L.E.A. level in different regions of the country. This was done in order to establish any national trends as regards such development and policy implementation (see Chapter 5). The summary of the main findings of the investigation in relation to the questionnaires i.e., the Interview Schedules for the Local Education Authorities, and for the Schools and Teachers (See Appendices 1 and 2) is as follows:

The sample of Local Education Authorities was very wide and the ten portrayed varied in their sizes, structures and the provision of educational services. Some of the L.E.A.s served rural as well as urban areas of the country (e.g., L.E.A.s C, F, J and K) while the others had responsibility to cater for the education of purely metropolitan districts of large conurbations (e.g., L.E.A.s A, B, D, E, G and H). The settlements of minority group populations also differed greatly in density and their origins or backgrounds. For instance, the ethnic minority groups formed 2.37 per cent of the total population within the L.E.A. C while in the L.E.A. B they constituted over 40 per cent of its population. These variations of different kinds seemed to have affected the L.E.A.s responses to the multi-cultural, multi-lingual development within their education services.

English was the only language used as the medium of instruction throughout all the Local Education Authorities of the study sample except the Welsh Authority. The Welsh L.E.A. K used also Welsh as a medium of instruction along with English. The scope of minority community languages as a means of imparting education was undermined with the exception of some L.E.A.s which supported children's bilingualism during the settling-in period in nursery and infant schools.

In spite of the obligations set out by the 1977 E.E.C. Directive (77/486) for the member states with reference to the children of migrant/immigrant workers, most of the British L.E.A.s seemed to have failed to develop firm policies consistent with the terms and spirit of that Directive, and relating to the provision within the school curriculum of mother-tongue/community language teaching (L.E.A.s, C, E, F, G, J and K).

The Local Authorities which had made efforts to formulate a policy for teaching ethnic minority community languages as a part of the multi-cultural curriculum did not provide sufficient resources and teachers to carry out their own policy statements i.e., to cater for the linguistic needs of all pupils from ethnic minority groups (L.E.A.s B, D, F, G and H). The portrayals of the ten Local Education Authorities indicated that this situation of insufficient provision for home language teaching was prevalent in all those L.E.A.s which represented the different regions of the country.

Some of the L.E.A.s had carried out language surveys to establish the size of population speaking languages other than or in addition to English whereas others seemed to have overlooked the educational needs of linguistic minorities in their areas. Similarly most of the Local Education Authorities had not kept any record of the teachers from linguistic minority groups who were able to teach ethnic minority community languages.

Where the L.E.A.s had made some provision for teaching ethnic minority mother-tongues, they did not seem to have any system for selecting pupils for mother-tongue teaching. One would have thought that some formal criteria for such selection were essential, given the demand being in excess of that which could be met by the very limited resources available. There were inconsistencies in the position of schools as regards selection; Local Education Authorities had no specific criteria for the inclusion of schools or colleges in mother-tongue/community language teaching programmes. The decision on such a crucial educational issue was left to the discretion and initiative of individual schools rather than being influenced by the overall linguistic needs of all minority group pupils in the Authorities' schools.

It was quite clear from the L.E.A.s portrayals that there was a shortage of appropriately qualified teachers to teach minority community languages. Consequently the level and range of mother-tongue language provision was insufficient and far from satisfactory in terms of meeting the linguistic needs of pupils of ethnic minority origins.

As the majority of the Local Education Authorities had failed to develop the mother-tongue teaching in their mainstream schools, ethnic minority groups had organised voluntary language schools to maintain their community languages. Voluntary languages classes took place either in the evening or at the weekends. With the exception of some Local Education Authorities (e.g., L.E.A.s B and H), formal liaison between the voluntary mother-tongue schools and the L.E.A.s seemed to be very little or of no consequence. Some Local Authorities offered financial and free accommodation to voluntary language classes and the others showed no interest at all in this development (e.g., L.E.A.s C and K). The Local Authority H's initiatives in appointing a co-ordinator for voluntary language schools, substantial cash grants and in-service training for voluntary language school teachers were imaginative and commendable.

So far as the supply and initial teachers' training for community languages were concerned, no L.E.A. has shown any real imagination and fore-thought as to the future development for this aspect of the school curriculum. Arrangements for in-service training for the servicing community language teachers and mainstream teachers were rather piecemeal in all regions of the United Kingdom.

When explored about the long-term planning and co-ordination of mother-tongue teaching and bi-lingual education development programmes, 70 per cent of the L.E.A.s in the research sample had no special strategy for multi-lingual initiatives and no extra budgetary allocation to cope with the financial implications of such educational enterprise.

Whatever the level of provision for ethnic minority community language teaching under the different circumstances among the Local Education Authorities, the important aspect of 'evaluation' seemed to have been ignored by nearly all the L.E.A.s. Public examinations were the only means of evaluating the pupils' success in community languages and these were limited to G.C.E. 'O' and 'A' level courses. The L.E.A.s had failed to devise their own methods of assessment in order to record pupils progress in mother-tongue learning.

The main problems encountered by the L.E.A.s in operating mother-tongue teaching policies are summarised below:

(i)   The apparent racism of the British society as a whole was the biggest hurdle in the advancement of pluralistic developments in the field of education (as admitted by the L.E.A.s A, H and K).

(ii)   The unavailability of suitably qualified and trained teachers for community languages was another obstacle put forward by the L.E.A.s for multi-lingual development in schools.

(iii)   Time-tabling on the basis of peripatetic teaching of community languages was considered as a main difficulty in the schools.

(iv)   Some L.E.A.s stated as their main difficulty convincing the politicians of the necessity for such development in education.

(v)   Indifference on the part of general public and some ethnic minority parents was another problem in making the required progress towards minority community language teaching in mainstream schools.

Asked about the future of mother-tongue teaching and bi-lingual education, the L.E.A. 'representatives' and teachers' responses were rather mixed. Some of them were very optimistic seeing such a development as an asset and an enrichment to the linguistic and cultural fabric of British society while others saw it as a transitional phase of the 'melting pot' situation in a wider context of assimilation.

Chapter 7

Educational Implications and Recommendations

It was apparent from the L.E.A. case studies that the practice of inter-cultural education in general and mother-tongue/community language teaching in particular was extremely diversified from one L.E.A. to the other i.e., in terms of content, quantity, quality and methods. The written documents presented by the Local Education Authorities and the subsequent interviews with the representatives of the L.E.A.s showed that no proper thought had been given with regard to the need for and the provision of minority community language teaching in the mainstream schools. Either the L.E.A.s had ignored their obligations with regard to the E.E.C. Directive (77/486) for the education of children of migrant/immigrant workers, or they had tried to play them down by offering lip service to the issues of languages of linguistic minority groups in their areas.

It seemed that there was a lack of comprehensive planning and resource provision with regard to the development of this aspect of mainstream curriculum. Although the L.E.A.s could seek to claim 75 per cent of the total expenditure for such educational developments from the Home Office under Section 11 of the 1966 Local Government Act, it seemed that they were not forthcoming even when they would only have to meet 25 per cent of the costs of such language teaching programmes.

There was enough evidence to suggest that there was some element of 'passing the buck' on the part of central government and the Local Education Authorities. It appeared that central government suggested that it was the responsibility of the L.E.A.s to develop the provision of ethnic minority language teaching within mainstream education. The L.E.A.s felt frustrated by the lack of financial resources and other guidance from the Department of Education and Science and blamed the central government for not granting additional funds to develop mother-tongue/community language teaching initiatives within the mainstream curriculum (L.E.A.s C, E, F, G and K).

The L.E.A.s' case study portrayals showed that wherever the provision of ethnic minority mother-tongue and community language teaching had taken place, it was far from adequate and satisfactory in scale and scope to meet the special language needs of all pupils from linguistic minority groups. It also seemed, with the exception of a few isolated cases, that the teaching of minority languages was confined to pupils of ethnic minority origin instead of making it available to all pupils in schools i.e., to give these languages some acceptable status and prestige by making them an integral part of the curriculum.

A vital educational implication of this research exercise relates to the training and supply of teachers for ethnic minority languages. The interviews with the L.E.A.s' representatives revealed that there was an acute shortage of suitably qualified teachers for the development of ethnic minority language teaching programmes in the mainstream schools. Some Local Education Authorities had to employ untrained instructors and the others had to recruit teachers with unqualified status i.e., their qualifications were not recognised by the D.E.S. (for example, L.E.A. H). At the same time some Local Authorities had teachers from linguistic minority groups whose services might have been utilised to develop this aspect of the cirriculum but the L.E.A.s had not shown the will or the imagination to tap this resource (e.g., L.E.A.s B and K).

The unavailability of up-to-date and suitably developed teaching resources posed another difficulty for teachers seeking to make desirable progress in the teaching/learning process of minority community languages. The books and other teaching resources had largely to be imported from the countries of origin of these languages. Teaching materials published abroad failed to reflect the British way of life and other immediate environmental aspects i.e., fauna and flora of Britain. The literary contents of the imported publications were divorced from the everyday life of the pupils born and/or brought up in this country.

The various interviews with the local authorities representatives and teachers showed that racism of the British Society, as a whole, was one of the biggest obstacles in the advancement of multi-ethnic, multi-lingual aspects within the mainstream education (L.E.A.s A, B, H and K).

The task of establishing an order of priorities among recommendations arising from any research study can be an almost impossible task. This is no less true in the case of this study and no such ordering has been attempted. Recommendations ought to be viable and valid in terms of their potential for execution and implementation. The author has endeavoured, in what follows, to put forward what he considers to be the most important and practical recommendations arising from the study:

(a) The E.E.C. Directive, the Department of Education and Science and the L.E.A.s:

(i)   The D.E.S. should issue guidelines for action with regard to the

European Economic Community Council Directive (77/486) on the teaching of mother-tongue/minority community languages i.e., for both language maintenance and active bilingualism purposes. It should invite the Local Education Authorities to participate in multi-lingual projects and relevant programmes which can be evaluated and monitored. Central government should also provide additional financial resources including Urban Aid, E.E.C. Social Fund, Inner Area Programmes, Manpower Services Commission language projects and Section 11 funding. Information on other resources available from central funds and other sources for mother-tongue support should be regularly up-dated and brought to the attention of the local authorities and ethnic minority community organisations. The Swann Committee (H.M.S.O., 1985) also emphasised the need for increased financial support for the education of minorities by saying: "...We would urge the government to demonstrate its commitment to the development of 'Education for All' by ensuring that the additional resources are made available". It should be mentioned here that the Swann Committee recommends that mother-tongue maintenance, at initial stages, should be left to the community with support from Local Education Authorities and in liaison with mainstream schools. It goes on to say, "We are however wholeheartedly in favour of the teaching of ethnic minority community languages within the languages curriculum of maintained secondary schools, open to all pupils whether ethnic minority or ethnic majority". The critics of the Swann Report reject this recommedation as it fails to take into account the logical progression of mother-tongue/community language learning and its development within the mainstream provision, i.e., both at primary and secondary stages.

(ii)   The Department of Education and Science should provide guidance to the L.E.A.s on the form in which and the method by which statistics could be collected which would provide data on the numbers and distribution of pupils from ethnic minority groups and their linguistic and educational needs i.e., by means of a survey of language diversity among both pupils and teachers for the development of minority community language teaching. The Local Education Authorities ought to have more comprehensive and long-term planning and co-ordination for supporting mother-tongues of most of the pupils than the present situation in which there is inadequate and discretionary provision for minority languages teaching programmes.

(b) Supply of teachers and In-service Training:
(i)   The initial training for the supply of minority community language teachers and the in-service training for the existing mother-tongue teachers are other important aspects which cannot be overlooked or

ignored. The range of ethnic minority languages is not inconsiderable and it will require a concerted action by the D.E.S., Local Education Authorities, teachers' training institutions, examining bodies and ethnic minority community groups, if any systematic progress is to be made in this direction. Craft and Atkins (1983) in their report 'Training Teachers of Ethnic Minority Community Languages' submitted for consideration by the Swann Committee recommended that, "The D.E.S. should call into being a small national working party to develop a co-ordinated policy in this field". They also recommended that provision in ethnic minority community languages should be offered some protection in the National Advisory Body review of higher education in the public sector. The same should, now, apply to the National Curriculum, under the 1988 Education Act.

(ii)   Another issue is that of teachers who have obtained their training and community language qualifications abroad but whose qualifications are not recognised in Britain. There is a need for appropriate intensive training courses for such teachers leading to recognition of qualified status by the D.E.S. In the long term it will be necessary to offer initial training through B.Ed. and P.G.C.E. courses in the languages of minority communities in Britain. There ought to be a community languages option component in B.Ed. courses not necessarily as a major subject whereby teachers could be turned out with qualifications to teach say Social Sciences as their major subject but one of the community languages as their subsidiary teaching subject.

(iii)   The Department of Education and Science in liaison with polytechnics and universities should explore the possibilities of collaborative work with campus language departments for minority community language teachers' training courses. Consideration should also be given to the provsion of complementary options for those students wishing to develop specialist skills in ethnic minority community languages.

(iv)   If teacher education is to take a fuller account of the needs of schools in a plural society, it will require a more systematic programme for training the teacher trainers than such that exists at present. Her Majesty's Inspectorate, L.E.A. advisers/inspectors, lecturers and teachers might all benefit from a fuller examination of the relative perspectives, concepts and curriculum initiatives now being developed in a number of local education authorities. This should include those relating to linguistic diversity. It is therefore recommended that H.M.I.s, L.E.A. advisers/inspectors and initial training institutions knowledgeable in this field with the support of the Centre for Information on Language Teaching and Research

(C.I.L.T.), the National Council for Mother Tongue Teaching (N.C.M.T.T.), the School Curriculum Development Committee (S.C.D.C.), the language associations and other relevant bodies consider the urgent need for the provision of appropriate short courses, conferences and seminars for teacher trainers and practising teachers.

(c) Teaching Resources:

(i)   The lack of resources for developing suitable teaching materials has already been mentioned as a major difficulty. The minority community language teachers face the realities of teaching in very difficult circumstances with inadequate resources. The majority of the imported texts published abroad are inappropriate and unsuitable in a British setting. Teachers of modern languages have in recent years had to develop new approaches with their classes of very mixed ability and motivation; their experience of this and their development and wide use of audio-visual materials, language laboratories and television and radio materials can be very valuable resources for teachers of ethnic minority languages. Production of books and other teaching materials suitable to the age and ability of pupils should be one of the priorities in this context.

(ii)   Access to typewriters in community languages, relevant word processing facilities and the trained typists to use them are also vital to develop up-to-date teaching resources in minority community languages. For instance, the L.E.A. H's initiative of the Harafgraphy Project with the assistance of Central Government, i.e., the development of 'word processing' facilities for Asian languages, is worth considering by all local authorities and institutions.

(d) Public Examinations:

(i)   As part of the evaluation process examination is an important aspect in the assessment of progress in any teaching/learning programme. Although entry to public examinations may not be appropriate to all pupils learning ethnic minority languages, these are desirable to encourage them to develop some skills in community languages. Examinations are nevertheless important in terms of the status that the subjects need to obtain in secondary and tertiary education, and in the development and supply of the future teachers of minority languages.

(ii)   There is also a need to develop graded objective tests in minority languages such as used in modern languages. These locally devised tests can be used for real applications of community languages either for the less able ethnic minority group pupils and/or for majority group pupils encountering ethnic minority languages on language awareness courses.

(iii) Which languages are to be examined has a major impact on the curriculum development of all schools in a multi-lingual society. A relatively short-term aim should be that a large number of minority languages are provided by most of the examination boards at 16 plus (G.C.S.E.) and advanced ('A') levels. Cost factors can be a problem for such an ideal development. It can be solved by a practice of 'loan' papers whereby a particular examination board agrees to provide an examination in a 'minority' language which it will 'loan' to other examination boards in return for their contribution in another area of the minority languages pool.

(iv)   Examination syllabuses that do exist in ethnic minority languages tend to be old-fashioned and out-dated compared to the more modern approaches now developed in the major modern languages such as French, German, Spanish and Italian. More emphasis should be placed on demonstrating practical life-oriented skills in these languages.

(v)   Ethnic minority languages should also be introduced as examination subjects in further and higher education. The Council for National Academic Awards (C.N.A.A.), the Business and Technicians' Education Council (B.&T.E.C.), the Royal Society of Arts (R.S.A.), the School Curriculum Development Committee (S.C.D.C.), and other validating bodies should recognise the importance of minority community languages when developing examination subjects and syllabuses.

(e) Miscellaneous:

(i)   There is a need for extensive in-service training for all teachers in language awareness i.e., to understand the linguistic diversity of contemporary multi-lingual British society.

(ii)   The language of the home and the local communities whether these are English dialects, West Indian Creole or of non-English origins must be recognised as having their own validity.

(iii)   Consideration should be given to the vocational aspects of minority languages both in training and work situations, in education and, in commerce and industry so as to accelerate the learning of new skills.

(iv)   The teaching of minority community languages should be made available to all children and adults who would like to learn these languages and not by virtue of their ethnic backgrounds only. In this sense they are not foreign languages but the languages of various communities in the United Kingdom.

Suggestions for Further Research:

Research is an essential part of Education in most of the British universities, polytechnics and colleges of higher education, but its scope and development seems to have been curtailed or at least temporarily limited because of the effect of the recent public expenditure cuts at all levels. In spite of all such limitations the on-going research in education affects directly or indirectly various aspects of the school curriculum. It should be stressed that research in mother-tongues of linguistic minorities and bi-lingual education is still in its infancy in Britain. This field of educational research certainly requires more encouragement and resources at different levels in order to influence the development of minority languages provision to meet the special linguistic and educational needs of ethnic minority groups in particular and of the mainstream population in general. The following areas, perhaps, ought to be given priority for further research in this context:

(i)   Initial training for the supply of teachers for ethnic minority languages in order to cater for the teaching needs at different stages of the curriculum including the re-training of teachers who have obtained their language and teaching qualifications abroad.

(ii)   In-service training for teachers already engaged in the teaching of minority languages in the public and voluntary sectors and also for mainstream teachers to support community languages and bi-lingualism.

(iii) Review of existing teaching resources i.e., books, publications and other teaching aids for classroom use and further development of suitable and up-to-date teaching materials in minority languages.

(iv)   More research intiatives into different aspects of bi-lingual education in the light of developments that have taken place in North America, Europe and Australia.

(v)   Further longitudinal research to study the progress of the development and implementation of mother-tongue/community language teaching and of related educational policies at local and national levels.

Appendices

1. Questionnaire: Interview Schedule for the Local Education Authorities

2. Questionnaire: Interview Schedule for Schools and Teachers

Appendix 1

Questionnaire: **Interview Schedule for the Local Education Authorities.**
Ref: Mother-tongue/Community Language and Bilingual Education

1. Name of the interviewee:
2. The Position of responsibility within the LEA:
3. The type of LEA County/Metropolitan District/Regional
4. Total number of school-age children (including sixth formers);
5. Number of children from ethnic minority groups: i.e., of:
    (a) European origin:
    (b) Caribbean origin:
    (c) South Asian Origin from:
        (i) India: (ii) Pakistan
        (iii) Bangladesh
    (d) African origin:
    (e) Far-East origin:
        (i) Chinese   (ii) Vietnamese
    (f) Others:
6. Total number of students in Further and Higher Education colleges/Institutions:
7. Number of students from ethnic minority groups:
    (a) European origin:
    (b) Caribbean origin:
    (c) South Asian origin from:
        (i) India   (ii) Pakistan
        (iii) Bangladesh
    (d) African origin:
    (e) Far East origin:
        (i) Chinese   (ii) Vietnamese
    (f) Others:
8. Languages used in teaching i.e., as a medium of instruction:
9. Home/Community Languages of Students. Please name these to the best of your knowledge:
10. Has the LEA any official policy for teaching mother-tongue/home languages or community languages?: Yes   No
11. Information about such policy:
    (a) Official documents/papers: (b) Personal notes:
12. Languages used for mother-tongue teaching:
13. Number of pupils learning each language at different stages:
    Name of Language/Nursery/Primary/Secondary/Higher Education
14. Number of teachers from ethnic minority groups:
15. What are the criteria for selecting these languages for curricular teaching?:

16. For how many years has the programme presently described been operating?
Is it experimental?   or operational regularly?

17. How many learners are involved in different languages? Please give details:

18. Are the indigenous pupils involved to learn ethnic minority languages? If yes, please give details:

19. How many teachers are involved to teach these languages?

20. Have the teachers qualified status? All/Partly/None

21. Are there some special provisions for teachers' training for this programme? If yes, give details:

22. Are there teachers for special languages?
Please give details:

23. Do you select pupils for this programme?

24. What are the criteria to select them?

25. How many schools and colleges are included in mother-tongue teaching respectively?

26. What are the criteria for including schools and colleges in this programme?

27. Are there supplementary schools run by minority voluntary organisations for mother-tongue teaching within the jurisdiction of the LEA?

28. How many of such schools are operating and for which languages?

29.   Is there any liaison between the LEA and the voluntary language schools?

30. Does the LEA give any assistance to these voluntary supplementary schools?
Finance/Staff Remuneration/Accommodation/Resources and materials
Any other

31. Are there provisions for adults to learn ethnic minority languages?
(a) for adults from ethnic minority groups
(b) for adults from indigenous population

32. Is there any in-service programme for teachers to learn these languages? Give details.

33. What are the provisions for the supply of teachers to teach these languages?
(a) Cooperation from the local ethnic communities for the supply of teachers.
(b) Efforts by the local colleges to train teachers for teaching these languages (e.g.; Bridge-over courses for suitable candidates from minority groups):

34. Planning and coordination:
(a) What are the explicit goals for this programme?
(b) Strategies for implementation of bilingual education/mother-tongue teaching policies?
(c) Coordination of resources (Teachers and other materials)?
(d) Funding provisions for these policies?
(e) Evaluation of the whole programme at the LEA level? e.g., Reports and Feed-back system.

35. Do the learners take public examinations in these languages?
(a) What proportion?
(b) At what level? CSE/GCE 'O' level/16+/GCSE 'A' level

36. Any other method applied by the LEA to assess the progress in these languages: If yes, please specify:

37. What are the main problems you have encountered in operating these policies? Please feel free to comment.

38. What are the responses/reactions of the teaching profession as a whole to these policies?
head teachers/Principals:
Heads of Department:
Teachers/Lecturers:

39. What are the reactions/responses of the professional bodies of teachers/lecturers at local level?

Comments on the attitudes, responses and reactions to this programme from:
(a) Governing bodies of the schools/colleges concerned:
(b) General Public:
(c) Parents of the indigenous pupils:
(d) Parents of ethnic minority pupils:
(e) Media coverage:

40. How do you foresee the mother-tongue teaching/bilingual education for future development in the whole curriculum and the education system?

41. Other comments:

Appendix 2

Questionnaire: **Interview Schedule for Schools and Teachers.**
Ref: Mother-tongue/Community Language Teaching and Bilingual Education.

1. Name of School/College: (b) Type of School/Group etc:
2. Name of interviewee:
3. The Position of responsibility within the school/college:
4. Total number of pupils (including sixth formers):
5. Number of children from minority groups: i.e., of:
   (a) European origin:
   (b) Caribbean origin:
   (c) South Asian origin:
       (i)   India: (ii) Pakistan
       (iii) Bangladesh
   (d) African origin:
   (e) Far-East origin:
       (i) Chinese   (ii) Vietnamese
   (f) Others:
6. Language(s) used for teaching, i.e., as medium of instruction:
7. Home/community languages of pupils. Please name these to the best of your knowledge:
8. Has the school/college any policy for teaching mother-tongue/community languages?
   Yes   No
9. Is this policy an independent one or in line with the LEA guide-lines?
10. Information about such policy:
    (a) Documents/papers   (b) Personal notes
11. Languages used for mother-tongue teaching: Please give details:
12. Number of pupils learning each language:
    Name of language   Number of pupils.
13. Number of teachers from ethnic minority groups:
14. What are the criteria for selecting these home/community languages for teaching?
15. For how many years has the programme presently described been operating?
    Is it experimental?   or operational regularly?
16. Number of months for instruction per year, i.e., Full-year/Part-year
17. How long are these languages taught, i.e., duration of teaching per week?
18. How many learners are involved in different languages?
19. Are the indigenous pupils involved to learn ethnic minority languages: If yes, please give details:
20. How many teachers are involved to teach these languages?
21. Have the teachers qualified status? All/Some/None
22. Are there special teachers for all languages? Please give details:
23. Do you select pupils for this programme?
24. What are the criteria of this selection?
25. Approximately what proportion of learners
    (a) understand their mother-tongue?
    (b) do not understand their mother-tongue?
26. Are there supplementary schools run by voluntary organisations for mother-tongue teaching in the neighbourhood of the school/college?
27. How many such schools are operating and for what languages?
28. Is there any liaison between the school/college and the voluntary language schools?
29. Does the school/college organise classes for adults to learn ethnic minority languages?
    (a) For adults from ethnic minority groups
    (b) For adults from the indigenous population

30. Has school/college any school-based programme for teachers to learn these languages? Give details:

31. The detail of cooperation from the local ethnic minority communities for this programme:

32. Planning and coordination:
    (a) What are the explicit goals for this programme?
    (b) Coordination of resources used? (Teachers and teaching materials)
    (c) Evaluation of the whole programme at school/college level?
        e.g., Reports and Feed-back.

33. Do the learners take public examinations in these languages?
    (a) What proportion?   (b) At what level?
    CSE/GCE 'O' Level/16+/GCSE 'A' Level

34. Any other method applied by the school/college to assess the progress in these languages? If yes, please specify:

35. Outside the class, how often do pupils use their mother-tongues to communicate?
    Never/Seldom/Sometimes/Often/Always

36. What are the main problems you have come across in operating this programme?
    Please feel free to comment.

37. What are the responses/reactions of the teachers as a whole to this programme?

38. Comments on the attitudes, responses and reactions to this policy from:
    (a) Head-teacher/Principal:
    (b) Governing body of the school/college:
    (c) Parents of the indigenous pupils:
    (d) Parents of the ethnic minority pupils:
    (e) Local media:

39. How do you fore-see the mother-tongue teaching/bilingual education for future development within the school curriculum and in the education system as a whole?

Bibliography

Adelman, C., Jenkins, D. and Kemmis, S. (1977).	'Rethinking Case Study: Notes for Second Cambridge Conference', Cambridge Journal of Education, Volume 6, pp. 139-150
Alladina, S. (1979).	The Relationship Between the Degree of Bilingualism Among Gujrati/English School Children and their Academic Performance. Unpublished Thesis, Department of Applied Linguistics: University of London.
Alladina, S. (1982).	'Multiculturalism and Multi-lingualism in Britain', Letras Soltas: Department of Linguistics, Universidade Nova de Lisboa.
Alladina, S. (1982).	'Languages in Britain: Perceptions and Policies'. London: National Convention of Black Teachers.
Allport, G.W. (1942).	The Use of Personal Documents in Psychological Science. New York: Social Sciences Research Council.
Anderson, E. (1969).	'The Social Factors have been Ignored' Harvard Education Review, 39, pp. 581-585.
Ashworth, B. (1983).	Careers Education: Some Dimensions and Perspective. Unpublished M.Phil Thesis: University of Bradford.
Ashworth, M. (1975).	Immigrant Children and Canadian Schools. Toronto: McClelland and Stewart.
Baetens Beardsmore, H. (1977).	'Anomie in Bicultural Education' in de Grove and Rossel, E. (Eds.), pp. 9-23.
Baetens Beardsmore, H. (1979).	'The Recogniton and Tolerance Level of Bilingual Speech', Working Papers on Bilingualism (Toronto), 19, pp. 115-128.
Bagley, C. (1975).	'On the Intellectual Equality of Races' in Verma, G.K. and Bagley, C. (Eds.). Race and Education Across Culture. London: Heineman.
Bagley, C. and Verma, G.K. (Eds.) (1982).	Self Concept, Achievement and Multi-Cultural Education. London: The Macmillan Press Limited.
Balkan, L. (1970).	Les effets du bilinguisme francias-anglais sur le aptitudes intessectuelles. Bruxelles: AIMAV.
Banton, M. (1954).	The Coloured Quarter. London: Jonathan Cape.
Banton M. (1970).	'The Concept of Racism' In Zubaida, S. (Ed.) Race and Racialism. London: Tavistock Publications.
Banton, M. (1977).	The Idea of Race. London: Tavistock Publications.
Barnes, J.B. (1960).	Education Research for Classroom Teachers. New York: G.P. Putnam's Sons.
Barzun, J. and Graff, H.F. (1970).	Modern Researcher. New York: Harcourt Brace.
Ben-Zeev, S. (1972).	The Influence of Bilingualism on Cognitive Development and Cognitive Strategy. Unpublished Doctoral Dissertation: University of Chigago.
Bernstein, B. (1961).	'Social Structure, Language and Learning', Educational Research, Volume 3, pp 163-197
Best, J.W. (1970).	Research in Education. Englewood Cliffs, New Jersey: Prentice Hall. Second Edition.
Bhatia, T.K. (1982).	'English and the Vernaculars of India: Contact and Change, Applied Linguistics, Oxford, Vol 3, No. 3, pp. 235-245.

Bidewell, S. (1976).   Red, White and Black. London: Gordon Cremonesi Ltd.

Bloom, B.S. (1966).   'Twenty-five years of Educational Research', American Education Research Journal, No. 3, pp. 212.

Bloomfield, L. (1933).   Language. New York: Holt, Rinehart and Winston.

Bohannan, P. (1966).   Social Anthropology. New York: Holt, Rinehart and Winston.

Boyle, E. (1965).   Ministry of Education Circular No. 7. London: D.E.S.

Broadbent, J. et al. (1983).   Community Language at 16+. York: Longman for Schools Council.

Brockway, F. and Pannel, N. (1965).   Immigration: What is the Answer? Two Opposing Views. London: Routledge and Kegan Paul.

Brown, D.M. (1979).   Mother-Tongue to English: The Young Child in the Multi-cultural School. London: Cambridge University Press.

Brown, J. (1970).   The Unmelting Pot: An English Town and its Immigrants. London: Macmillan.

Bruck, M. et al. (1977).   'Cognitive Consequences of Bilingual Schooling: The St. Lambert Project', Linguistics, The Hague, 187, pp. 13-35.

Bruck, M., Jakimik H. and Tucker, G.R. (1980).   Are French programmes suitable for the Working Class Children? In Engel, W. (Ed.) Prospects in Child Language. Amsterdam: Royal Vangorcum.

Bullock, A. (1975).   A Language for Life: The National Committee of Inquiry Report. London: H.M.S.O.

Burnaby, B. (1976).   Language in Native Education. In Swain, M. (Ed.) Bilingualism in Canadian Education: Issues and Research. Yearbook for the Study of Education, Volume 3, Edmonton, Alberta: Western Industrial Research Centre.

Butcher, H.J. (1966).   Sampling in Educational Research. Manchester: Manchester University Press.

Campbell-Platt, K. and Nicholas, S. (1978).   Linguistic Minorities in Britain. London: Runnymede Trust

Caradog-Jones, D. (1946).   Economic Status of Coloured Families at the Port of Liverpool. Liverpool: Liverpool University Press.

Carlyle, M. (1980).   Speech at the European Economic Community Colloquium on the Bedford Pilot Project on Mother-Tongue Teaching. 24th March, 1980.

Chapman, L. (1980).   'An Experiment into Mother-Tongue Teaching', Trends in Education. London: Department of Education and Science.

Charbonneau-Dagenais, A. (1979).   'An Attempt to Define Bilingualism', Bulletin of the C.A.A.L., Vol. 1, No. 1, pp. 31-38.

Chipman, L. (1980).   'The Menace of Multi-Culturalism', Quadrant, Vol. 24, No. 10, pp. 3-6.

Coard, B. (1971).   How the West Indian Child is made Educationally Subnormal in the British School System. London: New Beacon Books.

Cohen, A.D. and Swain M. (1976).   'Bilingual Education: The Immersion Model in the North American Context', T.E.S.O.L. Quarterly, 10, pp. 45-53.

Cohen, L. and Manion, L. (1980).   Research Methods in Education. London: Croom Helm.

Collins, S. (1957)   Coloured Minorities in Britain. London: Lutterworth Press.

Commission for Racial Equality (1981).   Mother-Tongue Teaching: Conference Report. 9-11 September. C.R.E./Bradford College: Bradford.

Commission for Racial Equality (1981).	National Survey of Local Education Authorities on Mother Tongue Teaching. London: C.R.E.
Commission for Racial Equality (1981).	Summary of the Main Issue of Regional Consultation with Voluntary Classes on Mother Tongue Teaching in U.K. London: C.R.E.
Commission for Racial Equality (1982).	Ethnic Minority Community Language: A Statement. London: C.R.E.
Commonwealth Immigrants Advisory Council (1964).	Second Report on Immigration from the Commonwealth Countries. Cmnd. Paper 2266 London: H.M.S.O.
Conservative Party (1983).	Annual Conservative Party Conference. Motion by Harvey Proctor for curbing immigration and compulsory repatriation.
Corey, S.M. (1953).	Action Research to Improve School Practices, New York: Bureau of Publications, Teachers' College, Columbia University.
Craft, M. and Atkins, M. (1983).	Training Teachers of Ethnic Minority Community Languages. Nottingham: University of Nottingham.
Cronbach, L.J. (1961).	Essentials of Psychological Testing. New York: Harper & Row.
Cronbach, L.J. (1962).	Educational Psychology. Second Edition, New York: Harcourt Brass.
Cronbach, L.J. (1966).	'The Role of University in Improving Education', Phi Delta Kappan, 47.
Cronbach, L.J. and Suppes, P. (1969).	Research for Tomorrow's Schools: Disciplines Inquiry for Education. New York: Macmillan.
Cummins, J. and Gulstan, M. (1973).	'Some Effects of Bilingualism on Cognitive Functioning'. In Carey, S. (Ed.) Bilingualism, Biculturalism and Education. Proceedings from the Conference at College Universitaire. Saint Jean: The University of Alberta.
Cummins, J. (1976).	The Influence of Bilingualism on Cognitive Growth. Educational Research Centre, St Patrick's College, Dublin.
Cummins, J. (1977a).	'Cognitive Factors with the Attainment of Intermediate Levels of Bilingual Skills', Modern Languages Journal (St. Louis), 61, No. 1,2, pp. 3-12.
Cummins, J. (1977b).	'Immersion Education in Ireland: a Critical Review of Macnamara's Findings', Working Papers on Bilingualism, 13, pp. 121-127.
Cummins, J. (1978a).	'The Cognitive Development of Children in Immersion Programmes', The Canadian Modern Languages Review (Toronto), 34, 5, pp. 854-883.
Cummins, J. (1978b).	'Immersion Programme: The Irish Experience', International Review of Education, The Hague, 24, 3, pp. 273-283.
Cummins, J. (1978c).	'Educational Implications of Mother-tongue Maintenance in Minority Language Groups', The Canadian Modern Languages Review, 34, pp. 395-416.
Cummins, J. (1978d).	'Bilingualism and the Development of Metalinguistic Awareness', Journal of Cross-Cultural Psychology, 9, pp. 131-149.
Cummins, J. (1980).	'Linguistic Interdependence and the Educational Development of Bilingual Children', Review of Educational Research.
Cummins, J. and Swain, M. (1983).	''Analysis by Rhetoric: Reading the text on the reader's own projections. A reply to Edel Sky et al', Applied Linguistics, Oxford, Vol. 4, No. 1, pp. 23-24.

Cunningham, W. (1969). Alien Immigrants to England. London, 1897. Reprinted (1969), London: Cass.

Daniel, W.W. (1968). Racial Discrimination in England. London: Penguin Books.

Darcy, N.T. (1953). 'A Review of the Literature on the Effect of Bilingualism upon the Measurement of Intelligence', Journal of Genetic Psychology, 82, pp. 21-57.

Davis, D. (1977). 'Everybody's Languages', The Times Educational Supplement, 18th November, 1977.

De Houwer, A. (1982). 'Second Language Acquisition: A Survey of the Recent Literture', I.T.L. (Louvain), 55.

Dennis, W. (1941). 'Infant Development under Conditions of Restricted Practice and of Minimum Social Stimulation', Genetic Psychology Monographs, 23, pp. 143-189.

Department of Education and Science (1977). Education in Schools: A Consultative Document. London: H.M.S.O.

Department of Education and Science (1980). An Opening Speech by the Secretary of State at the Bedford E.E.C. Project Colloquium. 24th March, 1980.

Department of Education and Science (1980). Matters for Discussion 11: A view of the Curriculum. London: H.M.S.O.

Department of Education and Science (1981). Curriculum Advice: The School Curriculum London: H.M.S.O.

Department of Education and Science (1981). Circular 5/81: Directive of the Council of E.E.C. on the Education of Children of Migrant Workers. London: D.E.S.

Department of Education and Science (1984). A Statement made by the Secretary of State (Keith Joseph) for the Introduction of New 16+ (G.C.S.E.) Examination from 1988.

Department of the Environment (1971). 'Social and Economic Deprivation' as mentioned in 'Race and School' in Five Views of Multi-racial Britain. London: C.R.E., 1978.

Dewey, J. (1933) How We Think. Boston: Raytheon Education Company.

Dipietro, R.J. (1980). 'Filling the Elementary Curriculum with Language: What are the Effects?' Foreign Language Annals, New York, Vol. 13, No. 2, pp. 115-123.

Douglas, J.W.B. (1967). The Home and the School: A Study of Ability and Attainment in the Primary Schools. England: Panther Books Limited.

Douglas, J.W.B. (1968). All Our Future. London: Peter Davies.

Doyle, A. (1977). 'Some Issues in the Assessment of Linguistic Consequences of Early Bilingualism', Working Papers on Bilingualism (Toronto), 14, pp. 21-28.

Drake, G. (1979). 'Ethnicity, Values and Language Policy in the United States', In Giles, H. and Saint-Jacques, B. (Eds.) Language and Ethnic Relations. Oxford: Pergamon Press.

Dube, N.C. and Herbert, G. (1975). St John Valley Bilingual Education Project: Five-Year Evaluation Report 1970-75. Prepared for U.S. Department of Health Education and Welfare.

Edwards, J. (1977). 'Ethnic Identity and Bilingual Education', In Giles, H (Ed.) Language Ethnicity and Intergroup Relations. New York: Academic Press.

Edwards, J. (1979). Language and Disadvantage. London: Edward Arnold.

Edwards, J. (1980). 'Bilingual Education: Facts and Values' Canadian Modern Languages Review (in press).

Edwards, J. (1980).   'Critics and Criticisms of Bilingual Education', Modern Languages Journal (in press).

Γ wards, V. (1979).   The West Indian Language Issues in Schools. London: Routledge and Kegan Paul.

Eggleston, J. (1979).   'The Characteristics of Educational Research: mapping the domain', British Educational Research Journal, Volume 5, No. 1, pp. 1-12.

Eggleston, J., Dunn D. and Purewal, A. (1981).   In-service Teacher Education in Multi-Culural Society. D.E.S. Research Project: University of Keele.

Eggleston, J. (Ed.) (1983).   Work Experience in Secondary Schools. London: Routledge and Kegan Paul.

Elizabeth II (1983) & (1987).   Her Majesty Queen Elizabeth II's Christmas Broadcast Messages to the British Commonwealth of Nations.

Encyclopaedia of the Social Sciences (1934).   Ref. Volume 13, New York: Macmillan.

Ervin-Tripp, S. (1964).   "An Analysis of the Interaction of Language, topic and listener", American Anthropologist, 66, pp. 86-102.

European Economic Community (Ref. NOC 38/2IV) (1976).   Resolution on Education of Migrant Workers and Their Families. Brussels: The Council for the E.E.C.

European Economic Community (1977).   Education of Children of Migrant Workers. Directive 77/486/EEC. Brussels: The Council for the E.E.C.

E.E.C. Bedford Project (1980).   Mother Tongue Teaching to Panjabi and Italian Children: A Pilot Project.

Evans, E. (1976).   'Bilingual Education in Wales', In Bilingualism and British Education: the Dimensions of Diversity. London: Centre for Information on Language Teaching and Research.

Eysneck, H. (1971).   Race, Intelligence and Education. London: Temple Smith.

Eysneck, H. (1973).   The Equality of Man. London: Temple Smith.

Ferguson, C.A. (1959).   'Diglossia', Word, Volume 15, pp. 325-340.

Firth, R. (1958).   Human Types. New York: Mentor.

Fishman, J.A. (1965).   'Who Speaks What Language to Whom and When?, Linguistique, Volume 2, pp. 67-88.

Fishman, J.A. (1966).   'Varieties of Ethnicity and Varieties of Language Consciousness', Monograph Series on Language and Linguistics, No. 18, Washington D.C.: Georgetown University Press.

Fishman, J.A. (1967).   'Bilingualism with and without Diglossia: diglossia with and without bilingualism', in Macnamara, J. (Ed.), 'Problems of Bilingualism', The Journal of Social Issues, Vol. 23, pp. 29-38.

Fishman, J.A. (1968).   'Sociolinguistic perspective on the study of bilingualism', Linguistics, 39, pp. 21-50.

Fishman J.A. (1972).   The Sociology of Language. Rowley, Mass: Newbury House.

Fishman, J.A. (1976).   Bilingual Education: an International Sociological Perspective. Rowley: Mass Newbury House.

Fishman, J.A., Cooper, R.L. and Rosenbaum, Y. (1977).   'English the World Over: A Factor in the Creation of Bilingualism Today', In Hornby, P.A. (Ed.), Bilingualism: Psychological, Social and Educational Implications. New York: Academic Press.

Fishman, J.A. (Ed.) (1977). Language Loyalty in the United States. The Hague: Mouton.

Fishman, J.A. (1980). 'Bilingualism and Biculturalism as Individual and Societal Phemonena', Journal of Multi-Culturalism and Multilingualism Development, Volume 1, pp. 3-15.

Flynn, J.R. (1980). Race, I.Q., and Jenson. London: Routledge and Kegan Paul.

Foot, P. (1965). Immigration and Race in British Politics. London: Penguin Books.

Freire, P. (1972). Pedagogy of the Oppressed. London: Penguin Education.

Frideres, J.S. (1974). Canada's Indians: Contemporary Conflicts. Toronto: Prentice Hall.

Gaarder, A.B. (1967a). 'Organisation of the Bilingual School', Journal of Social Issues, 23, pp. 110-120.

Gaarder, A.B. (1967b). Bilingualism and Education: Report of the Special Sub-Committee on Bilingual Education of the Committee on Labour and Public Welfare. U.S. Senate Nineteenth Congress: Reprinted in B. Spolsky (Ed.) (1972), pp. 83-93.

Garner, M. (Ed.) (1981). Community Languages: Their Role in Education. Melbourne: River Seine Publications.

Gateskill, H. (1962). The Parliamentary Debate: The House of Commons. Hansards: H.M.S.O.

Gekoski, W.L. (1980). 'Language Acquisition Context', An Occasional Paper.

Genesee, F. (1978). 'Second Language Learning and Language Attitudes', Working Papers on Bilingualism, Toronto, 16, pp. 19-39.

Genesee, F., Tucker, G.R. and Lambert, W.E. (1978) 'An Experiment in Trilingual Education: Report 3', The Canadian Modern Languages Review, 34, pp. 621-634.

Genesee, F., Tucker, G.R. and Lambert, W.E. (1979) 'An Experiment in Trilingual Education: Report 4', Language Learning, Ann Arbor Mich., 28.2, pp. 343-365.

Getzels, J.W. and Jackson, P.W. (1962). Creativity and Intelligence. New York: Wiley.

Gleitman, M. and Gleitman, F. (1970). Phrase and Paraphrase. New York: Norton.

Gibson, M.A. (1976). 'Approaches to Multicultural Education in the United States: Some Concepts and Assumptions', Anthropology and Education, 7, pp. 7-18.

Gowin, D.B. (1972). 'Is Educational Research Distinctive?', in L.G. Thomas (Ed.) Philosophical Redirection of Educational Research. Chicago: Chicago University Press.

Guildford, J.P. (1950). 'Creativity', American Psychologist, Vol. 5, pp. 444-554.

Guildford, J.P. (1956). 'The Structure of Intellect', Phychological Bulletin, Volume 53, pp. 267-293.

Gumperz, J. (1966). Language and Social Identity. Cambridge: C.U.P.

Haley, A. (1977). Roots. London: Hutchinson. Originally published; Garden City, New York: Doubleday, 1976.

Hancock, G. (1979). 'Why is Africa Poor?' New Internationalist, 71, January Issue.

Hartmann, P. and Husband, C. (1974). Racism and the Mass Media. London: Davis Poynter.

Haugen, E. (1956).
Bilingualism in the Americas: A Bibliography and research guide. Montgomery: University of Alabama Press.

Hicks, D.W. (1981).
Minorities: A Teacher's Resource Book for the Multi-ethnic Curriculum. London: Heinemann Educational Books.

Higham, J. (1975).
Send These to Me. New York: Antheneum.

Hilgard, E.R. (1954).
'A Perspective of the Relationship Between Learning Theory and Educational Practice', In E.R. Hilgard (Ed.), Theories of Learning and Instruction. Part I of the 63rd Year-book of the National Society of the Study of Education. Chicago: University of Chicago Press.

Hodge, J.J., Struckman, D.K. and Frost, L.D. (1975).
Cultural Bases of Racism and Group Oppression. Berkley, California: Two Riders Press.

Hodges, L. (1978).
'Review of the Schools Council's Multi-racial Education Project 1973-76,' in the Times Educational Supplement, 24 February 1978.

Horace, B. and English, A.C. (1958).
A Comprehensive Dictionary of Psychological and Psycho-analytical Terms. New York: Longman, Green and Co.

Hornby, P.A. (Ed.) (1977).
Bilingualism: Psychological, Social and Educational Implications. New York: Academic Press Inc.

Houlton, D. (1983).
Priority for the Multi-lingual Classroom. A Conference on Bilingual Education. London: C.I.L.T./I.L.E.A. 17 March 1983.

House of Commons (1974).
Educational Disadvantage and the Educational Needs of Immigrants. Cmnd Paper 5720, London: H.M.S.O.

House of Commons (1974).
Select Committee on Race Relations and Immigration: Education Report No. 405. London: H.M.S.O.

House of Commons (1975).
White Paper on Racial Discrimination, Cmnd Paper 6234. London: H.M.S.O.

House of Commons (1977).
Select Committee on Race Relations and Immigration: The West Indian Community, Volume 1, Report No. 180. London: H.M.S.O.

House of Commons (1978).
Select Committee on Race Relations and Immigration: The West Indian Community, Cmnd Paper 7186 London: H.M.S.O.

House of Commons (1981).
Fifth Report of the House of Commons Home Affairs Committee. London: H.M.S.O.

Hymes, D. (1967).
'Models of the Interaction of Languages and Social Settings', In Macnamera, J. (Ed.) 'Problems of Bilingualism', The Journal of Social Issues, Vol. 23, No. 2, pp. 8-28.

Hymes, D. (1974).
Foundations in Sociolinguistics. Philadelphia: University of Pennsylvania Press.

Independent Broadcasting Authority (1984).
The Jewel in the Crown. Manchester: Granada Television Series.

Ianco-Worral, A.D. (1972)
'Bilingualism and Cognitive Development', Child Development, Volume 43, pp 1390-1400.

Jackson, J.A. (1963).
The Irish in Britain. London: Routledge and Kegan Paul.

Jahoda, M., Deutsh, M. and Cook, S. (1951).
Research Methods in Social Relation. New York: Holt, Rinehart and Winston.

Jenkins, R. (1966).
'A Speech made on 23 May 1966 to a meeting of the National Committee for Commonwealth Immigrants' quoted in Essay and Speeches by Roy Jenkins (1967) London: Collins, pp. 267.

Jenkins, R. (1969).   'A speech made to a meeting of Voluntary Liaison
                                        Committee', Quoted in Rose, E.J.B. (1969), Colour
                                        and Citizenship. London: Oxford University Press,
                                        p.25.

Jensen, A. (1973).   Educability and Group Differences. London:
                                        Methuen.

John, V.P. and Horner, V.M. (1971).   Early Childhood Bilingual Education. New York:
                                        Modern Languages Association of America.

Jones, H. (1961).   'A Speech made to Birmingham Immigrant Control
                                        Association', in Foot, P. (1965). Immigration and
                                        Race in British Politics. London: Penguin Books.

Joos, M. (1959).   'The Isolation of Styles', in Harrell, R. (Ed.) The
                                        Report of the 10th Round Table Meeting. Washington
                                        D.C.: Georgetown University Press.

Joseph, K. (1984).   The Department of Education and Science Statement:
                                        The Introduction of 16+ (G.C.S.E.) Examination
                                        from 1988.

Kagan, J. (1969).   'Inadequate Evidence and Illogical Conclusions',
                                        Harvard Education Review, 39, pp. 1-123.

Katznelson, I. (1973).   Black Man, White Cities. London: Oxford University
                                        Press for the Institute of Race Relations.

Kerlinger, F.N. (1973).   Foundation of Behavioural Research. Second Edition.
                                        New York: Holt, Rinehart and Winston.

Kerlinger, F.N. (1977).   'The Influence of Research on Education Practice',
                                        Educational Research, 6, 8, pp. 5-11.

Koler, P.A. (1963).   'Inter-lingual Word Association', Journal of Verbal
                                        Learning and Verbal Behaviour, Volume 2, pp.
                                        291-300.

Kuhn, T.S. (1970).   'The Structure of Scientific Revolutions', Second
                                        Edition — International Encyclopaedia of Unified
                                        Sciences, Enlarged, First Published in 1962, Chicago:
                                        Chicago University Press.

Labov, W. (1966).   The Social Stratification of English in New York City.
                                        Washington D.C.: Centre for Applied Linguistics.

Lado, R. (1982)   Language Teaching. New York: McGraw

Lambert, W.E., Havelka, J.   'The Influence of Language Acquisition
and Crosby, C. (1958).   Contexts on Bilingualism', Journal of Abnormal and
                                        Social Psychology, Volume 56, pp. 239-244.

Lambert, W.E., Havelka, J.   'Linguistic Manifestations of Bilingualism'
and Gardner, R.C. (1959).   Journal of Psychology, Volume 72, pp. 77-82.

Lambert, W.E. and Rawlings, C.   'Bilingual Processing of Mixed Language
(1969).   Associative Network', Journal of Verbal Learning and
                                        Verbal Behaviour, Vol. 8, pp. 604-609.

Lambert, W.E. (1969).   'Psychological Studies of the Inter-dependencies of
                                        the Bilingual's Two Languages', In Puhvel, J. (Ed.),
                                        Substance and Structure of Language. Los Angeles:
                                        University of California Press.

Lambert, W.E. (1975).   'Culture and Language as Factors in Learning and
                                        Education'. In Wolfgang, A. (Ed.), Education of
                                        Immigrant Students, Ontario Institute for Studies in
                                        Education.

Lambert, W.E. (1977).   'The Effect of Bilingualism on the Individual:
                                        Cognitive and Socio-cultural Consequences', in
                                        Hornby, P. (Ed.), Bilingualism: Psychological, Social
                                        and Educational Implications. New York: Academic
                                        Press.

Lambert, W.E. (1978).   'Cognitive and Socio-cultural Consequences of
                                       Bilingualism', Canadian Modern Languages Review
                                       (Toronto), 34, 3, pp. 537-547.

Lamey, P. (1974).   The Impact of Bilingualism upon Ethno-linguistic
                                       Identity. Paper presented at VIII World Congress of
                                       Sociology, Toronto, Canada.

Lamey, P. (1976).   'Bilingualism in Montreal: Linguistic Inference and
                                       Communicational Effectivness', Paper on Linguistics
                                       (Campaign, III). Vol. 9, 3/4, pp. 1-14.

Larrabee, H.A. (1945).   Reliable Knowlege. Boston: Houghton Muffin.

Lenneberge, E. (1967).   Biological Foundation of Language. New York:
                                       Wiley.

Leopold, W.F. (1949).   Speech Development of a Bilingual Child. Volume 3,
                                       Evanston: Northwestern University Press.

Lewis, O. (1959).   Five Families. New York: Basic Books.

Lewis, O. (1961).   The Children of Sanchez. New York: Random House.

Lewis, O. (1966).   La Vida. New York: Random House.

Lieberson, S. (1970).   Language and Ethnic Relations in Canada. New York:
                                       Wiley.

Liedka, R.S. and Nelson, L.D. (1968). 'Concept Formation and Bilingualism', Alberta
                                       Journal of Educational Research, Volume 14, pp.
                                       225-232.

Lindman, R. (1977).   'Self-ratings and linguistic proficiency in bilingual
                                       subjects', Language and Speech, Hampton Hill,
                                       Middlesex, Vol. 20, No. 4, pp. 325-332.

Linguistic Minorities Project (1983). Linguistic Minorities in Englanda; a report for the
                                       D.E.S. London: University of London Institute of
                                       Education.

Little A., (1978).   'Schools and Race', in Five Views of Multi-racial
                                       Britain. London: Commission for Racial Equality.

Little, A. and Willey R. (1 81).   Multi-ethnic Education: The Way Forward. London:
                                       The Schools Council.

Little, K.L. (1947).   Ne
                                       oesin Dritain. London: Routledge and Kegan Paul.

Lockwood, W.B. (1975).   Language of the British Isles: Past and Present.
                                       London: Deutsch.

Lynch, J. (Ed.) (1981).   Teaching in Multi-cultural School. London: Ward
                                       Lock Eucational.

Lynch, J. (1983).   The Multi-cultural Curriculum. London: Batsford
                                       Academic and Educational Ltd.

Lynd, R.S. and Lynd, H.M. (1937).   Middletown in Transition. New York: Harcourt,
                                       Brace and World Inc.

Lyons, J. (1968).   Introduction to Theoretical Linguistics. Cambridge:
                                       Cambridge University Press.

Mackay, W.F. (1962).   'The description of bilingualism', Canadian Journal of
                                       Linguistics, Volume 7, pp. 51-85.

Macnamara, J. (1966).   Bilingualism and Primary Education. Edinburgh:
                                       Edinburgh University Press.

MacNamara, J. (1967a).   'The Bilinguals' linguistic performance: a
                                       psychological overview'. In J. Macnamara (Ed.)
                                       'Problems of Bilingualism', Journal of Social Issues,
                                       23, 2, pp. 58.77.

Macnamara, J. (1967b).   'The Linguistic Independence of Bilinguals', Journal
                                       of Verbal Learning and Verbal Behaviour, New York,
                                       6,5, pp. 729-736.

Magiste, E. (1979).   'The Competing Language Systems of the
                                       Multilinguals: A Developmental Study of Decoding
                                       and Encoding Processes', Journal of Verbal Learning
                                       and Verbal Behaviour, New York, 18, 1, pp. 77-89.

Martinet, A. (1982).   'Bilingualism and Diglossia: The Need for Dynamic Approach', Linguistique, Paris, Vol. 18, No. 1, pp. 5-16.

Mason, P. (1966).   'What do we mean by integration?' Social Studies Reader: Race and Immigration, New Society, 16 June, 1966.

Megarry, J., Nisbet, S. and Hoyle, E. (Eds) (1981).   Education of Minorities: World Yearbook of Education. London: Kogan Page.

Mercer, N. and Mercer E. (1979).   'Variation in Attitudes to Mother-Tongue and Culture', Educational Studies, Volume 5, No. 2, pp. 171-177.

Merton, R.K. (1949).   'The Self-fulfilling Prophecy', In Social Theory and Social Structure. New York: Free Press.

Milner, D. (1975).   Children and Race. London: Penguin Books.

Ministry of Education (1944).   The 1944 Education Act for England and Wales. London: H.M.S.O.

Ministry of Education (1965).   Circular No. 7. Dispersal of Immigrant Children.

Mitchell, R. (1978).   'Bilingual Education of minority language groups in the English Speaking World: Some Research Evidence'. Education Seminar, Stirling, paper No. 4.

Montagu, A. (1952).   Man's Most Dangerous Myth. Third Edition, London: Harper and Row.

M.O.T.E.T. (1981).   A Report by Olav Rees and Barre Fitzpatrick on the D.E.S. Sponsored Project on Mother Tongue and English Teaching to Young Asian Children in Bradford. Bradford: University of Bradford.

Mouly, G.J. (1978).   Educational Research: The Art and Science of Investigation. Boston (Mass.): Allyn and Bacon, Inc.

Mullard, C. (1980).   'Racism in Society and Schools: History, Policy and Practice', Occasional Paper No. 1. Centre for Multi-cultural Education. University of London Institute of Education.

Muller, H. (1979).   'Auslandisch Abeitkinder in der Bundes-republik', Kindbeit, Volume 1, pp. 169-184.

Murtaugh, K.O. (1982)   Study in Romance Language. Harvard: Harvard University Press.

National Association of Language Advisers (n.d.).   Foreign Languages in Schools. Quoted in the Working Party Programme of N.C.L.E. (1982).

National Congress on Languages in Education (N.C.L.E.) (1983).   The Minority Community Languages in School A Working Party Report.

National Union of Teachers (1978).   All Our Children. London: N.U.T.

National Union of Teachers (1982).   Linguistic Diversity and Mother-Tongue Teaching: A Policy Statement. London: N.U.T.

Newsam, P. (1983).   Fringe activities (tokenism) of multi-culturalism in Britain — Source: The Times Educational Supplement — October, 1983.

Nicholson, M. (1970).   Conflict Analysis. London: English Universities Press.

Nisbet, J.D. and Entwistle, N.J. (1970).   Educational Research Methods. London: University Press.

Nisbet, J. and Watt, J. (1978).   Case Study: Guide on Educational Research. Nottingham: University of Nottingham.

Oksaar, E. (1971).   'Sprakpolitiken och minoriteterna'. In I. Schwartz (Ed.) Identite onto Minoritet. Stockholm pp. 164-175.

Oliver, S. (1927).   The Anatomy of African Misery. London: Leonard & Virginial Woolf.

Orton, H., Sanderson, M. and Widdowson, M. (1978).   Linguistic Atlas of England. London: Croom Helm.

Osborne, C. (1961).

House of Commons Parliamentary Debate on Immigration — Hansards: H.M.S.O.

Osgood, C. and Sebeok, T. (Eds.) (1965).

Psycholinguistics: a survey of theory and research problems. Bloomington: Indiana University Press. (First published by Indiana University Publications in Anthropology and Linguistics, Mem. 10).

Page, E.B. (1975).

'Accentuate the negative', Educational Researcher, 5.

Pannel, N. ard Brockway, F. (1965).

Immigration: What is the answer? Two opposing Views. London: Routledge and Kegan Paul.

Parekh, B. (1978).

'Asians in Britain: Problem or Opportunity?' In Five Views of Multi-racial Britain. London: C.R.E.

Patterson, S. (1968).

Immigrants in Industry. London: Oxford University Press for Institute of Race Relations.

Paulston, C.B. (1975).

'Ethnic Relations and Bilingual Education: Accounting for Contradictory Data', Working Papers on Bilingualism, Volume 6, pp. 1-44.

Peal, E. and Lambert, W.E. (1962).

'The Relationship of Bilingualism and Intelligence', Psychological Monograph, Volume 76, No. 27, American Psychological Association Inc.

Perren, G.E. (1976).

'Bilingualism and British Education', In Bilingualism and British Education: The Dimension of Diversity. London: Centre for Information on Language Teaching and Research (C.I.L.T.).

Peters, R.S. and White, J.P. (1969).

'The Philosophers' Contribution to Educational Research', Educational Philosophy and Theory, 1, pp 1-15.

Pidgeon, D. and Yates, A. (1957).

Admission to Grammar Schools: The Third Interim Report on the Allocation of Primary School Leavers to Courses of Secondary Education. London: Newness.

Powell, E. (1968).

'Birmingham Speech on 20 April 1968,' In Smithies, B. and Fiddick, P. (1969). Enoch Powell on Immigration. London: Sphere Books.

Prashar, S.V. (1979).

'A Synchronic View of English Bilingualism in India', C.I.E.F.L. Bulletin (Hydrabad, India), 15, 1, pp. 65-76.

Prashar, S.V. (1980).

'Mother-tongue-English Diglossia: A Case Study of Educated Bilinguals' Anthropological Linguistics (Bloomington, Indiana), Vol. 22, No.4, pp. 151-162.

Pride, J.B. (1971).

The Social Meaning of Language. Oxford: Oxford University Press.

Pride, J.B. (1981).

'Native Confidence and Bilingual/Multi-lingual Speakers' English World-wide (Heidelberg), 2, 2, pp. 141-153.

Pringle, Kelmer (1971).

Deprivation and Education. For the National Bureau for Cooperation in Child-Care. London: Longman.

Putman, C. (1961).

Race and Reason. Washington, D.C.: Public Affairs Press.

Rado, M. and Lewis, R. (1980).

'Exploring Students' Attitudes towards Ethnic Language Maintenance in Australia', I.T.L. (Louvain), 49-50, pp. 117-136.

Rampton, A. (1981).

West Indian Children in our Schools: An Interim Report of the Committee of Inquiry into the Education of Children from Ethnic Minority Groups. London: H.M.S.O.

Rees, O. and Fitzpatrick, B. (1981).

Mother-Tongue and English Teaching to Young Asian Children in Bradford. Bradford: University of Bradford and Bradford College.

Rees, T. (1982).   'Immigration Policies in the United Kingdom' In Husband, C. (Ed.) Race in Britain. London: Open University and Hutchinson United Library.

Registrar General (1981).   Office of Population Censuses and Surveys Report. London: H.M.S.O.

Review of Educational Research   'Twenty-five Years of Educational Research'. Educational Research, New York, 26, pp. 323 ...

Rex. J. (1973).   Race, Colonialism and the City. London: Routledge and Kegan Paul.

Richmond, A.H. (1973).   Migration and Race Relations in an English City: A Study in Bristol. London: Oxford University Press for the Institute of Race Relations.

Richmond, A. (1974).   'Language, Ethnicity and the Problem of Identity in a Canadian Metropolis', Ethnicity, Vol. II, pp. 175-206.

Robb, G.P. (1968).   Simplified Statistics for Education and Psychology: a work text with feedback by B.G. Turner & G.P. Robb. International Textbook.

Ronjat, J. (1913).   Le development du langage observe chez un enfant bilingue. Paris: Champion.

Rose, R. (1970).   The United Kingdom as a Multinational State. Glasgow: University of Strathclyde.

Rosen, H. and Burgess, T. (1980).   Language and Dialects of London School Children. London: Ward Lock Educational.

Rowan, J. (1976).   Ordinary Ectasy. London: Routledge and Kegan Paul.

Roy, R. (1980).   'Immersion defined by strategy', The Canadian Modern Languages Review (Toronto), 36, 3, pp. 403-407.

Rummel, J.F. (1964).   An Introduction to Research Procedures in Education. Second Edition. London: Harper and Row.

Saifullah-Khan, V. (1980).   'The "Mother-Tongue" of Linguistic Minorities in Multi-Cultural England', Journal of Multilingual and Multicultural Development, Clevedon (Avon), Vol. 1, No. 1, pp. 71-89.

Saifullah-Khan, V. (1983).   Linguistic Minorities in England: A Report from the Linguistic Minorities Project for the D.E.S. London: University of London Institute of Education.

St Lambert Experiment (1972).   Bilingual Education of Children: A Report by Lambert, W.E. and Tucker, G.R. Rowley (Mass.): Newbury House Publishers Inc.

Saunders, G. (1980).   'Adding a second language in the home', Journal of Multi-lingual and Multi-cultural Development, Clevedon (Avon), Vol. 1, No. 2, pp. 113-144.

Scarman, L.J. (1981).   The Brixton Disorder: The Case for Community Policing. A Report of the National Committee of Inquiry under the Chairmanship of Lord Scarman. London: H.M.S.O.

Schools Council (1970).   The Humanities Curriculum Project: An Introduction. London: Heinemann Educational.

Schools Council (1973).   Working Paper No. 50: Education for Multi-cultural Society Project. London: Evans Brothers.

Scottish Education Department (1981).   Circular 1071: Directive of the Council for the European Community on the Education of the Children of Migrant Workers. Edinburgh: Scottish Education Department.

Scott, S. (1973).   The Relation of Divergent Thinking to Bilingualism. Unpublished research Report: McGill University.

Shuey, A. (1966).   The Testing of Negro Intelligence. New York: Social and Economic Press.

Simon, B.S. (1978).   'Educational Research: Which Way?' Research
                                        Intelligence, Volume 4, No. 1.

Simpson, G.E. and Yinger, J.M. (1972). Racial and Cultural Minorities. London: Harper and
                                        Row.

Sivanandan, A. (1976).   Race, Class and the State: The Black Experience in
                                        Britain. London: Institute of Race Relations.

Sivanandan, A. (1982).   A Different Hunger: Writing on Black Resistance.
                                        London: Pluto Press.

Skutnabb-Kangas, T. (1975).   'Bilingualism or Double Semilingualism: Who sets the
                                        norms?'. Papers for the Second Scandinavian
                                        Conference of Linguistics, University of Oslo,
                                        Norway.

Skutnabb-Kangas, T, and   'Teaching migrant children their mother-
Toukomaa, P. (1976).   tongue and learning the language of the host country in
                                        the context of the socio-cultural situation of the
                                        migrant family'. Tampere, Finland: Tutkimuksia
                                        Research Reports.

Skutnabb-Kangas, T, and   The Intensive Teaching of Mother-Tongue
Toukomaa, P. (1977).   to Migrant Children at Pre-School Age: Tutkimuksia
                                        Research Report 26. Department of Sociology and
                                        Social Psychology: University of Tampere, Finland.

Smith, D.J. (1974).   Racial Disadvantage in Employment. London: P.E.P.
                                        (Political and Economic Planning).

Smith D.J. (1977).   Racial Disadvantage in Britain. London: Penguin
                                        Books.

Smith, D.J. (1981).   Unemployment and Racial Minorities. London:
                                        Policy Studies Institute.

Smolicz, J.J. and Harris R. (1977).   'Ethnic Languages in Australia', International Journal
                                        of the Sociology of Languages, Volume 14, pp.
                                        89-108.

Smolicz, J.J. and Lean R. (1980).   'Parental and Student Attitudes to the Teaching of
                                        Ethnic Languages in Australia', I.T.L.: A Review of
                                        Applied Linguistics, Volume 35.

Smolicz, J.J. and Lean, R. (1980).   Ethnic Languages in Australia, I.T.L., Volumes
                                        49-50, pp. 91-116.

Smolicz, J.J. (1981).   'The Three Types of Multi-Culturalism' In Garner, M.
                                        (Ed.). Community Language. Melbourne: River Seine
                                        Publications.

Sparrow, J. (1973).   A Letter to 'The Times' (17 March 1973).

Steel, D. (1969).   No Entry: The Background and Implications of the
                                        Imigration Act 1968. London: Hurst.

Stenhouse, L. (1975).   An Introduction to Curriculum Research and
                                        Development. London: Heinemann Educational.

Stephen, F.F. (1948).   'History of the Uses of Modern Sampling', Journal of
                                        American Statistical Association, 43, pp. 12-39.

Stephens, M. (1976).   Linguistic Minorities in Western Europe. Gomer Press
                                        Ltd.

Stern, H.H. (1973).   Report on Bilingual Education: Study E7 of the
                                        Studies prepared for the Commission of Inquiry into
                                        the position of the French Language and the Language
                                        Rights in Quebec. Quebec: The Quebec Official
                                        Publishers.

Stewart, W.A. (1968).   'Sociolinguistic Typology of Multi-lingualism', In
                                        Fishman, J. (Ed.). Readings in the Sociology of
                                        Language, The Hague: Mouton.

Stoller, P. (1977).   'The Language Planning Activities of the United
                                        States Office of Bilingual Education', Linguistics, The
                                        Hague, 189, pp. 45-61.

Swain, M. (1978).   'French Immersion: Early, Late or Partial?' The Canadian Modern Languages Review (Toronto), Volume 34. No. 3, pp. 577-585.

Swain, M. and Cummins, J. (1979).   'Bilingualism, Cognitive Functioning and Education: Survey Article', Language Teaching and Linguistics Abstracts, Cambridge, Vol. 12, No. 1, pp. 4-17.

Swain, M. (1980).   'Home-School Language Switching', In Richards, J.C. (Ed.), Understanding School Language Learning: Issues and Approaches. Rowley, Mass: Newbury House.

Swain M. (1981).   'Time and Timing in Bilingual Education', Language Learning (Ann Arbor, Mich.), 31, 1, pp. 1-15.

Swann Committee (1985).   A Report of the National Committee of Inquiry into the Education of Children from Ethnic Minority Groups under the Chairmanship of Lord Swann: 'Education For All'. London: H.M.S.O.

Tajfel, H. (1978).   'Social Psychology of Minorities'. In Husband, C. (Ed.), Race in Britain. London: Hutchinson University Library, 1982.

Taylor, D.M. (1977).   'Bilingualism and Inter-group Relation', In Hornby, P. (Ed.) Bilingualism: Psychological, Social and Educational Implications. London: Academic Press Inc.

Taylor, I. (1976).   Introduction of Psycholinguistics. New York: Holt, Rinehart and Winston.

Taylor, P.H. (1966).   'The Role and Function of Educational Research', Educational Research, 3, 9, pp. 11-15.

Thatcher, M. (1978).   A Television Broadcast Interview expressing fears for British Culture and Values being swampped by people with different cultures.

Thorndike, E.L. (1918).   'The nature, purpose and general methods of measurement of educational product'. In Seventeenth Yearbook of the National Society for the Study of Education, Part II. The Measurement of Educational Products. Bloomington (Illinois): Public School Publishing Company.

Thouless, R.H. (1969).   Map of Educational Research. Slough (England): National Foundation for Educational Research.

Thurstone, L.L. (1935).   The Vector of the Mind. Chicago: Chicago University Press.

Tierney, J. (Ed.) (1982).   Race, Migration and Schooling. London: Holt, Rinehart and Winston.

Titone, R. (1978).   'Some psychological Aspects of Multi-lingualism', International Review of Education, The Hague, 24, 3, pp. 283-293.

Tomlinson, S. (1981).   Special Education: Policy, Practices and Social Issues. London: Harper and Row.

Torence, E.P., Gowan, J.C., Wu, J.M. and Aliotti, N.C. (1970).   'Creative Functioning of Monolingual and Bilingual Children in Singapore', Journal of Educational Research, Volume 61, pp. 72-75.

Tosi, A. (1979).   'Mother-tongue Teaching for the Children of Migrants: Survey Article', Language Teaching and Linguistics Abstracts, Cambridge, Vol. 12, No. 4, pp. 213-231.

Toukomaa, P. and Skutnabb-Kangas, T. (1977).   The intensive teaching of mother-tongue to migrant children in the lower level of comprehensive school. Helsinki: The Finnish National Commission for UNESCO.

Travers, R.M.W. (1978).   An Introduction to Educational Research. New York:
                                     Macmillan Co. Inc. Fourth Edition.

Trudgill, P.J. (1978).   Sociolinguistic Patterns in British English. London:
                                     Arnold.

Tsushima, W.T. and Hogan, T.P. (1975) 'Verbal Ability and School Achievement of Bilingual
                                     and Monolingual Children of Different Ages', Journal
                                     of Educational Research, 68, pp. 349-353.

Tucker, G.R. (1977).   'The Linguistic Perspective in Bilingual Education:
                                     Current Perspective', Linguistics, Volume 2,
                                     Arlington (Va), Centre for Applied Linguistics, pp.
                                     1-40.

Tyler, R.W. (1949).   Basic Principles of Curriculum and Instruction.
                                     Chicago: University of Chicago.

Tyndall, J. (1977).   As Quoted in Walker M. (1977). The National Front.
                                     London: Fontana Books.

UNESCO (1953).   The Use of Vernacular Language in Education.
                                     Monographs on Fundamental Education.

Van Dalen, D.B. (1966).   Understanding Educational Research. New York:
                                     McGraw Hill.

Verma, G.K. and Bagley, C. (Eds.) (1975). Race and Education Across Cultures. London:
                                     Heinemann Educational.

Verma, G.K. and Bagley, C. (1979).   Racial Prejudice, the Individual and Society.
                                     Farnborough: Saxon House.

Verma, G.K. (1980).   The Impact of Innovation: Evaluation of Humanities
                                     Curriculum Project, England, CARE, University of
                                     East Anglia.

Verma, G.K. and Beard R.M. (1981).   What is Educational Research? Aldershot (Hants):
                                     Gower Publishing Company.

Verma, G.K. and Ashworth, B. (1981). 'Education and Occupational Aspirations of Young
                                     South-Asians in Britain', In Verma, G.K. and Bagley,
                                     C. (Eds.) Self-concept, Achievement and
                                     Multi-cultural Education. London: Macmillan.

Verma, G.K. and Bagley, C. (Eds.) (1984). Race Relations and Cultural Differences. London:
                                     Croom Helm Ltd.

Vygotsky, V.S. (1934).   Thought and Language. Reprinted by M.I.T. Press in
                                     1962 and 1975.

Walker, M. (1977).   The National Front. London: Fontana Books.

Ward, A.W., Hall, B.W. and   'Evaluation of published educational
Schram, C.F. (1975).   research: A national survey', American Educational
                                     Research Journal, 12, 2, pp. 109-128.

Washburn, S.L. (1966).   'The Study of Race', In Jenning, J.D. and Hoebel,
                                     E.A. (Eds.) Readings in Anthropology. New York:
                                     McGraw Hill.

Webb, C. (1969).   'Survey of London Life and Labour', In Elman, H.F.
                                     and Elman, R.M. (Eds.) Charles Booth's London.
                                     London: Hutchinson.

Weinreich, U. (1953).   Language in Contact. New York: Linguistic Circle of
                                     New York.

Weinreich, U. (1974).   Language in Contact. The Hague: Mouton.

Whitehead, A.F. (1954).   Dialogues of Alfred North Whitehead. New York:
                                     American Library of World Literature.

Whittingham, E.S. (1982).   The Place of West Indian Dialects in Language
                                     Teaching. London: National Convention of Black
                                     Teachers.

Wilson, C. (1970).   'The Immigration in English History', In Plant, A. et
                                     al., Economic Issues in Immigration. London:
                                     Institute of Economic Affairs.

Wirth, L. (1945).

'The Problems of Minority Groups'. In Linton. R. (Ed.). The Science of Man in World Crisis. New York: Columbia University Press.

Wise, J.E., Nordberg, R.B. and Reitz, D.J. (1967).

Methods of Educational Research. Boston: Heath and Company.

Wragg, E.C. (1979).

Conducting and Analysing Interviews. Oxford: TRC-Rediguides Limited.

Wren, B. (1977).

Education for Justice. London: SCM Press.

Wrigley, J. (1976).

Social Science Research Council Newsletter. October 1976. Quoted by Simon. B.S. (1978) 'Educational Research: Which Way?' Research Intelligence. Volume 4. No. 1.

Young, P.V. (1966).

Scientific Social Surveys and Research. Englewood Cliffs. New Jersey: Prentice Hall Inc.

Index

absorption   See assimilation
achievement   See under achievement
Adelman, C.   85
advantage   See disadvantage
advisers/educational   76, 92-160, 168
Africa/African   9, 22-25, 27, 65, 76, 126-127
   131, 150, 152
Afro-Caribbean   126-129, 142
Aliotti, N.C.   59
Alladina, S.   8, 10, 12-13, 39, 63-65, 122
Allport, G.W.   87
America   61-67, 76, 150-152, 171
Amin, Dada   44
Anglo-phone   61
apendices   172-175
Arabic, language   12, 65, 69, 91, 99-100, 108,
   113, 158-159
Ashworth, B.   41, 45
Ashworth, M.   60
Asia, Asians   3, 4, 11, 13, 16, 23-25, 32, 36, 39,
   41-44, 65, 68-69, 72, 74, 76, 79, 105, 113,
   124-128, 131-133, 143, 145, 150-152
aspects/policies, curriculum   13, 91-160
assessment   91-160, 164
assimilation   4, 7, 9, 11, 64, 67-68, 118, 164
Atkins, M.   75, 168
attitudes   22, 25, 41, 46, 49, 91-160
Australia/Australian   2, 8, 40, 49, 62, 67, 77,
   79, 81, 85, 117

Baetens-Beardsmore, H.   49, 61
Bagley, C., and Verma, G.K.   4, 28, 31, 36
Balkan, L.   60
Bangladesh-Bangladeshis   9, 25, 108
Banton, M.   28-29, 31, 33, 35-36, 38
Barnes, J.B.   83
Barzun, J.   83
Basic Inter-Communication Skills
   (B.I.C.S.)   62
Beards, R.M.   78, 80-81, 84
beliefs   46
Bengali, language   15, 72, 91-92, 98-99, 100,
   102, 113-117, 119-124, 127, 131-140, 143,
   147, 149, 158, 159
Ben-Zeev, S.   60
Bernstein, B.   52, 53
Bhatia, T.K.   52
biculture/biculturalism   53-54, 62, 67-68, 75,
   161-171
bidialectalism   11, 23, 52-54, 65, 127, 170
Bidwell, S.   17, 19, 20
bilingual/s   15, 51,-77, 92-171
   balanced   52
bilingualism   4, 13-15, 49, 51-71, 85, 93-171

Bilingual American Education Act   77
bilingual education   15, 51-87, 95-171
black (children/immigrants/pupils)   16, 20-23,
   26-29, 31, 37, 42-47, 65, 104
biliteracy   62
Black Studies   3
Bloomfield, L.   51
Bohannan, P.   34
Boyle, E.   10,41
British Broadcasting Corporation (B.B.C.)   126
British Educational System   58
Broadbent, J. et al   14
Brockway, F.   29,38
Brown, D.M.   74
Brown, J.   10, 23
Bruck, M. et al   61
Bullock, A.   13-14, 66, 70-71, 93, 129
Burnaby, B.   62
Burgess, T.   10, 14, 65
Business & Technicians' Education Council
   (B.TEC)   170
bussing of children   10,41
Butcher, H.J.   89

Campbell-Platt, K. & Nicholas, S.   15
Canada, Canadian/s   2, 17, 30, 40, 57, 60, 65,
   76, 79, 81, 85, 100
Cantonese, language   99, 107, 137-138, 143
capitalism   37
Caradog-Jones, D.   21
Caribbean, islands/people   9, 21-22, 42
Carlyle, M.   12, 42, 69, 72
case study/studies   82-86, 91-160, 162-171
Caucasian/s   31, 34
Celt/Celtic languages   9, 64
census/es   30, 37, 45, 93, 106-107
Centre for Information on Language Teaching
   and Research (C.I.L.T.)   15, 75, 168
Chapman, L.   14
Charbonneau-Dagenais, A.   51
China, Chinese (language/people)   65, 75, 91,
   100, 105-108, 113, 119, 137-40, 147,
   152-153, 158
Christian/s, Christianity   24, 43
Circular/s, Departmental   10, 41, 109, 155
class, social   98
Coard, B.   10, 38
code/s, language/linguistic   55
cognition   58, 60, 66
cognitive, development/growth/skills   55, 57,
   60-63, 130, 161
Cognitive, Academic Linguistic Proficiency
   (C.A.L.P.)   62
cognitive performance   57, 60

194   INDEX

NOTES

NOTES

NOTES

NOTES